WHAT WE'VE FORGOTTEN

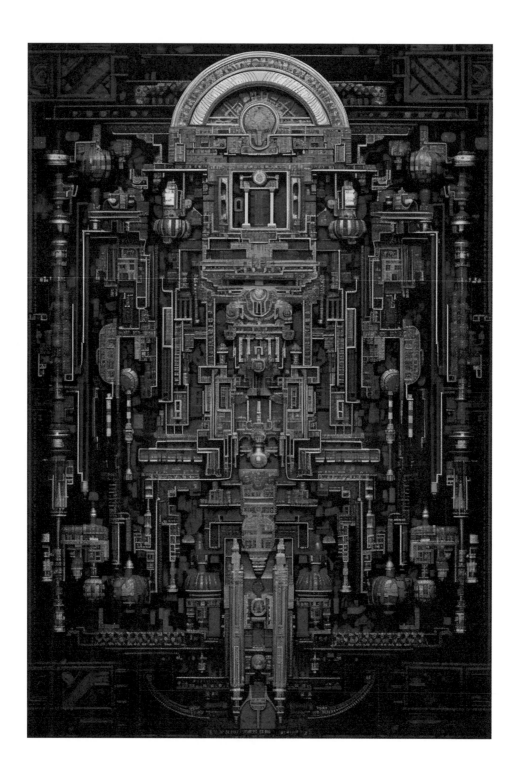

AMY MIRANDA

WHAT WE'VE FORGOTTEN

AN INTERDIMENSIONAL ADVENTURE TO REMEMBER THE WONDER WITHIN

RISE
BOOKS

RISE BOOKS

Jacket design by Thunderwing Studio
Cover & Interior Art Concept Design by Amy Miranda
Sirius Astrophotography Donated and Supplied by Peter Roth
Interior design by Thunderwing Studio and Neuwirth & Associates, Inc.

Library of Congress Cataloging-in-Publication Data Available Upon Request

ISBN 978-1-959524-01-4 (hardcover)
ISBN 978-1-959524-06-9 (eBook)

Printed in the United States of America

First Edition
10 9 8 7 6 5 4 3 2 1

To my temple of wonder, my spectacular jackpot, my other half, my great cackler, and creator king of my heart. There's no one else I'd rather be on this interdimensional adventure with.

Thank you for knocking on my window, pulling back my veil, and being my consort in life, practice, love (and wonder). I hope the world finds the same love, joy, commitment, and fierce compassion you've reminded me to carry every single day.

Goose, this one is for you. I loud love you forever, by every name we've ever had.

CONTENTS

I
KNOWING

II
RECEIVING

III
BECOMING

I

KNOWING

THE INTRODUCTION

This book is about the magic that lives inside of us. I'm going to let you know, right here at the beginning, that if you're not quite ready for it yet, it will find you when you are; it will wait. Magic can do anything and unlock anything because it's *in* everything. It's already in you. It has been all along. We're born with magic. All of us. So don't do that thing where you think I'm not talking about you, or where that voice in your head is already saying, *Not you.*

I've been doing this magic thing pretty exclusively for a long time, and here's the thing about it. It doesn't (and can't) exist without wonder. Wonder is the space we make in our consciousness to leave room for the possibility of magic. It lives in the being that is you and inside the places you're about to visit on this adventure. In all this time, I haven't met one person who couldn't access magic, because as long as you have met wonder, you have danced with magic. I have met lots of people who think it *"won't work,"* or who think they are too broken to receive it. *You* might even be one of those people. I was. That's exactly how we got here, you and me (yep, it's back to you and me again).

I once thought I was too broken to be fixed. I tried to hide it from everyone, with cool outfits, addictions, money, and makeup. I ran such a good show that most people never had any idea that there was anything much going on behind the curtain. I'd had too much trauma to be able to feel or to recognize any real magic that was running through me. I was a vessel who'd run aground. Progress was stalled. I was stuck, and much like humanity right now, I was in need of a major overhaul.

Humankind is in a healing crisis. We've lost our kindness and we've forgotten our magic because we closed the door to wonder. Some of us slammed it shut.

The magic in our lives didn't leave on its own. It didn't just slip from our consciousness. *It was taken.* And we are going to bring it back. This is not a serious book about magic, but it is a *serious* book about magic.

Magic is sacred stuff, don't get me wrong, but it also has a sense of humor (*because humans*), so this book does too. Laughter creates a lightness of being. That's good for light work, and it's going to help us on this quest. And since humanity has been wandering along kind of aimlessly for hundreds of years now in a state of denial, we could certainly use a good adventure. We've been pretending we're running things on Earth; meanwhile, all our systems, built on a foundation of capitalism, patriarchy, colonialism, and white supremacy, are failing. Crumbling. Collapsing. We are watching the downfall of Western civilization. So many of us feel as if we're too far gone, or that we're "too broken to be fixed." As someone who once felt exactly those two things, I now know differently. I know that we have simply forgotten.

And this book is here to help you remember. Together we're going to shine a new light on some of the old ways, and although there are still books being burned, there is something more tangible at work here. No, not the internet. The real information superhighway: consciousness.

Here's what I know about energy: It speaks in symbols and visions and downloads and transmissions. I also know that when working with Source, in Spirit, it's like seeing underwater. It's like tuning into specific channels on the radio and we are the antennae. It is the signal. We are able to connect to people using our ordinary senses, and then we have the capacity to remember to use our gifts and experience messages and guidance from non-ordinary reality. We live in ordinary reality, but outside of that is a place where we can reach through our consciousness to a non-ordinary reality. Spirit World. The Heavens. As above and so below. On Earth as it is in Heaven. Or, if you prefer, celestial and terrestrial.

You don't need to *believe* in it, you just have to try to be open to it. This adventure won't work without wonder, so we're going to start by just practicing the wonder of *maybe*s. If you can do only five minutes of wonder at a time, start there.

You don't have to move into Spirit Town, you can just start with some day trips, or a quick lunch.

But first . . .

Let Me Take You to Nerd Town

In order to help us to remember, we're going to reframe some things on this adventure. The concept of Source, or Spirit, is one of them. Do you know where the word *Spirit* originated? It's Latin. It comes from *spiritus*, "to breathe." That's how we should be looking at it too. It's as important as breathing. Not acknowledging our Spirit, or soul, is indeed akin to not breathing. It is like a breath that fills our being. How could it be any clearer? Yet here we are, most of us feeling like Spirituality is attached to something it isn't. We think it's woo-woo for being too out there, when in fact, it's not out there. It's in here. It's in *us*.

Not using our Spirituality is like ignoring the accelerator in a vessel that's been designed to move. It's time we recognize how we got here, how we got stuck, and that this resurgence of real magic on the planet and the rising interest in the old ways of shamanism, witchcraft, and other Nature-based root spiritual practices of humanity isn't an accident. It's a remembering.

We have misplaced our connection to ourselves for so long that as people are finding their pedals, they are reminding others how they can find them too. Traditional wisdom-keepers from across the globe are traveling and sharing teachings to spread ancient medicine, because shamanism is universal, and witches come in all traditions. We can all find medicines in our lineage if we're willing to look.

It's time to remember that the real magic is us. The star stuff that lives inside of us. The little voice of intuition nudging to just do that thing or take that different path home. This *is* what we've forgotten. It's our birthright on the planet as long as breath is moving through our bodies. In fact, I've seen it continue after that breath (and soul) have left. It's never been woo-woo; it was always you. You.

Magic isn't about rabbits coming out of hats (though we may go down some mind-bending rabbit holes on our way to Wonderland, Alice) or booming voices coming from the sky (although we're not crossing anything out). Wonder is about remembering that synchronicity is the language of Nature. When we're connected to our Spirit, we are connected to the source of everything. Except systems of power don't usually support that connection, because when humans are connected with our souls and communicating with Nature, it makes it hard for The Uninvited to take advantage of people with systems of oppression.

The Uninvited are who you may previously have known as the oppressors, abusers, the white supremacist-capitalist-colonial-patriarchy. These were the men (and women) who were agents of density, rage, separation, and hatred. They had no room for wonder because they were full of hurt, anger, and division. They weren't invited to our sacred suppers, so they broke in and caused total devastation. They lit it all on fire to dissuade others from stepping out of line. The ways of light turned dark through their lens and under their gaze. The Uninvited soon sat at every table, dominated every meal, and ultimately, they put themselves in charge of who was fed.

They soon realized that in order to maintain their tables, they needed to infiltrate the most sacred of circles. Organized religion became a tool for monetization and control. This is why people have been (and still are) murdered for their voices and for their magic. Burning witches, murdering medicine people, and persecuting healers has been part of our collective consciousness for far too long. We all carry the ability to commune with Nature because we all come from Nature. Some of us have just forgotten because we've gotten so far away. Being a witch inherently means being connected to the natural world. That's what Spirituality has always been about, congregating for community. That's all a coven is. It's a gathering to create and raise power for the greater good.

The Uninvited have only worked harder, telling us it's all dangerous (*and worse*). But as we rise, we're getting louder and stronger, and they are losing their control of the tables. We're beginning to connect the dots to see the commonalities. We're beginning to realize that not only can we take back the tables, but we can also turn them, and this time, *everyone* gets fed. This also brings us to an important point. We have to consider The Uninvited's mark on the history books. Some things in this book may be credited to people who may (or may not) have been the first to have shared the thought. Yet, they were the first ones who got attribution because of who they were in society. May we recognize and give credit to all the medicine people and wisdom keepers whose names we may not know because of the marks left by The Uninvited.

I've read many books about magic, some that carried magic and many others that made very little sense to me until I had the capacity to understand them. That's part of how magic works. It joins in when we've made the room and laid the foundation to hold it.

One day after really focusing on my practice, it was like suddenly I had a secret decoder ring that enabled me to connect the dots. These books that had never made much sense to me suddenly made perfect sense. Everything looked *different*. Magic came to me, it came through me, in ways that required witnesses to believe. Some of those people will even tell you that sometimes the magic was simply *too much* for them. The only possible response to it all was the simple phrase, "You can't make this shit up," and more often than I care to admit, people said, "Well, I'm probably going to head out now."

We need to acknowledge that wonder and magic come with awe as a built-in side effect. Most of us aren't used to that. It's refreshing but also like drinking out of a firehose. *Too much refreshment at once.* Awe can sometimes take some time to process. Don't worry, our adventure includes simple instructions for the foundation (but building it is up to *you*). Sound familiar?

"Magic" is the non-ordinary reality of energy; it is interaction directly with the divine. It is the merging of worlds. We are standing at the intersection, we are directing the traffic of our energetic fields, and we get to decide what direction they're going. Are they going to crash—or are they going to take us where we need to go? Where our souls brought us here to go?

This book is going to take you deep into both your soul and the cosmos. Think of it as an interdimensional treasure hunt. Together, we are going to experience an adventure, one that might even become part of the story of your life. You're being invited into a place that exists not only in print but in consciousness. As we move through this journey together, we will remember our own unique superpowers, reclaim wonder, creativity, connection, *and* collaborate with Source. This is another place where we'll need to leave some room for wonder. We're going to entertain that there *is* a Source to this whole life thing. We can call it a Creator, a Spirit, an Energy, or even Rick—if you want. But we're going to entertain that there's something out there, in here, and everywhere that wants to collaborate with us. *Because* love.

Source is love.

Way better bumper sticker.

If life is a magical intention-driven scavenger hunt, it means that if we don't have the first clue right, the rest of it can be kind of confusing. A real nonstarter. So we want to track this adventure like a scavenger hunt, and that means we should probably write things down. There might be some wonder to be found in the corners and details of divine timing. And listen, before you go too far down *that* particular rabbit hole, *divine timing* doesn't have to translate to "God," it can also mean "excellent" or "delightful." So why not make room for some delightful timing in your life? You might want to write that down. MAKE ROOM FOR DIVINE TIMING. It's a good reminder to have around when you're stuck.

On this adventure there are breadcrumbs, treasures, *and* gifts. The rabbit hole is deep and full of sacred objects and secret caverns. Rites, rituals and remembering. The real 3 R's How many you discover will be entirely up to you.

What We've Forgotten doesn't promise that life is going to be all rainbows and unicorns. Life is hard in this Ocean of Consciousness. Our job as human beings is to remember how to swim, and then to find *and remind* the others. Hard things are going to happen here, but when we use all the tools available to us, and the gifts we'll discover along the way, it becomes easier to ride those waves and handle the surf when things like grief, pain, and trauma hit. Although we may be separate souls on separate journeys, the pendulum always swings an equal amount on both sides. We can have more ease and grace in this life—and beyond. We just have to ask for it; most have forgotten how.

So let's remember, shall we? It's clear that humanity is on a crash course, and we're going to run out of real air if we don't fix this and fast. We need to use our collective magic. Employ our Spirits. Engage our souls to help steer our little beings out of the muck to exactly where they need to go. We are going to remember that there is an easier way to live life on planet Earth.

We may not be in the same physical space right now, but try to use your mind's eye and imagine that it's just you and me. We're going to spend some time knowing, reclaiming, and becoming your magic. This is our adventure and our treasure hunt. We'll make some pit stops in Wonderland, Spirit World, and Nerd Town. We're going to remember that wonder and magic were always a part of you. You *knew* it when you were a kid. It *is* our birthright. We did magic. We made wishes. We imagined we could fly. *What We've Forgotten* is going to get you back to that place of wonder, that inner knowing, our intuition. The voice of our soul that used to run the whole show.

This book is going to reintroduce us to our magic *and* to the magic of life. It's illumination, it's wonder, it's goosebumps, shivers, and moments when the feeling of certainty moves through every fiber of our beings. When we just *know* that yes, this is the way. We're on the adventure moving through the Ocean of Consciousness in search of lost treasures and ancient knowledge. We are basically Goonies. If you haven't seen *Goonies*, this is part of your homework. If you have seen it, you know the Goonie motto, *"Goonies never say die."*

We don't say that here either.

We say, *"Welcome home."*

CHAPTER ONE

THE INVITATION

THE MAGIC BOOK

Since this book *is* self-care, try to get into a space where you won't be disturbed. We're going to call this sacred space, and before you get all worried that this is going to be too "woo-woo" for you, know that when we want the world to progress forward. We are willing to do the sometimes weird and uncomfortable work it takes to get there.

We're going to get comfortable with the uncomfortable parts because in order to work with magic, we must acknowledge the appropriation of medicines across the world, and that the people who are still being murdered are the same ones who have been keeping magic alive for thousands and thousands of years. People of color are persecuted across the world by the systems of The Uninvited. We have to do more than just acknowledge the magic of the oppressed, we all have to accept responsibility for the ongoing genocide of marginalized people all over the planet until every single system of theirs is rebuilt in balance.

We all carry the burden and the honor of reconciliation. Civilizations have existed all over the planet since our inception who have worked with the healing arts. As we refuel our wonder tanks, we'll remember and honor some of the origins of magic on the planet. We're going to review some of the clues and visit some of the peoples with pyramids (and mountains). A core component of what we're going to be remembering on this journey is that the commonality of energy is light and that light in the Universe comes from the celestial realm. We're going to entertain that maybe these pyramids all over the globe could be arrows pointing to the sky. Maybe all these great civilizations around the world just wanted us to look up, to look into the wonder of what we're made of.

The triangle pointing upward still means "up." Check any elevator. We're all just little triangles ourselves. Beings of mind, body, and Spirit. A holy little trinity holding light. A little breadcrumb here as the alchemical symbol for fire *is* a triangle.

Grand-Mother Ayangat, of the Mongolian Union of Ancestral Traditions, offers this wisdom: "We have neglected our ancestral knowledge and dishonored the law of Nature. Let's respect each other and revive Indigenous knowledge on how to live in harmony with Nature."

We all have to do the work to be of service and educate ourselves in our local communities. We have to be clear about our own connections and histories in new practice of the old ways. I'm a descendant of both settlers and colonized people. Unhealed colonial violence that occurred in my family eventually dripped its blood down onto me. My precolonial last name remains unknown; the name on this book came via colonization. My Filipino ancestors hold those truths.

Together, we'll all practice letting go of whatever understanding we may have previously had about Spirituality, witches, shaman, and prophets like Jesus. This is foundational for practice. We are going to imagine clearing our minds of clutter, unconscious bias, judgment, or worry, and we're going to set about forgetting our collective conditioning and instead remember our collective humanity.

In order to learn, we have to release our conditioning. We've got to do our own research, and we've got to trace our own webs. To change it, we have to acknowledge that like life, this adventure is an ongoing education. A part of this journey is to remember and understand our own individual and unique origins. That's what we're going to try to do here together. We're going to remember that our shared lineage is light and that's the thread we're going to be focused on tracing through the foundation, practice, and application.

The Malian ethnologist, poet, and historian Amadou Hampâté Bâ shared the advice elders would give to outsiders who came to experience their ancient hunting rituals: "You shouldn't bring back what I tell you by comparing it to what you know; you have to absolutely forget, you have to empty yourself of everything you know, in order to learn. That's where we tell you to know that we don't know. If you know, you don't know, you will know. If you know that you don't know, you won't know."

Hard Resets Aren't Just for Electronics

We're going to start our adventure together by doing what I call "dropping in." Try to give yourself permission to let yourself be still. Try to let your mind clear. Try to see it as a blank slate—a blank chalkboard—and just focus on your breathing for a moment. Maybe put your hand on your heart, maybe both hands. Breathe in and out. Hold on to each breath, in and out, for a count of four until you feel grounded. Our nervous systems are typically on high alert, *because life*. These breaths are helping to let your body know you're safe. Also, please do yourself a favor and turn off your notifications—you'll thank me later. Airplane mode is a fantastic friend for your nervous system.

Be somewhere that you can relax and feel comfortable. If you want to lie down, lie down. If you want to get a blanket, get a blanket. If you like candles, or oils, or crystals, go grab them.

If you don't have those things and you don't feel safe, all is not lost. We can use any objects at our disposal that bring warmth and grounding, or no object at all. And lean on the safety that comes with each breath that shows up. The air in our lungs, the heart that's been keeping us alive all these years. In this moment together we are safe. If you don't feel safe in this moment, come back when you are ready.

Let's flex our visualization muscles now, as you're going to need them for our adventure. Close your eyes if that's comfortable. If you're thinking, *How am I supposed to read this and close my eyes?* You can try recording this next part in a voice memo for yourself so that you can close your eyes, or check out the audiobook version. Or if you're a visual learner, read on ahead and then put the book down to do the work. This *is* choosing your own adventure.

Imagine a light source at the very top of the Universe, as if at the very beginning of time. Imagine it, the light of a star hundreds of times brighter than our own sun. Feel the warmth of it, like our own sun on your face. Feel that warmth and imagine a strand of that light, a thread, like a current moving through your body. As if it's rolling through you like a wave. You may want to adjust how you are sitting, or lying, as you let this beam, this Source fuel, move through you.

Through every cell, every fiber, and every fragment of your being there is light. As you breathe in air, imagine you are also breathing in light. And as you exhale, the air goes out, but imagine that the light is staying in. As this warmth moves through you, you may hear the whistling of birds. The faint sounds of a rattle. Wind rustling through the leaves and then, the sound of a drum, the heartbeat of the Earth. Then feel the rolling thunder that moves through your own chest. As it does, it reminds you of *something*.

It reminds you of *everything*.

You are not separate from it. You *are* it. You are a walking star. And the thing about stars is, they don't worry. They don't just shine in one spot. They are being and doing their magic all the time. We weren't put on the planet to worry or to create division or pain for other beings. We are here to shine. We are here to learn. We are here to remember how to use all the tools available to us, how to work the controls of our vessels. We are here to use our own unique magic as part of the collective.

If you still can't remember what magic feels like, imagine it's warm. It's alive. It's like the feeling of a warm fire, a light emanating from somewhere deep inside your chest. That's the real you. It's where you're from and to where we all return. As we imagine ourselves floating in this warm sanctuary, let's start to come back into the now. You can bring that warm feeling with you. You may be ready to open your eyes, or you may need a moment before you want to be back in your day. Do what works for you as we take a few moments to ground ourselves back, to imagine rooting into the earth. This is why people hug trees; it's a shortcut. They're about as grounded as a being can get, and by hugging them, we can ground our own energy. You can imagine doing it now as part of this grounding. Acknowledge the energy moving through your body and imagine it moving down through the earth, like the roots of the tree. Imagine you are soaking up that grounding energy and extending it back up through the top of your head. You're like a little antenna primed for transmissions.

I hope you're feeling more grounded and open now. This was part of what magic does. It calms and reminds, awakening a curiosity and bringing such wonder that makes it almost impossible to not follow the breadcrumbs.

The Initiate

Since we're having an adventure together, this is where I tell you about how magic found me, about my breadcrumbs. I was in my mid-thirties when the amazing life I had painstakingly built for myself had started collapsing. It turns out this is what happens when you build on a foundation of unhealed trauma.

I was a successful executive producer. I was working in advertising and media, making cool stuff for global brands. I *should* have been happy. I was a single female entrepreneur working with incredible artists and meeting my literal heroes. So why didn't I feel *well*? Because I was hiding out behind the Trauma Shed. You know the Trauma Shed: It's that place in the back of our mind where we sit with all the awful memories and thoughts. I wasn't just visiting the Shed, I'd basically moved in.

I may have been at the top of my career goals, but I was breaking under the weight of what I was carrying around. I finally had to admit that I was totally and completely exhausted. Way beyond not-being-able-to-take-the-garbage-out exhausted. I was burned out. Part of it was that it had never really occurred to me that I'd even live as long as I had. I'd had so many things happen in my life by then that I was constantly braced for impact. You know how they say trauma puts you in fight, fright, or freeze mode? I was all of them at once, I was at war, and yet I was literally dragging myself to what I thought felt like some kind of success-based finish line.

I learned how to work around the increasingly heavy backpack of emotional baggage I'd been carrying for as long as I could remember. I was so afraid to take it off that I grappled with addiction to drugs, to work, to anything that numbed the pain. I didn't know what was in it, and I didn't want to know. I just knew that I wasn't the one who packed it. I was a ball of tension who barely slept and had never had a massage (*the emotional backpack would have had to come off!*). Instead, I just dragged around all this abuse and trauma and addiction and self-harm and wondered why I was so fucking exhausted.

I knew I needed to do something different. I set my intention, as if I were at the controls of my being, and I asked for help. I wrote that request down. I asked to be shown what was next. I asked for it to be made clear. *PLEASE MAKE IT CLEAR.* Then I did what I now do every day: I followed the breadcrumbs.

The term comes from the Hansel and Gretel fairy tale where the characters create a trail of breadcrumbs to help them find their way back home. It's also a term in user experience design that refers to the navigation sprinkled across big websites, helping us find our way. Source leaves us breadcrumbs to help us find our way back to the home of who we are and why we're here. In treating and tracking these as clues, we can begin to piece together where our purpose lives. Breadcrumbs are synchronicities or events that might seem as if they're unrelated, but they are experienced as occurring together in a meaningful manner. They are not coincidences; they are omens, signs, guideposts. They are how divinity interacts with us. It's how they let us know we're not alone. Someone is looking out for us enough to give us little surprises when we are on track. There *is* an intelligence greater than us.

It's part of the assistance we have access to that helps us live our lives on the planet. We must also get some clues on what we're here to do, right? Synchronicity and tracking breadcrumbs are how we begin to figure it out. How does this actually translate? Because, sure, it all sounds good while we're here, but what about real life?

Well, by asking something outside of myself for help, I learned something big about the Universe: When people say it finds a way, they mean it. *Especially* when you ask Source to make it clear.

It was 2006 and I'd just bought a house with my partner. The real estate agent was my longtime friend Ben. After we bought the house, I mentioned to him that

I wanted to do a little interior design work. Ben gave me a designer's number, but I never called him.

Two years later, I was in that house alone, after my partner became my ex. I was on a crash course, again. I'd realized my traumas were catching up to me. I couldn't seem to maintain relationships. I pushed everyone away. I got fired. I treated my body like a trash can. I fought every kind of authority like a warlord. When I'd finally started to connect the dots, I realized the common denominator in it all was me. So I started to lean into the idea that maybe I needed a massage after all. I also needed someone to help me make sense of myself.

When I finally found the right massage therapist, I kept it up. I'd previously sat in capitalist judgment of people who took time for themselves, the wellness community, and now, somehow, I was a *massage person*. I noticed something one day in the lobby of the beautifully designed wellness center. It may as well have grabbed me by the shoulders. There was a menu of services beside the reception desk. It offered all different kinds of wellness services, most of which I recognized (and tried)—except for one, and as a result it was as if someone had circled it in fluorescent yellow highlighter. I repeated the words in my mind so that I'd remember. As soon as I was lying down, I mumbled with my face planted in the donut hole of the massage table, "Who is Daniel and what is shamanic healing?"

"Oh," said my massage therapist, as she got to work on my tension ball muscles. "He's amazing. He's a shaman. You should see him. He designed this clinic."

In retrospect that didn't really tell me anything, but it was a *breadcrumb*. It was enough for me to latch on. I'd found my massage therapist through someone who had helped get me back into my body enough to even be able to get a massage. Every time I intentionally followed the clues in my life, I was being rewarded with someone great. There was a precedent, so that was all it took: *You should see him.*

We can't and won't talk about shamanism any further without honor and reverence for the Indigenous peoples around the world who have not broken the chain of succession in carrying the wonder and keeping watch of the wisdom. This wisdom is potent medicine and must be heard, respected, and honored. The hard truth is that colonial settlers committed genocide out of fear of what this ancient knowledge could make possible. As Dr. Grace Nono, an artist and cultural scholar of shamanism in the Philippines, says so succinctly in her book *Babaylan Sing Back,* "When the European colonizers arrived in the sixteenth century, they observed voice to be an important tool of cultural reinforcement in the lives of Indigenous peoples. They wasted no time in transforming this voice into a site of colonial control."

Carrying and protecting this wisdom through thousands of years was an arduous and dangerous journey. Countless people lost their lives because a segment of the population tried to erase them. This is still happening. From a Spiritual perspective, all of our human knowledge contains appropriative elements. We have to begin by tracing the lineages and searching for the sources of our stories, in order to reconcile the violence so many of us hold within our ancestries.

The Uninvited stole our name, our original Spiritual beliefs, and tried to take our pride. They tried to assimilate us. They also brought some of my own settler ancestors to Canada from Scotland and England. I didn't grow up knowing anything about my Asian ancestry, and even less about my Puerto Rican roots, but I knew a lot about the colonial pieces of myself. I knew that looking like a European granted me access to a world where my other ancestry was unseen. That's what white supremacy does. It erases everything but itself. It permeates with its self-sabotage and unconscious bias. Colonialism inserted itself into the fabric of humanity on purpose, amplifying itself and flooding the system. In advertising, it's what we call a "Pay and Spray," dominating media by being everywhere and buying up everything. The difference is that, here, no one paid. No one was Invited. They just stole. They distributed their own invitations. They made sure to eliminate the people who had the most powerful stories and voices from the list, and the Earth: the wisdom-keepers, medicine people, shamans, witches, and healers of history became public enemy number one because they held the most *knowledge*. The word *shaman* is likely Siberian in origin and came from the root word *sa*, or "to know."

It's time to amplify these voices and the wisdom-keepers who carry them. They carry the knowing to save the planet. Shaman are known to be able to see in the dark; they are the teachers we need to help light the way. They have the training. The medicine is traveling, and we are remembering. Shamanic healing is sacred. It has been sacred since we got to the planet. Part of reconciling this gift is making reparations for the horrors of the past and present. That is how we change the future.

While we're here, let's cover a crucial teaching. One does not typically refer to themselves as a shaman; a shaman is named by their community, by those who visit. There are incredible human teachers all over the planet teaching this work and carrying the wisdom.

To quote twenty-seventh-generation wisdom-keeper and shaman Bhola Nath Banstola of Nepal, who teaches the practices and traditions of his ancestors around the world, "All of my work depends on how people feel; if they feel good, that means I believe what I do. If they say that it is good, I believe that it works."

Little did I know but that was my first clue that Daniel was the real deal, as he never once called himself a shaman. It was his community who told me he was a healer; it was his community that referred to him as a shaman. From a bit of internet research after that massage, I learned that he focused on working to bring back power that had been lost to trauma. By then, I knew that I'd lived through some heavy shit, but I also knew there was heavy shit I didn't know. There was something that was too heavy for me to name, comprehend, or even acknowledge. I was starting to drown in it, so I booked a session.

When I went for my soul-retrieval ceremony with Daniel, I didn't know what to expect. I brought in all my bias, I was all 3-D, all-mind. As a result, I'd envisioned he'd be in some kind of elaborate *Lord of the Rings* robe and there'd be weird things being sprayed in my face. I grew up in the rave scene, so you'd think I wouldn't be worried about costumes or shit being sprayed in my face, but I was. I was afraid, I was anxious, and I couldn't have been more off-base.

Because when I walked into the room that day for the ceremony with Daniel, it felt more like a womb. The room was scattered with pillows, blankets, and a few small soapstone statues of dancing bears, and the lighting was low and calming. He was wearing a plaid shirt and jeans. No costumes. Nothing sprayed in my face except for the truths I was about to find. I felt totally safe. Totally at home in a way I hadn't ever remembered. I closed my eyes—something I'd always had trouble doing, especially in a space with men. As he got going, his voice filled the room. He rattled and drummed around me, and I seemed to fall into a lucid dream. When it was done, he began to speak, and I felt as if I were going to come up off the floor. The visions he described were somehow the same ones I'd seen as I laid there hanging between dimensions. I was awestruck.

The whole thing took less than two hours, and somehow, I came out feeling more like myself than I ever had. I'd been to lots of appointments trying to fix myself. Somehow, this time, in this space, I was welcoming myself home. I felt like for the first time in a long time I was in my body versus hanging by a cord outside. I was floating in a different way. In the ceremony I received my first animal totem or guide. Our power animals are expert translators because Spirit doesn't speak the same language we do. A key component of a journey is having a guide who speaks the language to guide us through the journey. Daniel did work to help me begin to call myself back home. That was the day I met the man who changed my whole life.

I wasn't exactly sure what had happened in that time in that room, but I knew I felt better, and I wanted to try to understand why. It was as if Daniel had *magically* flipped through the index cards of my memories, of my soul, and somehow brought me back to myself (with some percussion).

My massage therapist was right. His clients were right. He *was* amazing. I knew in my bones that he was also the person, the teacher I needed.

What do you do when someone becomes your Spiritual teacher? Well, I decided to find him on Facebook. But when I connected with Daniel, I saw he was also friends with Ben, my friend and real estate agent. I was totally perplexed. How would *they* know each other? I'd known Ben since I'd been in the rave scene. Maybe it was that. Maybe Daniel *raved*? I messaged Ben.

"How do you know Daniel?" I typed into Facebook Messenger.

He typed back, "He's my next-door neighbor." Then he added, "I introduced you to him when you moved into the house and wanted a designer."

Wait, WHAT?

Time folded in on itself, like one of those *MAD Magazine* fold-ins. The designer I never called, the same person who had just now retrieved part of my soul on a blanket down the street, *had been living right next door to one of my oldest friends.* Holy shit, but also, as I've learned since, *of course.*

In this case, the Universe made quite sure that I didn't miss the call.

I promise, it will do the same for you. The Universe is kind of like a worried mom—it'll keep at it until we pick up. So please don't worry that you've missed your window. There will be more windows—think a Burj Khalifa number of windows. Here's what I mean; not very long after we met, Daniel moved across the country to a tiny island. His next-door neighbor this time? My ex's father—the one I bought the house with, the one I was living with when Ben first gave me Daniel's details. A wink from Source as if to say, *Clear enough for ya?*

You just *can't* make this shit up.

The more work I did with Daniel, the more I was being reintroduced to myself and less time I began to spend in the Trauma Shed. It was a special kind of remembering. A homecoming. After a while, I had enough energy back in my body to be able to look inside. I finally had enough foundation to move out some of the heavy shit. To look at who was hiding. My body told me. It spilled out of me like lava, and as it did, the most beautiful realization was that I wasn't alone. I was with Daniel, lying down on the treatment table, with my teacher sitting beside me. He had his hand on my shoulder in the moment it all came flooding back.

I'll tell you, the brain does us a favor when we are hurt this badly. It seems to do its best to take the worst parts of the picture and just leave the fuzzy edges. The memory is almost completely blurred out, burned out. Sometimes we get nothing, sometimes it comes back in a dream, or a smell. We may get only pieces at a time because the whole of it is so awful that our brain knows how much we can handle; it knows to take away the rest. It's like the mind stops recording, but the body doesn't. The body always knows. The soul knows. Suddenly, the full picture flooded back, and I could finally name it.

It spilled out of me: what I'd been carrying in that backpack. That I'd survived one of the worst things a human being can experience.

My father had started sexually abusing me before I could even talk. It wasn't just asthma that had tried to take my breath.

Fun fact: Fear manifests in the lungs. My asthma attacks resolved themselves when we stopped living in the same house as my father. Breadcrumbs.

That's what I mean about everything changing in an instant.

The immediate side effect of this revelation was that every aspect of my life got shuffled. In an instant, everything I ever thought I knew about my life changed, and I had a decision to make. Let this kill me or choose life . . . again. Sobriety or addiction. Survive or succumb. Life or death.

I guess you probably know what I chose.

When you remember something traumatic that has long been buried, you become a human excavator trying to dig through all of your moments of memory, looking for more of what hurt you. I had to put those tools down and finally accept that there was no archaeological tray for this. There would be no further artifacts to uncover. To choose to live through this, I *had* to look at everything with a fresh perspective. I had to choose to throw open the doors of the Trauma Shed and blast it with light. I looked at it all from a ten-thousand-foot view. Every single moment had to be viewed through a new lens, so I zoomed out on the timeline of my life as if on a map. As I looked over the experiences at a distance like this, a shift happened.

A Holy Shift.

I gained more perspective, and I began to become an active participant in healing my trauma. Then it wasn't just my Trauma Shed, which is a terrifying and lonely place, it was the Sheds of my family, my ancestors, all that led to this moment in my life. What came out of the darkest moments of my life were the most amazing gifts.

I found the others. The Remarkables as I call them. The survivors of The Uninvited. The ones who've left hell behind but will go back in to pull another out. The ones who've slayed demons since they were babies and who operate in service for each other and the ones who didn't make it. When I found my voice, I found the other Remarkables, and they found me. The weight of what I'd carried got spread out between us all, and we can carry the weight of it into the light. We can shine a light on men like my father. We can eject them from the tables where they eat and leave no places for them to hide.

We can allow trauma to freeze us, frighten us, or send us flying off and disassociating, or we can choose to ask for help, to find the others. We can lead the adventure. Because inside the Trauma Shed was actually always the doorway to Narnia, talking lions and all. Are you ready, because I want to officially and cordially invite you to start this adventure.

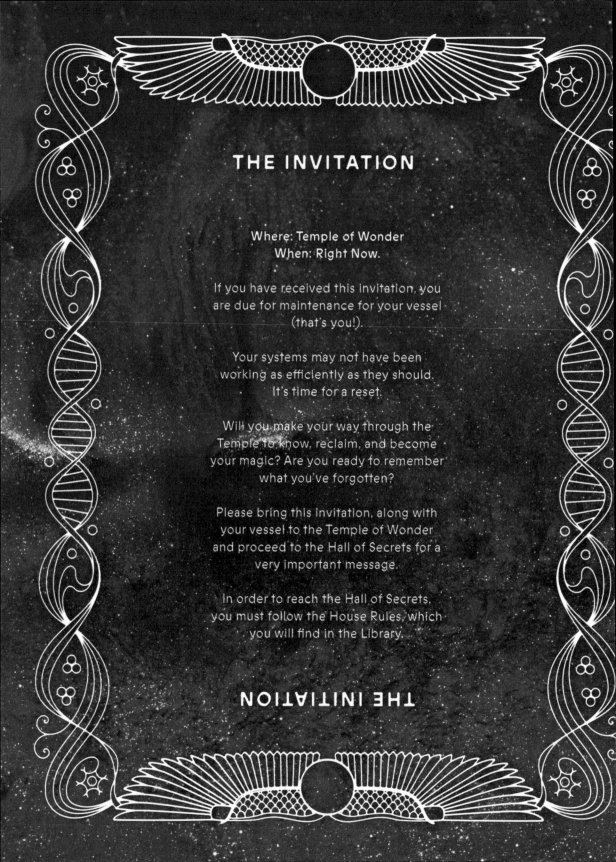

THE INVITATION

Where: Temple of Wonder
When: Right Now.

If you have received this invitation, you
are due for maintenance for your vessel
(that's you!).

Your systems may not have been
working as efficiently as they should.
It's time for a reset.

Will you make your way through the
Temple to know, reclaim, and become
your magic? Are you ready to remember
what you've forgotten?

Please bring this invitation, along with
your vessel to the Temple of Wonder
and proceed to the Hall of Secrets for a
very important message.

In order to reach the Hall of Secrets,
you must follow the House Rules, which
you will find in the Library.

THE INITIATION

Into the Wonder

To start this adventure together, I want you to give yourself the gift of tracking your experiences as you remember them, to reignite your sense of wonder. This is our first practice: Create a journal for this remembering, for all the things you may have forgotten about your own magic. I'm going to ask you to find or create a notebook that is especially for your magic, for the practices in this book and beyond. As you remember and reignite your sense of wonder and magic, you're going to create a journal for your soul. It's not for shopping lists or anything else but magic. It's to make note of the special stuff that happens. It's for your own personal scavenger hunt. You're going to track *your* clues and note *your* sacred treasures. This notebook will be for recognizing and recording *your magic only*. This practice is to find (or create . . . or both) a notebook especially for your magic and for the practices during our adventure. Use your intuition to choose the right book. It may be one you already own, it may be one you are going to make, you may buy it, or you may take something you have and customize it. The only rule to this and all the practices in this book is to follow your instincts. You may decide that this is your first intention and see what you may find by following those instincts. That's what you'll do before we start. It's all we're going to need in terms of supplies. A pen (or pencil, or marker, or pencil crayon . . . whatever makes you happiest) and our magic notebook.

Let's be open to the idea that magic is already happening and that the breadcrumbs of our lives have led us both to this very moment together, and that this was how it was meant to be all along. This is your invitation to reclaim your magic.

As we move through this adventure and through the keyhole, we will explore a Temple of Wonder. It is full of rooms containing secrets, rituals, and treasures. Each room will take you deeper into the realm of magic and down the hallways of illumination and deep remembering. Bring your invitation, and I will meet you on the steps of The Temple to experience the light and magic that lies ahead.

CHAPTER TWO

THE ENTRYWAY

THE VESSEL

Together we're going to remember The Temple. It is a building unlike any you've ever seen, a place built by the cosmos, just outside of time. It's surrounded by clouds and the massive gold rampway that leads up to the door. It is held perfectly in space. We're going to imagine ourselves standing together on the massive ramp that leads up into The Temple door.

Maybe your vessel traveled here as a result of someone else, or maybe you came on this journey completely on your own. Maybe you came on a ferry from the Ocean of Consciousness. I know we're just getting started, but I invite you back into The Temple as many times as you like, because the magic found within the adventure (and you) will be different based on the timing of energy itself. Energy changes just like we do.

If you're carrying a heavy backpack of your own, this is the place you can set it down. There are interdimensional helpers here. You can trust them to take good care of it. We don't need to carry anything inside but our beings. As human beings, we are all three components: mind, body, and Spirit (or energy if you prefer). Most of us are spending a lot of time on just two of those components, right? Or maybe just one? For me, I was focused on just my mind for most of my life, and even that was dicey. I couldn't manage anything else. I didn't even feel safe in my own body, and I had lost so much of my Spirit, lost touch with so much of my energy, that it was almost impossible to imagine there was anything else but that heady place where I lived all the time. It was one-dimensional. Everything was flat and scary. Fight, flight, or fright begins in the mind. So you get stuck there because it's the brain owning that state of being. Trauma traps us in the more primitive parts of the brain, and until we get out of that state, we're stuck. When that happens, we can't operate in the higher-functioning parts of the brain. You can't get any more in your head than vibrating in that space. That's what trauma does to the brain, and you don't have to survive the things I have to live in that space full-time. Trauma is trauma. It's not a contest. It all impacts the brain the same.

When I started to realize there were whole worlds that I'd missed by being locked in one place, it was like a roof I never even knew existed blew itself right off. Denial is a side effect of being out of balance. I had forgotten there could be any kind of harmony because it was stolen from me before I knew what it was. That's where we're seeing some of the density in humanity: the flat Earthers, the pandemic deniers, the climate-emergency deniers. I don't mean *dense* as in stupid, I mean *dense* as in there's not enough light getting through to enable the truth to permeate. You can't shine a light through every type of rock. Things are confusing and sometimes frightening when we don't use all the information available to us. Instead of dividing us further, we need to start asking what happened to the ones who became so deeply stuck that they're doing donuts before our eyes. We can see more clearly if we actively and intentionally use *all* the parts and systems we have available to us— mind, body, and Spirit. Things do in fact get easier and, much of the time, smoother. We can spend less time guessing. We become clearer on what is next when we become aware of whether or not we're actively employing our whole beings.

You Are an Emotionally Complex Triangle

We're going to get familiar with our three main components. Try to imagine that you're like a supercomputer. Your mind is the processor, your Spirit is the fuel or the electricity or juice, and your body is the vessel.

This is where I tell you what you may already know: Consciousness isn't something science has completely accounted for. It's one of the great mysteries. It's magic. Agent Mulder from the *X-Files* proved this. Consciousness is like an ocean and our little being, our vessel, is floating through it inside a human body (for now). Our heart sends the messages and sets the tone, and the brain operates the controls. We are souls, or energy, or the Universe having a human experience. We are all connected because we're all made of the same stuff. We're cookies from the same batch whether you like it or not.

But if we human beings are like vessels moving through life, especially through an Ocean, then we all have parts that require routine maintenance. I'm not just talking about brushing our teeth. I'm talking about the systems that make this being actually *go*. You probably know that it's hard to navigate when you're out of balance. Right? Not to mention when the waters of life get rough. Yet we collectively seem to be driving right into an inferno instead of steering away from it. In fact, we seem to be lighting more fires along the way, both figuratively and literally. Maybe this wasn't meant to be so hard, and maybe it's possible for us to reset these previous perceptions or thoughts. What if it's possible to not only steer away from catastrophe but eliminate it? We do it all the time in movies. The thing we don't seem to do all the time in movies—or life—is talk about the things that have kept us out of balance. Because those things were put there intentionally, impacting everything around us.

But when we team up with the Universe, with the Divine, with Source energy itself, we co-create. Now before you're like, *Oh, that's never going to work for me*, it *does* work for you because you are a part of the Universe. Whether you want to be or not, you are. Remember, cookies. Same batch. I want you to stop worrying about whether you're connected to Source or not, because you always have been. Even when you're not trying. And yes, even the jerks are connected to it. So why not entertain the idea that you have more influence within the Universe than you've been led to believe? That makes the idea that we maybe missed the boat on how some of this stuff works even more plausible. Historical paintings of prophetic events, visions, angels, and gods were representations of the parts of life we couldn't explain. We painted them, we wrote on walls, we carved things into rocks. We left clues for each other. Unfortunately, The Uninvited decided that they knew better. So this is where we remember that we received the manual; we've had it this whole time. We just were told we weren't allowed to use it. They lied. It's with you right now. It's in the invitation you were just given.

But this is more than an invitation; maybe it's an intervention for humanity. We've all seen that show, the one that's like a surprise party that no one wants to have. You walk in and it's a room full of people you like and love, maybe some you haven't seen in a long time, a bunch of people who care about you enough to corner you somewhere, along with the help of an overly sympathetic stranger, as they tell you, *It's time to get help, because we're worried you're going to die.* You ever been to that party? No? Well, that's where we are.

This is where you realize that as healthy as you think you might be, the family you are a part of is very, very out of balance, out of sync, and as a result, critically ill. Mortally wounded. You may not be bleeding directly, but humanity is. We all rely on the same resources (Nature), and we can no longer trust unbalanced hu(man)-made systems. We have to make new ones. The good news is, we have all the answers for how to do this. Lately, most of us have just been tuned in to the wrong channel. We all know that channel. It's full of rage, incessant division, what-ifs, not-enoughs, and competition based on inauthentic power. This is the moment where we realize that it's never been us versus them; it's always been us *and* them. Us and Us.

We're going to get into the science and the magic of that, but the first thing we're going to do, now that we've received an invitation to the intervention, is bring ourselves in for service. Maybe your vessel doesn't need any maintenance. Maybe you're in tip-top shape. In that case, this is a reminder that you also have a responsibility to the collective, and that by taking yourself in for a tune-up, your actions will have a compounded positive impact on the other vessels in the sea. Maybe a rising tide really does float all boats?

We're going to entertain the idea that maybe as we bring ourselves into The Temple of Wonder for a recalibration, a rebalancing, since we are all connected by the same Ocean of Consciousness, that the individual action might eventually impact the whole.

Reharmonize? Maybe. Pretty sure. Definitely.

Because eventually, 1:1 becomes infinity. You can tell although I have walked through hell, I'm still an eternal optimist. If anyone in The Temple of Wonder asks you where you got the invitation, you can tell them that *Optimist Prime* sent you. Sort of like the main guy from Transformers but less truck, more wand.

Into the Wonder

I'd like you to close your eyes if that's comfortable for you, and imagine that you are a triangle, or a pyramid, and that you are naming all three sides. Each is equal. Each has the same weight and focus. When you feel pointy and balanced, we're going to take our little vessels into The Temple of Wonder for some maintenance. You've got your invitation, and I want you to imagine this is a place you can go when things get hard. Here is a place where you can decide to hang your keys. A place where you can practice your magic before you hit the road again, back to being you and doing all the things you wanted to, and more, but better. It's a place where you can plant your own little corner of wonder.

When you need a refresher, a reminder, a recalibration, you can return to The Temple and remember the spectacular system that you are a part of. The system that isn't human-made, the one that precedes words and forms. The place where everything that is, ever was, and ever will be exists for eternity.

You're going to wear a lot of different hats on this journey (figuratively, not literally, but I am big on adornments), and it's going to lead you to some of the most beautiful places you've ever seen, even in the darkest of times. And you're going to see it all through your mind's eye. How's that for an adventure?

I know you may be thinking, *I don't know how to be creative,* or *I don't think that way,* or *I don't even remember my dreams.* We're going to reframe all those *I don't*s into *I am remembering how to.*

And to help, let's imagine we have the map, we have the rooms, and we have the way. If you can't see it yet in your mind, we'll get you a copy to use for as long as you need it.

Let's entertain one more idea before we go inside. Maybe it seems like we're the only "intelligent life" because the actual intelligent life is not only avoiding our Solar System, but they're also locking their doors when they drive by. It's no wonder they rarely stop in. Because if we can't get along with each other, how can they expect not to be greeted with murder? I don't blame the Universe for communicating with us through magic. It's safer for the moment. Hopefully there will be a time when this book is shown to them and we can all have a good laugh around the cosmos about how we humans used to shoot rockets at each other, and how we developed enough toxicity to destroy everything. Not to mention how we didn't *start* with solar power after the ancient Egyptians left us literal signs, and wonders of the world, letting us know *exactly* where to plug in to power up civilization. Oops.

When I say the ancient Egyptians left us literal signs, they weren't the only ones. Civilizations all over the planet left us arrows pointing at the sky. From Gunung Padang (Mountain of Light) in Asia, to the Teotihuacán (Pyramid of the Sun) in the Americas, pyramids were human-made mountains. It's time we make the connection that peoples with pyramids were pointing at the sky, trying to teach us about the importance of connecting to light, to Nature, and to the ocean within that connects us all.

We all know there's some rumors out there about the origin of the pyramids being from some off-planet civilization, and I'm not going to go all guy-with-the-wild-hair, but we know from all of what's been left behind—and thanks to Egyptologists and wisdom-keepers—that ancient Egyptians did not distinguish between religion and magic. They believed that the manipulation of written words, images, and rituals could influence the world through a divinely created force. We're going to try being open to that idea too. The ancient Egyptians often explained things as occurring "by magic," and maybe we're still trying to figure out how they built the pyramids because we haven't accepted that they already told us. We're setting the idea down that we can't use wonder as a tool.

Before we proceed into the lobby of The Temple, know this: You can't bring money, inauthentic power, or hatred inside. So think of this as the place to empty your pockets before you go through The Temple's security system.

You can bring anger, because it's okay to be angry about where you've found yourself. Most of us haven't had it easy. We're typically just trying to do our best to survive our daily lives. I hurt myself before I learned how to love myself, and I learned that the self-inflicted wounds can sometimes be the hardest to heal. It's okay to feel angry. We're going to take care of remembering what to do with it inside. We are in the process of growing as a species. It's normal to have growing pains as we learn to develop a wider multidimensional perspective. Greed, envy, and rage are part of the old paradigm. We don't need them where we're going; they don't even exist there.

Ready? We're going to move through the door.

Portal of Entry

As we step inside, the room is warm as if there's a cozy fire that you can't see. The Entryway is wide open with high ceilings. There aren't any windows, but somehow there's light coming in, streaming through the door like high beams. As we adjust to being inside, we realize everything here feels like it's built for a giant. Our vessels are tiny in comparison to our new surroundings. There is a long wall running the length of the back of the room. We can perceive what feels like every single atom of this place. It also feels a bit like we're floating. As a result, we realize how heavy and tense your body has been feeling lately. Suddenly our shoulders are so relaxed that we can't even feel them. Now that we're here, we begin to recognize that your nervous system has felt like it was carrying all the weight of humanity. All those notifications piled up. You notice that along the back wall appear two doorways framed with heavy curtains and flanked by two huge statues. Our voices are coming out of our consciousness instead of our mouths now. All we can seem to feel or say is, *WOW*. There is awe. You haven't felt like this since you were a kid. Maybe even before then. What is this feeling?

You are remembering.

Since we're going to be traveling through thousands of years of stuff, we need key translators with thousands of years of experience. You may already know that traveling to far-off places without a translator doesn't usually provide the best experience. So, we're going to have two of the best there are. You may already know them as gods or deities. Here's the thing about ascended masters: They're omnipotent. They span space and time and human dimension. Terrestrial and celestial. Their impacts and teachings are rooted in their places of origin, but communication and connection with deities crosses all borders and cultures, because deities are designed to help all humanity.

And two helpers who are here for our particular adventure *really* like to help. They have been showing up for humans seeking knowledge and change for a long time *all over the world*. Humans first came to know them through Egyptian mythology as Thoth and Anubis. Since then, they found themselves as part of Greco-Roman mythology as Hermes and Hermanubis. They have continued to appear throughout mythology and popular culture (and in Spiritual circles) all over the planet for thousands of years now. Thoth and Anubis have become widely recognized as important Spiritual beings. Thoth, keeper of knowledge with the head of the ibis bird, brings lightness and the element of air, and Anubis, with the head of the jackal, brings guidance, grounding us to the Earth. We're in good hands (maybe even god hands?).

They protect the knowledge and balance as they've done throughout history (and in Neil Gaiman shows). Through thousands of years, and after centuries of theft, looting, and the destruction of so many cultural treasures, it's amazing that any of us still know the names of these two. But here, we see Thoth standing beside The Library as Anubis stands beside The Archives. Of course they do.

Let Me Take You to Nerd Town

The Global Consciousness Project, which was originally created in the Engineering Anomalies Research Lab at Princeton University, has grown into an international, multidisciplinary collaboration of scientists and engineers. This project examines subtle correlations that may reflect the presence and activity of consciousness in the world. The data illustrates that when human consciousness becomes coherent, it may change random systems. Random number generators (RNGs) produce completely unpredictable sequences of zeros and ones, known as binary, but when a great event synchronizes the feelings of millions of people, the Global Consciousness Project data shows that RNGs change. This collective of scientists and engineers calculate one-in-a-trillion odds that the effect is due to chance. We actually do react to disturbances in the force and the data seems to show that shocking events do vibrate through the collective consciousness globally even if they originate from one location. The studies available on the Global Consciousness Project site are a rabbit hole worth exploring. This evidence suggests a unifying field of consciousness. This has been a part of the belief of so many wisdom-keepers: that we are connected through unseen forces, through Energy, through Source, through light.

The remarkable thing about Energy is the longer we tune into it, the clearer it gets. All it wants is for you to pay attention, to be in the moment, to use your sense of wonder. As the mystic, poet, and Sufi scholar Ibn Arabi shared, "When the secret of one particle of the atoms is clear, the secret of all created things, both outward and inward, is clear; and you do not see in this world or the next, anything except God."

Light is part of most creation stories (including the Big Bang). In Aztec cosmology, the Sun God was worshipped as the Source of all Life. In Shinto, Amaterasu Omikama is the sun goddess and most important deity. In Egyptian cosmology is the idea that everything was being created from the Light of Ra, or Amun-Ra. Light is the Source of our adventure and that means The Temple of Wonder is a Temple of Light.

There is so much to look at and take in here. It all feels very bright. The space between the doors looks to be made of solid gold. It includes symbols of the sun. As we focus on the back wall, the beam of light follows, and we notice a pedestal has appeared. On the pedestal is a shimmering stone tablet, but it's hard not to be captivated by the golden part of the wall. We're being drawn into the door of The Archives, as if there's a magnet pulling us.

We feel something like a nudge to our consciousness, maybe a beak. We're not sure if the statue of Thoth moved off the pedestal, but it feels like he is pointing us back to the tablet. As if to say, *Not yet.*

We notice that the tablet has changed. It now reads, "The House Rules." Yes, there was mention of this on the invitation (which now seems to have disappeared). We focus on the tablet as the rules appear one at a time.

The House Rules

After agreeing to the house rules for our adventure, we prepare to enter The Library.

We already know not to wear our shoes into The Temple of Wonder, but we also can't bring a messy vessel into The Library. This isn't a Trauma Shed. We're going to do a little cleanse before we pass through the curtain. To do this, we'll need our magic books. A little note to self, from the soul. For this first entry the aim is just to get your soul talking. You might have to get quiet first for that to happen. Again, you feel a little nudge, a gentle peck at your back. When you turn to look, there's now a little stool sitting in front of the pedestal. If you want to rest here while you make this entry, make yourself at home.

Take a breath, imagine centering yourself in the middle of your being, in all of its magnificence, the collection of your cells.

Try to imagine for this entry that we're reviewing what we know about our souls, our beings, our purpose, *and,* yes, our magic. Try to also share any existing perceptions you have around Spirituality, the soul, or the concept of magic itself. Try to consider any experiences you may have had so far in your life with these things. Think about how these things may have shown up.

After you've made your list, consider how you came to know or feel this way about these things. You may want to make a *"How do I know this?"* column beside the items you've listed. Did you learn it? Did you experience it for yourself? Did someone tell you? We aren't looking for judgment around this list (or its sources). This is a brain dump. A cleanse. We are just noting clues so that we can follow

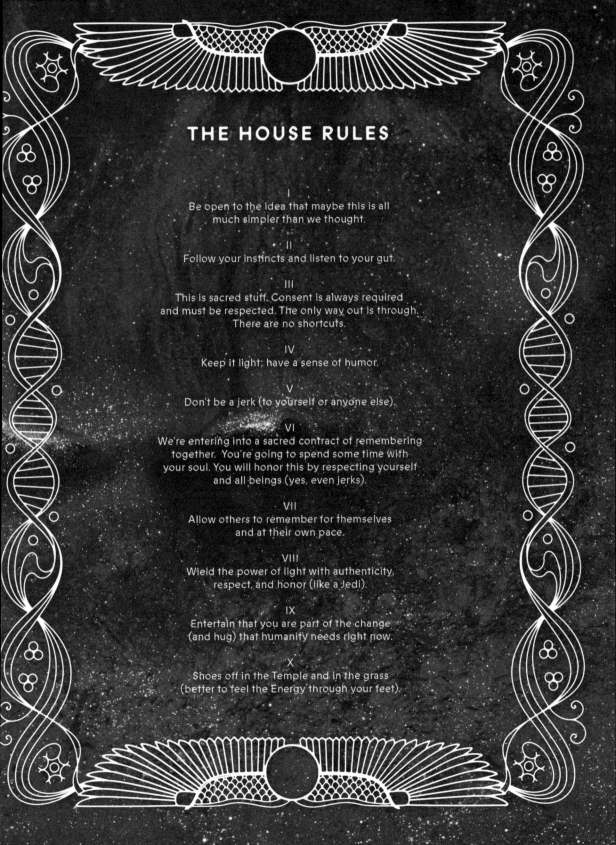

THE HOUSE RULES

I
Be open to the idea that maybe this is all
much simpler than we thought.

II
Follow your instincts and listen to your gut.

III
This is sacred stuff. Consent is always required
and must be respected. The only way out is through.
There are no shortcuts.

IV
Keep it light; have a sense of humor.

V
Don't be a jerk (to yourself or anyone else).

VI
We're entering into a sacred contract of remembering
together. You're going to spend some time with
your soul. You will honor this by respecting yourself
and all beings (yes, even jerks).

VII
Allow others to remember for themselves
and at their own pace.

VIII
Wield the power of light with authenticity,
respect, and honor (like a Jedi).

IX
Entertain that you are part of the change
(and hug) that humanity needs right now.

X
Shoes off in the Temple and in the grass
(better to feel the Energy through your feet).

them. As we finish the entry in our book, we notice the tablet now displays *a map* of The Temple. A map of our *adventure*. Past The Library is a Green House and a Garden, a Hall of Mirrors . . . *Was that wonder we just felt?*

You haven't just been invited here; you are needed here. That's why we're here in this particular space and time. How we got here *is* part of this adventure. This world *needs* our particular brand of magic to help rebalance the scales. As we move through the rooms in this Temple, we're going to remember how. We're going to follow our breadcrumbs to retrace our steps and honor the steps of those before us. We're going to find the clues left behind. The Universe knows what to do; meaning it knows what's possible and not possible. It knows all the routes available to us, whether *we* can perceive them or not.

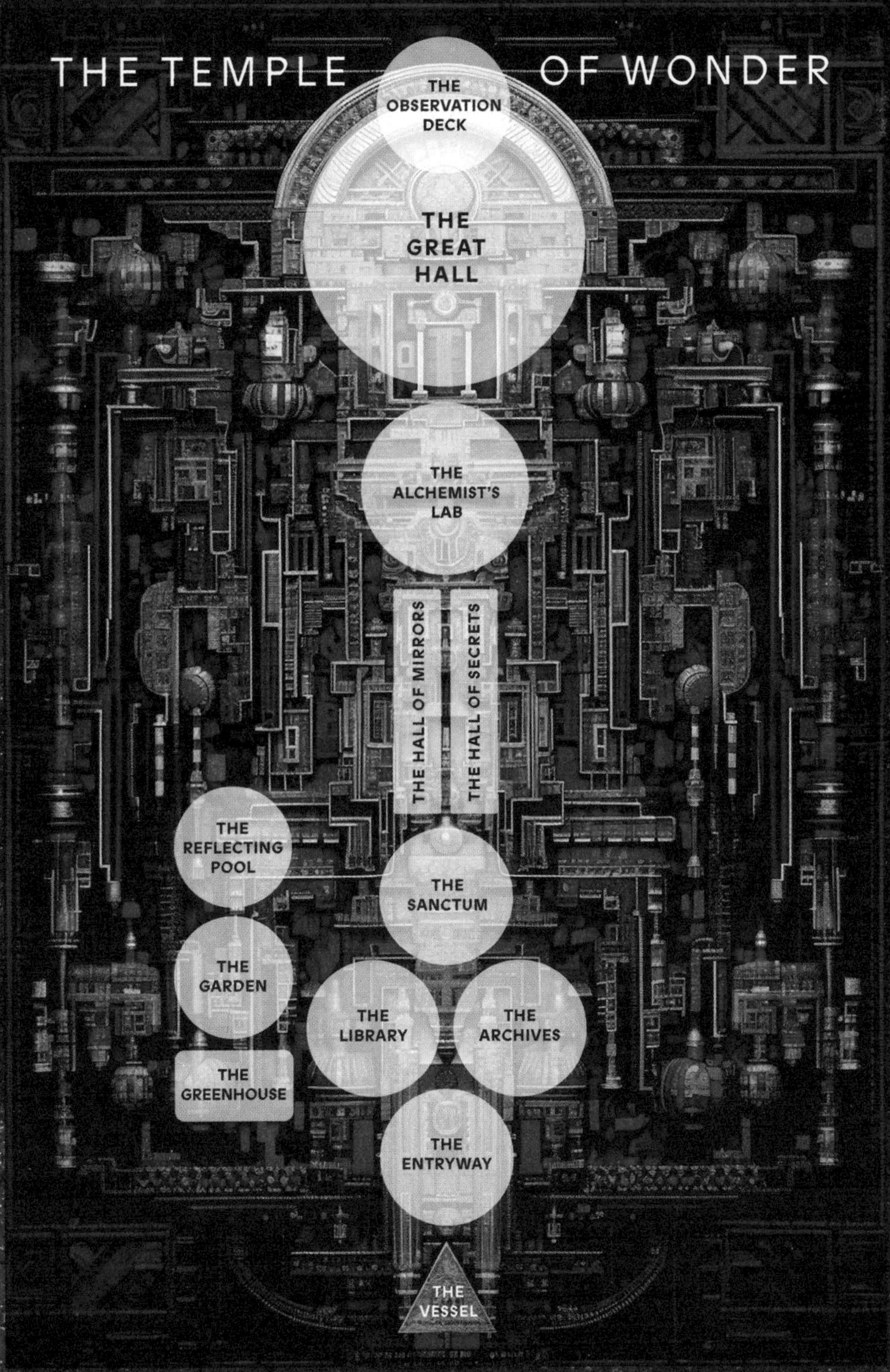

THE TEMPLE   OF WONDER

THE
OBSERVATION
DECK

THE
GREAT
HALL

THE
ALCHEMIST'S
LAB

THE HALL OF MIRRORS

THE HALL OF SECRETS

THE
REFLECTING
POOL

THE
SANCTUM

THE
GARDEN

THE
LIBRARY

THE
ARCHIVES

THE
GREENHOUSE

THE
ENTRYWAY

THE
VESSEL

CHAPTER THREE

THE LIBRARY

THE RESET

A s we walk through the curtain (shoes off, of course), we enter a two-story space with shelves upon shelves of books. It's the biggest library you've ever seen, let alone been inside. There are rows of columns lining the space leading up to the vaulted ceiling housing a dome of light surrounded with wings. It felt as if Thoth winked at you on the way in, and you realize now he probably did. Although the space is sacred, there seems to be a sense of humor about it. If he has all the knowledge ever available to him, of course things wouldn't seem so serious, or dire. He'd probably know all the systems and reasons, the context, architectures, and frameworks. No heavy burdens of trying to answer burning existential questions. No need for search engines. To be the steward of all that wisdom and intelligence throughout time. To *still* have to watch us humans hunting around for clues to who we are when everything we needed to know has been right there, in front of us this whole time. It's probably a little funny.

Everything would be lighter, as light as a feather.

This Library of knowledge that we stand in together is a place untouched by human systems of oppression.

What do we know, really, about being human? What might The Uninvited have had us miss? Since this whole adventure is rooted in intention, the only thing you need to do right now is set your intention to reset and be open to the idea that this whole life thing has been made so much more complicated than it ever was, on purpose.

It's a good thing we have a map, both for this adventure and this whole Spirituality thing. If we go back to the beginning, and to this idea of being on an adventure of light, we stumble upon another clue. *Let there be light* and *in the beginning was the word*. Light, frequency, and vibration are foundational elements of life in the Universe. We know this because of science. As Nikola Tesla said, "If you want to find the secrets of the universe, think in terms of energy, frequency, and vibration."

If we're talking about light for a moment, and the things we can see and the things we can't, it was alchemist Sir Isaac Newton who used a prism to break white light into a spectrum. Light is made of a spectrum of components. That's not just the cover of a Pink Floyd album. It's science. It's also a breadcrumb from Source.

It's a clue that there *is* more than meets the eye and that sometimes we need tools from our environment, like a prism or a quill, to help us decipher all the parts, to help us take note of what may be under the surface, or behind the curtain, if you will. As you make notes, you notice that there's a little chart carved into the side of where you're sitting. Ancient graffiti. It's rough, as though it's been pecked by a beak. It's a little cheat sheet for The Library.

It feels a little bit like the Dewey Decimal System. We can almost hear Thoth: *Which came first, the ibis or the egg?*

Noted.

Deity Decimal System

- 000–099 = General Information

- 100–199 = Collected Philosophy

- 200–299 = Religion & Spirituality

- 300–399 = Culture

- 400–499 = Language

- 500–599 = Science

- 600–699 = Medicine & Technology

- 700–799 = Creativity & Divinity

- 800–899 = Literature of Civilizations

- 900–999 = History & Geography

You realize we're in the 500s: astronomy.

Working on Our Light Moves

According to NASA, our galaxy, the Milky Way, has over 200 billion stars in it, with most of them being larger than the star we call our sun. Our galaxy measures over one hundred thousand light-years in size. The light-year is a measure of distance, *not time*. A light-year is the distance light travels in one year (5.88 trillion miles). That means it would take light *one hundred thousand* years (*light speed is 186,282 miles per second*)—to go from one end of our galaxy to the other—and our galaxy is just one tiny part of the Universe. *If* we were *able* to successfully travel at the speed of light, time would stop, because at the speed of light, there is no passage of time. Proxima Centauri is the closest star to us (other than the sun). It's (*only*) 4.25 light-years away. It *still* would take us approximately 6,300 years to get there from Earth if traveling at the speed of light.

There are *trillions* of galaxies in the Universe (that we know of). NASA's James Webb Space Telescope has produced the deepest and sharpest infrared deep field image of the distant Universe to date, which has helped show us the sheer vastness of space. Known better as Webb's First Deep Field, the image of galaxy cluster SMACS 0723 is overflowing with detail. Thousands of galaxies—including the faintest objects ever observed in the infrared—have appeared in Webb's view for the first time. This slice of the Universe covers just a patch of sky that NASA has

estimated is "approximately the size of a grain of sand held at arm's length by someone on the ground."

Some of the pictures we're seeing of star systems and galaxies from the James Webb telescope are finally showing us things as they were 4.5 billion years ago. In these images we humans get to see what happened in the past. In everyday life, we tend to think of the Universe in three dimensions (up, down, north, south, east, and west). In the theory of relativity, there's actually four dimensions. Spacetime is a model that combines the three dimensions of space and one dimension of time into a single four-dimensional continuum.

String theory, which originated from particle physics of the twentieth century, theorizes there at least ten dimensions.

So let's not act like there's no room for wonder. We've got lots of dimensions to hold it. When we leave room for mystery and discovery, we find surprise and delight. Everything that is, ever was, and will be is a part of this system. The Universe is constantly expanding. We can move through it because we're made of this stuff.

Star Children

You've probably heard this next thing before. Maybe it was from someone in a tie-dyed tank top at a music festival, or maybe from astronomer Carl Sagan or physicist Stephen Hawking. We are made of literal star stuff: oxygen, carbon, hydrogen, nitrogen, calcium, phosphorus, potassium, sulfur, sodium, chlorine, magnesium, and trace elements. As we move through The Temple, we will reconnect, reclaim, and refuel with the light—but just like in Earth school, in order to practice it, we first have to study it.

We are lights in a body. We are stars in a vessel. Lightning in a bottle. We are all made of light, we all emanate frequency, and we all create vibration. Your "vibration" is how we might describe your state of being. Everything in the Universe is made up of energy vibrating at different frequencies. *Even jerks.* Human beings

and everything in the natural world have a resonance. We all vibrate, and as the Global Consciousness Project has illustrated, sometimes we even sync up.

You may already be rolling your eyes, but energy isn't really so hippy-dippy or ambiguous. *It's science, man.* In a 2018 article featured in *Scientific American* aptly titled "The Hippies Were Right: It's All about Vibrations, Man!," the author discusses the now-accepted resonance theory of consciousness. In his 2003 book *Sync: How Order Emerges from Chaos in the Universe, Nature and Daily Life,* mathematician Steven Strogatz found that massive systems can somehow synchronize themselves from the tiniest of electrons in a superconductor to pacemaker cells in our hearts or the millions of neurons that must fire together to control our breathing. All these things happen spontaneously. He illustrates that although these phenomena might seem unrelated, at a deeper level there is a connection, as if the Universe has an overwhelming desire for order. At the heart of our universe is a steady, insistent beat, even some of the static on TV sets or the radio comes from deep space. The clues point to the Universe having a resonance that seems to have a connection with consciousness itself.

So while we're here in The Library, we're going to set down any judgment that the term *vibes* may bring, because the science is simple. We're all made of natural elements, and it's time we remember how to act like it.

We lost our sense of wonder when we separated from Nature. I'm sure you've heard (or had) the concept of life *flashing* before our eyes when we have near-death experiences or trauma; maybe the light at the end of the tunnel is somewhere in, or through, the stars. We don't need to wait until the moment of transition to know energy. To know the source of creation. When we think of these images in our minds—the light, the floating, the magic, and the majesty—it could be similarly described as flying through a nebula, a place where stars are said to be born. Maybe it's where souls are born too? Should we bring up how much the most detailed and recent photo of a black hole looks a lot like a human cervix? Talk about breadcrumbs, both key tools for creation.

Now that we've recognized that we probably know some things from science, some things from a person in a tank top at a music festival, and some stuff from our families or lived experience, we can start to catalog it. There is some other stuff we know as human beings, and we know some of those things because someone in history decided to carve them into a rock. If not for the Rosetta Stone, we would not have been able to translate whole languages. Hieroglyphs would have remained a total mystery had people not taken the time to literally spell it out. We leave clues for each other. It's what we've always done. It's also time to return the Rosetta Stone to Egypt. Returning all sacred objects to their original owners is a part of reconciliation of the hard truth. They're stolen.

Anatomy of Spirit

We seem to be getting nudged over to another section in The Library. It's just beyond the ones near where we were. As we move between two giant stacks of bookshelves in the 900s section, there's a sign: ALL HISTORY. ALL DIMENSIONS. We're standing among the collective history of every civilization in every dimension that has ever lived. How many thousands, or hundreds of thousands, or more years of history may exist here? As you lean in more closely to the shelves, you notice that these books are made of light. They're like holograms. You are entranced and move to touch one of the books, *Ancient Civilizations*. We hold the holographic magical light. We *are* the magical light.

If we imagine that we can shift into that *star stuff of ours*, we can restore our sense of wonder. We can consider that we used to be able to hear things we don't hear now. We used to get help from Nature and animal beings. We used to talk to everything that was a part of Nature. We used to be able to pick up vibrations and frequencies. See things with our eyes closed. We are built to dream on demand.

We used to live in societies that didn't need to play Broken Telephone because everyone was listening to the same source, or channel. We knew when something wasn't true in our bones, in our souls, and in our minds *all at the same time*. We worked in collaboration and balance with Nature. We had tribal law, we did ceremonies, we honored Nature, its beings, and each other. When we got an omen, we worked together to decipher the clues. When we worked as a collective to put it all

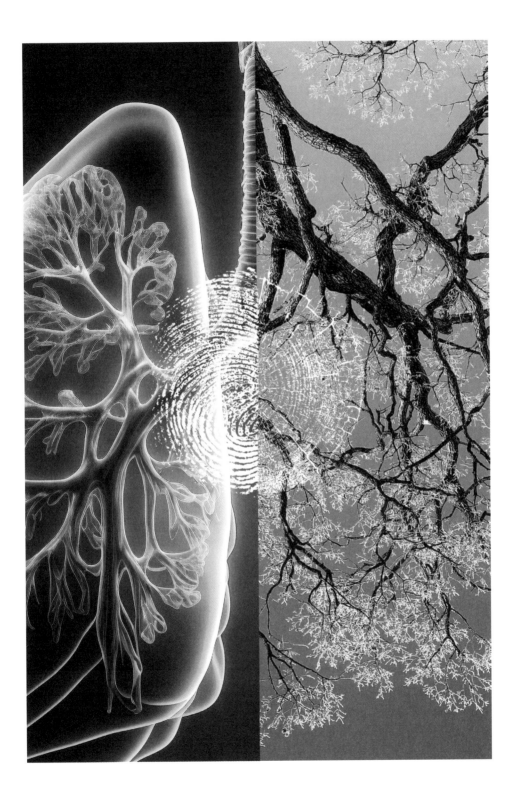

together, instead of muddying the water, it became clear what we needed to do, and we did it together. As a result, we made magic all over the planet.

This was how all those pyramids got built. They were never tombs. They were temples to the light.

To further enrich the adventure, we each get a unique brand of potion to bring to the party. We each carry a power, a magic absolutely unique to you. You know that good old human thing we call "chemistry" where you "hit it off with someone"? That's called alchemy, but we'll get more into that later.

For now, we're on the move again and we're following the nudge across the aisle of The Library into the 600s section. A sign hangs over this particular row: 611: HUMAN ANATOMY & 612: NEUROSCIENCE. There's a table in between these two stacks of books. The light shimmers over a book full of photographs.

Let Me Take You to Nerd Town

There are images of commonalities among human beings and natural systems placed side by side: an image of a human lung side by side with the extended branches of a tree; another shows a cross-section of a tree trunk side by side with a human fingerprint.

In three photos shown side by side there is a close-up image of a leaf, its channels and networks illustrated; in the next image there are blood vessels in the human heart; they look exactly like the next image of a network of rivers in the Amazon. Differential geometry in Nature, oscillating curves of flow in Nature. The human brain even mirrors the Universe, two of the most challenging and complex systems in Nature. The cosmic network of galaxies mirrors the network of neuronal cells in the human brain.

Our brain functions thanks to a wide neuronal network that is estimated to contain approximately 69 billion neurons. The observable Universe is composed of a cosmic web of at least 100 billion galaxies (and counting, thanks again NASA). Within both of these seemingly completely different systems, only 30 percent of each are composed of galaxies and neurons. Within both systems, galaxies and

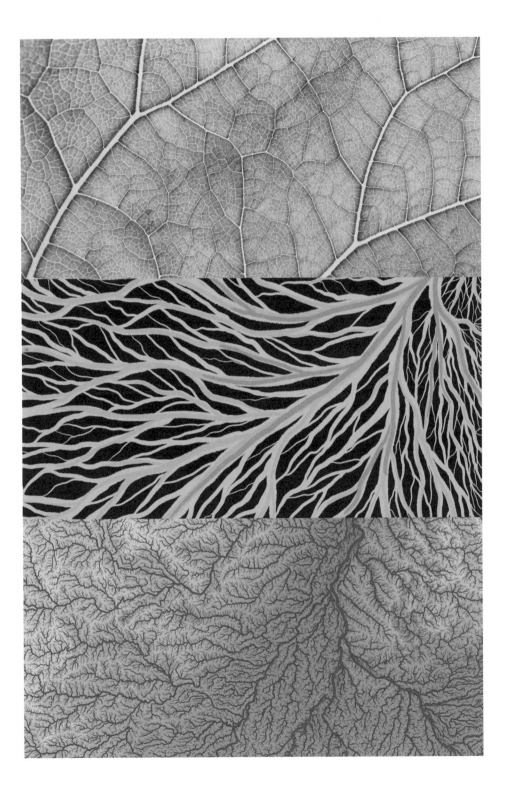

neurons arrange themselves as long nodes between the filaments. Filaments, yes, like a light bulb. Gives new meaning to the light bulb being used as a symbol for an idea, doesn't it? The most fascinating (and wondrous) piece of this is that in both systems, the brain and the Universe, 70 percent of the distribution of energy is composed of components playing a mysterious role. Water in the brain and dark energy, or dark matter, in the observable Universe. We are both made of 70 percent mystery.

We're now being nudged back to the 500s section, to the place where we left our things. On the table beside the carved chart there are now three objects: a small pine cone, a snail shell, and a baby pineapple. Nature is a phenomenal architect. These little objects all contain big math. The Fibonacci sequence (0, 1, 1, 2, 3, 5, 8, 13, 21, 34 . . .) can be found across all of Nature: plants, animals, weather structures, star systems—it is ever-present in the Universe. The sequence doesn't just appear at a high level in Nature but right down to the number of petals on flowers. Most have 3 (lilies), 5 (rose hips), 8 (Cosmea), 13 (daisies), 21 (chicory), 34, 55, or 89 (Asteraceae). Go ahead and try counting the petals (gently!) the next time you meet a flower and just try not yelling "Fibonacci!"

The Fibonacci sequence can also be found in computer algorithms, search techniques, heap data structure, and graphs. It's everywhere. It even helps create organic-looking compositions for human designers as in ikebana floral design. Nature is a masterful mathematician *and* a phenomenal art director. Speaking of which, let's move out of the stacks and toward the entrance to The Greenhouse. We approach a massive iron and glass door that has varieties of flora and fauna etched into its various panes. Beyond the door is a sea of green—quite a shift from Nerd Town.

I know this has all been a lot to consider, so we're going to pull our little vessels over for a second before we move into The Greenhouse. We are beginning the process of reading a deeply ingrained instruction manual that we didn't know we had. We're able to imagine what these similarities mean and what might actually be just through the keyhole. I hope you're already feeling a little lighter and full of wonder than when you came into The Library. You may want to imagine leaving the desk and sitting down in one of the comfier chairs, maybe one near the

window. Once you've found your spot, imagine that you're reviewing the fundamentals of what you may have picked up as we made this trip through The Library.

Think about what you know about your soul, your being, your purpose, and by default, *your* magic. What ingredients might make up the potion that is you? What lights you up? Write about the first memory you have of the feeling of wonder. When was there a time where you got goosebumps or a shiver because something struck a chord so deeply inside of you that you just *knew* something? What was it? Are there any other times you can remember where this happened? Write them down. Make the space for the wonder to come.

Next, try to think about any perceptions you may have about Spirituality or magic. Did anything in this overview trigger a certain reaction or feeling? Write down both your perceptions and the feelings you got as part of those perceptions.

Are you able to think about how you came to know these things? What parts may you have learned by yourself and what parts have you been told? How might you overcomplicate situations in your own life where some of the simplicity of Nature could assist you? Another way to look at this is to think about what Nature might do. How might you be able to apply similar principles to your life in order to stand more firmly in your wonder?

It's time to spend some time with Nature. When you're ready, I'll meet you in The Greenhouse. No surprise, we'll be keeping our shoes off.

CHAPTER FOUR

THE GREENHOUSE & GARDEN

THE GREAT SEPARATION

As you begin to connect the dots and follow the breadcrumbs, you're going to notice a lot of new things about the world. Nature is going to suddenly feel as if it's reaching out to you for a hug. But the first thing I want to make clear before we move farther into The Greenhouse is that Nature doesn't take cash. You can't build a relationship with Nature by buying it. The investment is time and energy. As I promised, the return on investment will make you rich . . . in wonder.

As we stand here in The Greenhouse, we are separated from The Garden by glass. This pane of separation prevents us from deep connection. We exist at a surface level as long as we are inside The Greenhouse. We weren't always separated from Nature; we used to be in unison, but it wasn't in the best interest of The Uninvited to have us communicating directly with Source. You can't have inauthentic power and control over humans who are in communion with the real power of Nature. If we are connected to Source and we eliminate the broken telephone, that means we're not going to be motivated by what's being sold to us.

Wisdom keeper Ayan Ayangat, of the Mongolian Union of Ancestral Traditions, shared a powerful message for our times from her ancestors:

Indigenous people are rooted in their ecosystem. Because they are deeply and closely connected with nurturing the environment, they have their own unique lifestyle, education, and cultural heritage . . . Our vivid earth needs diverse cultures to sustain its brilliance. There are significant advantages to having Indigenous cultures come from their unique and close connection with Mother Earth. If mankind realizes this connection, it can drop the globalization efforts then only focus on gains and profits, and instead start creating harmonious places for everybody, to let their own unique cultures flourish in the eternal circle of life . . . So please return to your consciousness before it's too late.

And with that, we move into The Garden.

Healing Nature

Stepping out of The Greenhouse and into The Garden, it feels like the first time you noticed how much everything in Nature *moves*. As we move into The Garden, the scent hits you. The rich earth. Greenery and wildlife. You may see or feel other Nature beings.

How many sounds it makes without the hum or buzz of the human voice, or without all the noisy (and often beautiful) things we've created. There are trees of every kind, and the birds are singing high in the branches. There are flowers of every color in every state of bloom, being tended to by butterflies and bees. You are witnessing collaboration *and* reciprocity personified. Close your eyes and imagine yourself there. You can settle into the grass if you like, or you may decide to sit with your back against one of the trees, just like Alice . . .

How could we have ever separated ourselves from this? Think about what it means to be separated from Nature, to be separated from one another. Western society's perception of the natural world in particular has changed greatly over time. In ancient civilizations, there was the idea of a cosmology that viewed the

Universe as one unified organism. Human beings were only one aspect of the overall function of Nature. We all lived within the system: It was us; we were it. This was the time where humans knew that the Universe was sentient, that Nature was synonymous with our lives.

The second phase started to take shape as modern science did. In this phase, the natural world was no longer viewed as an organism, but as a machine. And humans began to believe that we could learn the inner workings of that machine. We thought we might be able to figure out how it worked by dismantling it. We didn't understand that it might be *us* who needed the maintenance, not Nature. That perhaps we weren't meant (or able) to understand life by taking it apart and trying to put it back together again. We began to see ourselves as apart from and outside of Nature. We took ourselves out of the frame. We began observing instead of experiencing.

In the third phase we began to treat Nature as a resource we could exploit. We began to do the same to other beings, including each other. We stopped leaving room for wonder.

This is where humanity kind of lost our keys, where we separated from Nature. No wonder. Literally. No wonder. No keys. Wonder is the sacred knowledge of Source. The path leads us back here to reconnect us with the natural world, to reignite our spark. In the beginning, Spirituality and magic weren't separated. Spirituality *was* magical.

Speaking of keys and wonder, Eastern philosophy and Nature-based practices like Taoism and Shinto give us insight into how a relationship with Nature can become a way of life. Taoism has a unique sense of abundance. If all things in the Universe are well and balanced, then a society is a community of abundance. This view encourages both systems and people to take care of our connection to Nature. Shinto also holds the view that Nature is a presence that is inescapable and that our individual relationships with the environment are a portal to our higher selves.

Nature is inherently full of magic. It is in everything, everywhere. Source energy and many Nature beings aren't male or female. They are nonbinary, like me and maybe like you or someone you know. Energy is nonbinary. It is a perfect balance of the Taoist principle of yin and yang. When we are in balance and harmony, the magic occurs. This is where energy lives. If we entertain that human-ity is getting back in sync with Nature, we can entertain the idea that maybe the concept of energy being nonbinary is a bigger part of Nature than The Uninvited ever wanted to acknowledge. The nonbinary, gender-fluid, two-spirit people have been part of Nature-based civilizations throughout history. Part of reconnecting is remembering that this is entirely natural.

How do we do that? How do we go back and forward at the same time? We follow Nature. We trust its speed. We leave room for its wisdom. We have ignored its cycles and therefore ourselves. We haven't been slowing down in the winter. Most of us don't and many of us can't slow down at all. We have been in a state of constant production. We have lived in a society where productivity is king, and self-care is either scoffed at or turned into its own industry. Another engine for selling products that trick us into believing we've found (temporary) happiness. No wonder we're exhausted. We have a beautiful planet and yet a crisis for people to find housing. Species are being made extinct because we are removing ecosystems. You'd think it might be enough to make The Uninvited stop and think about what happens when we don't rest. If we don't sleep? If we don't reset? Maybe that's why they seem to like robots so much?

There is great meaning behind Nature's cycles and systems that can help us live better, more gently, and with more grace to help us glide easily through the chal-lenges of life. Without the seasons, the bleak desolation of winter, the time of rest, Nature wouldn't have the energy for the needed growth spurt in spring. Same for us. We have ignored the cycles and therefore ourselves. We haven't been slowing down in the winter. No wonder we can find ourselves in a depression, in the cavern created from the hole we've dug into the Earth (or a couch). When we work in connection with Source energy, the world opens up—and offers healing. And not just us, but every being who lives here. We awaken one of the most powerful forces in Nature: consciousness. This is part of what we've forgotten: how to connect to Nature, how to be in a relationship with the Universe.

We have been conditioned to see the Earth as somehow less alive than it is, as if Earth isn't as creative and purposeful as we are.

Every moment of every day the Earth creates crystals, gems, and minerals under the surface, by alchemy, by wonder, by magic. As we continue to wander down the garden path, we notice there is a formation of rocks ahead. They're cloaked in ivy and moss, but you see there's an opening. You make your way toward it.

Caves have great mystical importance to civilizations far beyond the shelter they provided. Shamanic teachings speak of the idea that these are gateways to the Spirit world: the Shaman's Cave. We have recognized the majesty and divinity of Nature since we could carve things into rocks. Some of the earliest discovered pieces of art—in caves, no less—were depictions of Nature. Animals, plants, and ourselves. There is nothing but magic to come from creating a relationship with Nature. Many of us have begun to remember that where the planets are in relation to where we are impacts us.

Let's anchor ourselves here in this rock formation. Imagine your hands touching the cool stone surface. We sat near a tree that was likely hundreds of years old and now we're touching something millions, billions of years old. We can imagine the energy of the ancient rock helping us ground and connect back into the real information superhighway. Nature.

Let Me Take You to Nerd Town

We are meant to be in communion with Nature. We are meant to be connected with each other and to care about each other. The whole "hippy dippy" approach is actually the way forward. And in fact, what is in our hearts is more important than what is in our brains, literally. The HeartMath Institute is a nonprofit organization whose work has not only been peer-reviewed but also validated by successful outcomes across childhood education, the military, and health care institutions like the Mayo Clinic. The Institute finds fault with the medical focus of the last few decades that says the body is there to carry our brains around. We've been told most of our lives that the brain is in control of everything. However, studies done at the Institute, referenced in Tom Shadyac's amazing documentary *I Am*, have shown that it's actually the opposite: 90 to 95 percent of our nerves are carrying information from the body to the brain, not the other way around. Our heart sends way more information to our brain than our brain sends to our heart. The ancient Egyptians seemed to know this well before we all figured it out. During mummification, the brain was essentially thrown away; it was the heart that was the focus. It was the heart that got the jewels.

We know our hearts beat, but what most of us don't think about is that there's a space in between each beat, a pause. By taking readings of the interstitial beats of the heart, HeartMath discovered that those pauses actually contain a lot of information. They can even reveal a person's emotional state. If you think of the heart as a carrier wave, our emotions are actually modulating the heart signal. Positive emotional states, particularly compassionate states, are the healthiest for humans. Research shows that experiencing positive emotional states can actually renew our physiology. Positive feelings and emotions such as love, connection, care, gratitude, and compassion actually have a positive impact on our body. When we are happy and feeling connected, we actually receive healing from our own bodies. Our heart beats out a very different message in its optimal state versus if the heart is sending a stressful or a negative emotional message. Research shows that those negative patterns have an impact on how our body processes. They also seem to inhibit our brain, and as a result we can't think as clearly. It's as if stress and negativity produce interference. Have you ever been angry and said something hurtful that you didn't mean? I'm going to assume you said yes to that question, or there's a good chance you *might* be a robot.

When we've calmed down and the anger has subsided, we get moments of clarity where we can't fathom that we said whatever awful thing may have come out of our mouths.

Anger is actually the body's equivalent to having blown a gasket—and likely why we call it that when someone flies off the handle. When a car blows a literal gasket, it means the channels are no longer sealed and different fluids, oil, and gases contained in the car escape the combustion chamber. When the engine gets overheated, an increase in thermal pressure puts too much strain on the gasket. I know you're probably thinking, *Is this witch also a mechanic?*

So what happens when we get angry in our own vessel? So much negative force or energy floods our system that our hearts pump out messages to our brain that the body can't process. Our thinking is impacted. It's not clear. Anger literally makes us less intelligent until it passes and the heart recovers its natural rhythm. Our positive emotions, however, lead to increased inner harmony, clearer thinking, and better performance. This is because it's the mode from which we are designed to operate. We function better when we process our anger, when we are in harmony with not just ourselves, but others.

This is the science of separation. What does it do to us when we're separate from each other, from Source, from Nature, from ourselves? What does it do to us when we're in a near-constant state of rage or pain? We know what it does because we are living in a world where we are so close to the edge that we are being bombarded by trauma. But when we go into Nature, it's possible for us to reconnect with the Spirit of everything. We can ask for help. We can create connection and actively and intentionally participate in the greatest and most powerful relationship we will ever have.

Archaeological evidence of civilizations before and after the Neolithic era shows a long-held sense of identification with the well-being of the Earth. This was exemplified by noticing the way the planets had a connection and relationship to the sun. People who live close to the land today also notice our connection to and reliance on insects, animals, plants, and especially trees. This relationship once resulted in a mutually beneficial and reciprocal world. In many parts of the globe, that chain of wisdom still hasn't been broken. It is now up to us, as descendants of colonizers, immigrants, and settlers, to amplify the voices of the wisdom-keepers, the language-keepers, and those who have always stood in service to Nature. They hold the wisdom to right our collective ship. Time is up for The Uninvited.

Part of this work is energetic. Remember, celestial and terrestrial. Along the way on this journey through The Temple, we will look back and work through how we can begin to do the work to transmute the horror of the energy we can hold in our ancestries. Now that we have begun to understand what happens when we introduce anger into the system, we are going to set ourselves on the path of reconnecting with Nature without anger, grounded and rooted in our own intention of reconnecting with respect and reverence. As we continue through the rock formation we stand in a clearing of old cedars. There is a scattering of logs, and instinctively we move toward them to be in the center of the circle with these ancient trees. We know they're alive, but we don't often think of trees as being as sentient as humans.

A core piece of resetting and reconnecting to Nature is recognizing and honoring that non-human beings are *not* lesser beings; they are fellow biological beings living within an intricately woven and connected fabric. We're all on the same web. Yes, spiders too, and they're not creepy; their medicine is creativity, and their web is part of their consciousness. Favor please: They're just making magic in the world. Don't kill them, just put them outside.

The days of assuming that what we do on one end doesn't impact the other are over.

Just because Nature may not speak with words doesn't mean we shouldn't learn how to speak its language. All beings in Nature possess a connection to consciousness. We have always been partners. We just forgot how to act like it. We forgot how to connect. Yet we still seem to know how to recognize sacred spaces in Nature all over the planet. There are more magical rocks than just mountains and pyramids. Some even come from above.

As we move out of the circle of cedars, we notice a trail of stones leading farther into the garden.

Rock, Paper, Symbology

As we follow the trail, we notice the stones are progressing in size, and we're standing in another circle, this time surrounded by huge rocks stacked on end. A rock garden. Humans have been arranging stones for sacred purposes for thousands of

years. We've also been visiting them. Mecca in Saudi Arabia is likely a sacred place you've heard of. What you may not have heard is that a key component of the pilgrimage to Mecca is centered around a sacred black stone from the heavens. It's said to be meteorite, the spent remains of an asteroid coming through the Earth's atmosphere. Islamic tradition holds that this sacred stone was placed there by the Prophet Muhammad five years before his first revelation. The treasure is now framed in silver in the eastern corner of the Kaaba in Mecca. Approximately 2 million visit each year to touch or kiss the black stone, as Muhammad himself was said to have done centuries ago. The stone is seen as a marker of the center of the world and also the Gate of Heaven.

Human beings have not only had a long history of visiting and collecting sacred rocks, but also of exploring living in harmony with the Spirit of Nature by way of geomancy. *Geomancy* comes from Latin, meaning the practice of seeking knowledge of the future or the unknown by supernatural means, through the divine. Divining isn't just for earth; you may have heard about it for water. In dowsing, or water divining, two rods or a single forked stick can be used to detect underground water sources. We've been doing this around the world for a long time.

One of the oldest of systems is the Chinese tradition of feng shui, a practice that uses energy to harmonize individuals with their surrounding natural environment. The term *feng shui* translates to "wind-water." We may have begun to remember that the practice of geomancy might be as crucial to our survival as air and water. As climate change wreaks more and more havoc in our lives and ecosystems, many of us are realizing the importance of prioritizing the health of our environment. This ability to work in meaningful collaboration with Nature has always been part of us; it's part of our Spirit. It's always been right there. Yet most of us take it for granted, as it's always there and it's largely unremarkable to us because we've forgotten how to communicate with it.

While we're in this part of The Garden, I want to reintroduce you to our closest allies. There are five of them, not four: earth, air, fire, water, *and* Spirit. You can count them on your fingers. Five points, like a star, like a pentacle. Because that symbol of the star with the circle around it isn't actually a symbol of evil or darkness, as too many of us have been led to believe; it is representative of the five elements (including Spirit) all within a circle of protection. No wonder The Uninvited didn't like it, right? It probably didn't make them feel so hot because it was designed to protect us against them. No wonder they wanted it out of here; the elements are powerful allies.

Water is the first element we meet in the womb. It knows us, it soothes us and cleanses us, but it can also rise up and become a force so destructive it impacts the seemingly immovable element of earth. You're probably figuring out we started with earth here. It's terra firma. Our foundation, the cornerstone. It is as much a magician and alchemist as there's ever been. And do you know why it feels so good to sit around a campfire? Because we've been doing it since the beginning. We held rituals and connected (in a circle) around fires. Sometimes we burned our dead. Sometimes we simply used it to cook our food. Fire collaborates. It is the most transformative element. The light. Air is a more ethereal element that prepares us for acceptance of Spirit. The only times we can perceive air is when it's cold and we can see the breath from our lungs, or when we feel the breeze—or are hit with the brutal winds and force it is capable of exerting. Without it, without this thing we cannot see that surrounds us, we would not be experiencing life. The fifth element, Spirit, is going to get its own space in The Hall of Secrets. That is who is going to deliver the message that called you here. Surprise!

So, why did The Uninvited play such a big role in shutting all this down? Because it's impossible to control and manipulate people when they are in direct communication with Source. All these system failures we are witnessing the last few years are because they're against Nature. They were never sustainable, and Nature *always* wins.

Let's sit down for a minute here on the rocks to ground all this information. Part of reconnecting to Nature is making space to enjoy its education in a Garden.

Raves, Plants, and Shamanism

The wisdom of Nature includes plant medicine, but it isn't a mandatory component to the journey of reconnecting to Nature. Ayahuasca, though recently seen as being synonymous with shamanism itself, is a specifically South American plant medicine. The shaman of Peru, known as P'akkos, wisdom-keepers of Nature-based practices, are now traveling *and* having people travel to them to share their medicine.

Practitioners of earth-based healing techniques are known by all different names around the world: Shaman, Babaylan, Yuta, Bruja, Dukun, Curandero, Hogon, Druid, Babalawo, Völva, Wu, and Taltos, to name just a few. Though all these local magical people are called different names and may utilize different medicines, what they all have in common is sound—the tones, the chants, the rattle, the drums. Some things require that a vibration be met with sound and word. This is the meaning of oral tradition of wisdom-keeping; some things are too sacred to be broadly published.

When a human being hears percussion at approximately 220 beats per minute, they enter a shamanic state of consciousness. Can you believe it? No wonder I went to raves and loved jungle music (*200 bpm on average*). It literally raised me up from the depths of my teenage pain and angst. DJs have, in fact, saved my life. I had transcendental experiences back then *because* of the drum (*okay, maybe a bit because of the drugs*).

How did humans know about this? How did we figure out that we could get into a higher state of consciousness and deeper alignment with Nature using a particular beat? Here's how: Plants told us. Maybe people were smoking them, or maybe people were just communicating with them, but they told us. Eventually a local magical person, or a woodpecker, decided to tap out that beat. Whomever it was, it was knowledge we were given by Nature. By the divine. There is nothing negative about being able to commune with Nature.

We can get started with our own percussion as part of our journey through The Temple. Here's an actual witch craft: Create a rattle using found objects from

Nature, pebbles, sand, or rice, beans, or beads in an empty can, glass, or plastic container. We can remember how to connect with plants without having to ingest anything.

These days I don't just like jungle music, I have a jungle. I have over one hundred plants. Somehow, they're so happy they seem to just keep multiplying. I used to not be able to keep a plant alive, but now, I listen to them. They tell me what they need. It's not just "my" plants. It's other people's too. I spend so much of my time these days talking to Nature and working in collaboration with Spirit, that they *know* I'm listening. They *know* I can translate. Science is finally starting to listen too.

A study by Tel Aviv University found that tomato and tobacco plants made sounds at frequencies humans cannot hear when stressed by a lack of water or when their stem is cut. Microphones placed 10 centimeters from the plants picked up sounds in the ultrasonic range of 20 to 100 kilohertz, which the team says insects and some mammals would be capable of hearing and responding to from as far as five meters away. The research suggests that a moth may decide against laying eggs on a plant that sounds water stressed. Plants might even hear that other plants are short of water and react accordingly. Imagine the things we can learn from this kind of conscious communication. It *is* magic and wonder that's been happening for thousands of years.

Rabbits, Pools, and Sacred Cows

We have to note that just like people, some plants just don't thrive. That's nothing to do with you, sometimes they just don't make it. I try to make something with them, more opportunities for witchcrafts. Every natural being I meet I try to communicate to. I have honed my vibration and Nature sees me. This was a slow process, otherwise I would have been afraid to leave the house.

Nature is gentle when we ask for ease and grace, delivering the medicine in the slow doses. It takes time to build relationships.

Most of us don't meet people on the street and then immediately ask them for their advice on our most personal matters. I wasn't far from that when I was in my trauma; I didn't know what boundaries meant. I didn't know I could have any. It took me tuning in slowly. I started with the Nature beings I lived with, pets. I'd always talked to animals as a kid. They may not have spoken in words, but they certainly understood them. I know now it was the energy that came along with the words, not the words alone. It was the feelings. Animal communication *is* feelings. As I leaned into other Nature beings, I realized (and remembered) that everything communicates!

Sounds a lot like *Alice in Wonderland*, right? Lewis Carroll was probably doing some shamanic journeying (or some good psilocybin). He also seemed a bit creepy with those kids, but that's for a different book. Those of you who've experienced journeying know that it is a lot like going through the looking glass. The white rabbit that Alice followed down the hole is what journeying is. Rabbits *are* magical medicine, or totems. They appear typically at dusk or dawn. They are mostly unseen but are prolific creators. Rabbit medicine would be helpful for the planet right now given how quickly we need to produce new systems. They're part of the fairy realm, and they're quite literally associated with magic. Rabbits out of hats . . . rabbits down holes . . . When we think about that, we can remember maybe it was Nature who first told us all these things? Animals can and do tell us what their magic is, whether through their actions or through their beings.

We have just forgotten how to ask. We've forgotten how to listen.

I have come to a point in my life where everywhere I am in Nature, I feel like Snow White. I have had some of the most meaningful and astounding experiences of my life with Nature beings. It wasn't long after my parents divorced, and my mum had moved us to the country. We rented a house on a working apple orchard and lived across the street from a dairy farm. This was the closest I'd ever lived to what felt like real Nature.

I quickly met some new friends. Cows.

After school when I got off the bus I'd go over and stand at the fence. I just wanted to be with them. Dairy cows are, of course, female. I was drawn to them.

They made me feel safe and secure. I stood there after school at the fence and talked to them. It didn't take long for one of the Holsteins to recognize me. She had big brown eyes with long eyelashes. Her face was mostly white with the trademark black splashes across it. She was a perfect specimen. She had a red tag in her ear that read #20. So that's what I started to call her. She would come running to the fence when she saw me and then eventually it just took my voice to bring her over. Through this experience I figured out that I loved cows. This was a breadcrumb. I needed that medicine back then. They probably needed mine too. Those dairy cows perpetually produce milk for babies they didn't get to keep, or see (this is just one of the horrible side effects of the dairy industry), so this human kid loving them through the fence gave us both the medicine we needed.

Nature beings are known for self-rescuing, so now that you have reconnected, be aware of beings coming into your life. When in trouble, they can seem to identify who will be safe to help them.

If you consume meat you can say, *Thank you for giving your life so that I may live.* You can also add that you are sorry for any pain or suffering endured on the way to your plate. Simple. Nature has solutions for everything, even waste. We just haven't been using the right materials. Again, if we listen to the wisdom-keepers, we can begin to remember that this way of life pre-existed the trouble we're in now.

When humans communicate and collaborate with Nature, two things happen. We can learn and do some wonderful things. How did the ancient Egyptians know what the cardinal directions were to build the pyramids? How did they know where to put them, or how to construct them? This is part of why science is still so captivated with ancient Egypt. It's because we still can't fully explain how they knew these things (without wonder).

It's simple.

They came together to ask Energy, and Energy told them. Spirit has always told us everything we wanted to know. When it was torn from us, we forgot part of our ability to translate the magic of life. When human beings remember (and work together) to commune with Source, we tend to get the same message. If you have a group of people doing the same shamanic journey and asking Spirit the same question, they will get iterations of the same answer.

The irony, right? That maybe it takes more than one of us to get all the instructions. We all count. This isn't a one-person job. Although we are each in our own relationship with the divine, how we connect is different for all of us. This is part of reclaiming our individual magic, part of walking this path of remembering. Walking in light. That we are literally following the breadcrumbs to our own power, our own method of being in alignment with the All. It is in you; it is around you. It is with you. We know all these stories of survival. People calling on Nature, or Spirit, to save them, to help them. Having these profound experiences and turning into motivational speakers spouting tales of close encounters with death (I am realizing what I've done here, *like me*). Because we *know* that Energy can and usually *does* show up. We *know* miracles happen. Nature knows how to make them. We've been hearing about it for thousands of years; we can remember how to invite more of them into our lives.

Let's move out of the stone circle and into the edge of The Garden to formalize our reconnection. Beyond the stone circle is a row of hedges, and just beyond them we can see some kind of structure. It's The Reflecting Pool, but before we go there, we're going to make a pledge and plug ourselves back in.

Into the Wonder

This meditation and visualization practice will invite you to find a place in Nature to begin to reconnect with what you've forgotten. If you made a rattle or have a drum, you're going to want to shake it fast, as if you were jumping double Dutch or imagine the beginning of Queen's "We Will Rock You."

We're going to use our mind's eye and we're going to visualize a place in Nature. Maybe it's somewhere where you grew up. Maybe it's somewhere that you go or somewhere you have a connection to but haven't been. Wherever it is, you're going to imagine that place as your point of reconnection. The point you're choosing is the place where you'll reconnect with all that you may have forgotten about Nature. It's your anchor. It might be a tree, a stream, a mountain.

As you imagine this place, see yourself there in Nature. Ask Nature in your mind, while you feel it with your body. When we think about vibration and frequency, it's not always about saying it aloud, it's about sending the intention and vibration in your mind. If it helps as you get started to speak aloud, do that until you're comfortable enough to do it with your consciousness.

We must start by asking for permission to return and reconnect: *May I step into your field of energy?*

We do the same and grant the same: *You may step into my field of energy.*

We apply consent to Nature and energy just as we should apply it to everything else. As you do this, imagine that you're plugging back into Nature. That means you're restarting your experience of Nature in a state of consent, openness, and respect. As you're setting that intention with that being in Nature, you may want to revisit a moment you've had with Nature. If there's something you'd like clarity or insight on, you can imagine going back to that moment.

Notice what comes through.

Visualize this great reconnection you're making after hundreds or thousands of years and imagine Nature sharing this news. How does it feel? Ask yourself and Nature if there is something that you can do in your life as a physical extension and representation of this reconnection. Is there a place nearby you can start to visit? Is there an activity you can do, a way you can be of service in Nature?

When you're finished with your reconnection, take a moment to thank Nature. Write about your experience. If you had something come through, great. If it didn't show up this time, you can try again another time, or try visiting another place or moment. Asking Nature for support and reconnection is your birthright.

Trust that Nature will let you know when it's time. It may be holding a special moment for you in the coming days. You may not have had anything come through today, but you may find a feather of your own. Pay attention, because if there's a "delay," this can also be a breadcrumb indicative of your own cycles. Yes, we all have them and not just people with periods.

Consider you can create a ritual, a mantra, or an offering as an extension of your reconnection. Part of this work is following the breadcrumbs through the natural world *and* the internal one. This may include leaving something for beings in

Nature, apples for deer, seed for birds, or donating or volunteering to a wildlife sanctuary or nonprofit. How each of us chooses to be of service is as personal a practice as any.

Taking your magic book into Nature or simply recording your interactions will bring a world of wonder, breadcrumbs, and clues.

When I started asking Nature for permission, as well as granting it mine, I began to have profound experiences. I started to have hawks visit me, pigeons landing on me, and squirrels treating me like I was one of them (they're not wrong).

Teachers come in all forms.

Remember when Nature delivers a message, it speaks clearly. It even has its own language. When you're ready, we'll start remembering how to speak it. We can move through the hedges and toward The Reflecting Pool. Until then, enjoy the magic and wonder of returning to a long-lost embrace with Nature.

It's been waiting for you.

CHAPTER FIVE

THE REFLECTING POOL

SYNCHRONICITY

As we move through the hedges, we're met with a colorful welcoming committee. Butterflies. They seem to dance like a curtain as we come to another structure. This one is open, and running along the length of it is a long reflecting pool framed with stone. A dragonfly whirs past and we notice there are some lily pads floating toward the middle of the pool. Lotus blossoms dot the surface like purple bubbles. Otherwise, the water in the pool is like glass, the light dances across it as the pool reflects every leaf and flutter. As we explore the walkway beside the water you notice that overlooking The Reflecting Pool is a little gazebo off to the left. It's midway and almost divides the pool in half. Its four stone pillars hold a dome of glass and under the dome sits a stone bench.

We move toward it, and as we do we see THE REFLECTING POOL carved carefully along the edge of the bench. Well, that's a good sign because this is a perfect place to reflect. Let's take a moment here. How are you doing? We've come through some big remembering since we arrived at The Temple of Wonder. We've had a reset, we've reconnected to Nature, and now we're here to begin to remember its language. What have you noticed so far as we get deeper into The Temple? Are you leaving space between exploring the rooms, or are you doing the rituals and going to the next chapter? This is a breadcrumb too. While we're in The Reflecting Pool we're going to talk about exactly what those are, what they mean, and how to collect them. Sometimes you will even find a whole loaf or a baguette. Your choice. *How* you are going at this particular journey, or adventure, is as important as deciding to go on it. This is a clue about how your energy operates. Some of us permeate, we marinate, we stew in things, and others devour it all in one sitting. Some of us are right in the middle or throttle between both. All these are perfect as long as it is what's natural for *you*. Take notice of your own rhythm. It will help as you move deeper into the journey inside The Temple.

We all carry unique skills within our vessels. How we mix and match the pieces and how we process the breadcrumbs is totally unique to *you*. You're perfect for your purpose—just like all those Nature beings we just talked about (*and to*). We are all components of a complex system—and we are perfect for what we're here to do. Earth is a busy place with lots of choices. You may have signed up to be here to clear out old ancestral patterns, you may be a teacher within your community, you may be a change agent, you may be raising one. As a vessel in the world, we are all meant to balance between experiencing the role of teacher *and* student. We're all learning and teaching. There's bound to be some growing pains (feel free to put on the theme song, it works for this next part). We are all in this human thing together. We're in school while we're on Earth. We're here to learn and to grow. We've got each other. So let's learn something new.

The Interdimensional Scavenger Hunt Begins

I always had some synchronicity in my life; I'd had déjà vu. I had moments where it felt like I knew something before it happened, or times where I thought I saw the future. Times where I actually had. I was someone who was always open to the prospect that there was something out there. I grew up leaving room until trauma filled it in, and I shut all the windows. Boarded them up, even. Life had taken up the space where wonder used to live. That was how it began for me when I first went down The Garden path. As I reconnected to Nature, I found myself again. My own authentic power. I remembered a faith in myself and my instincts that was

being rubber-stamped by Energy itself. When I was on track, it was smooth, and magic happened. When I was off track, it was as if everywhere I turned there was a brick wall. For years, I didn't understand what that meant. It was because I didn't speak the language and I didn't have a translator.

I was getting all kinds of messages, but there was no way for me to decipher them. Unfortunately, the Rosetta Stone isn't going to help you learn Spirit, and if someone could have carved this into a rock for you, they already would have. But we have to acknowledge that as human beings when we travel we often need a translator; sometimes if we travel really far to different places, we need a bunch of translators. This is what is really meant by a "helper," or a "power animal," or totem. They're typically animals. I think it's because Spirit is smart, and talking to an animal in the ether is way more palatable, approachable (and fun) than finding out, for example, that your helper is some older man named Craig. Though, I can't promise that you won't have a helper animal named Craig. (Sorry, Craigs.) It might take some time and practice, but helpers *will* tell you their names. I've received some pretty good ones from clients over the years, from Murray to Malachi. A small teaching here: it is *power animal,* not *spirit animal* (*unless you're Indigenous*). Using the term *spirit animal* to describe a helper is cultural appropriation when you're not Indigenous. So don't do that! #TheMoreYouKnow

When we begin to be in communication with Nature again, with Source, it may feel as if you missed a lot. It might feel as if you slept through some of the trip. You may feel annoyed. *Why didn't anyone tell me this? How did I not know I had help? What amazing things could I have done if I knew this earlier?*

This is where time comes in.

Remember how I mentioned that Spirit was outside of time? It is. There is no time in Spirit world. From my practice, it seems to be all moments. Everything is *now.* This means that the more aligned we are with Energy, the more in practice we are with being in balance and keeping our sunroofs open, so to speak. The more the light gets in, the more enlightened we and our environments become. Carl Jung, the founder of analytical psychology, was also the person who coined the term *Synchronicity.* He stated that, "Synchronicity is an ever-present reality for those who have eyes to see." A breadcrumb here for this adventure together (which we'll explore later) is that when Jung first used the term, he was actually discussing Chinese philosophy.

The Universe leaves breadcrumbs for us to remind us how to find the clues it drops, back to the idea that this is all just one big intention-driven scavenger hunt. We have to make sure we get the clues right to progress and to find the clues we need to follow the breadcrumbs left by synchronicity. We can practice reading synchronicity and its guideposts by starting to look for them. Sometimes you may find there may be several instances or layers of synchronicity that you may need to connect, or string together, to glean the meaning. This practice is following *the breadcrumbs.*

Some of my own scavenger hunts last months, years, and even decades. Let's take a look into The Reflecting Pool at some of mine. My clues started early; yours probably will too. Look for patterns. Mine were as clear as yours will be. My first breadcrumb and memory here was of being in the womb. I described the sounds to my mum, and she looked as if she were going to fall off her chair. When I was two, I asked for my first witch costume, drawing my first witch around the same time. It was that same year I had my first experience with telepathy. We'd moved to a new subdivision where there weren't any fences built between the backyards. She had spotted me from her back patio doors. A little girl with big brown eyes and a face shaped by light brown hair. I saw her from my own back door, and I said "Hello" in my mind. I heard her say it back, and then she raised her hand and waved at me. I waved back. A very tall tanned blond woman appeared beside her. I watched them exchange words and then they both smiled at me. Her name was Erin and she had just told her mum that I was her best friend. She knew it before I did. She always seemed to know everything before I did. She was as good a witch as there ever was. She rivals Glinda from *The Wizard of Oz*, but with even better hair. She got that and her Spirit from her mum. She carries Sisu, the Finnish quality of guts, courage, and determination, and with it, the connection to Nature and wonder. I had gained not only a best friend but a teacher who exuded a Spirit and confidence and it was infectious. Her famous line, when we'd get into something we knew we didn't have permission for, was, "If we get caught, we'll just say we didn't know *because we're little kids.*" It worked every time.

I started using my "magic powers" on my parents when I was four and by the time I was seven, I found one of the biggest breadcrumbs and clues to what I was doing here. Luckily it came via TV. A book came on the TV in the form of a commercial, and it blew my mind. Maybe *that's why* I ended up working in advertising! The ad was a montage of different people having conversations about mysterious events. It was intercut with facts about the mysteries, before a booming male voice came on, announcing: *Time Life Mysteries of the Unknown Books*. It wasn't until I saw the cover of the first book—*Mystic Places*—as they were laddering up to the sales pitch that I froze.

The front cover had an image of the Sphinx and the pyramids with light coming from behind them. It was magical and I needed it *immediately*. It was the eighties and there was no rewinding, no recording. The announcer was already saying that I needed to "Act now!" My jaw dropped open as I prepared to yell the one word every kid in my generation yelled when they saw something on TV that we wanted: *"Muuuuummmm."*

As my mum arrived in front of the TV, I was already in sales mode. They were now saying this came with a *free* gift: "a bag of crystals"?! I added it to my pitch. The deal just became sweeter.

"Mum, we need to call right away to get the free gift," I told her, now a tiny capitalist soldier working for *Time Life*. Seeing the Sphinx and the pyramids had activated some kind of switch inside of me; I recognized something. It was familiar. I remembered.

Try to think about what kinds of things captured your interest in that way as a kid. What things or activities really lit you up? Write them down. These are clues where your unique brand of magic might come from.

When that first book, *Mystic Places*, finally arrived. I devoured it. Just a little girl carrying around a *Time Life* book about sacred places on the planet. Not weird at all. When it arrived and only covered a little bit of the pyramids, I went deeper into the stacks, I went directly to the card catalog at our elementary school library, and I started learning about Egyptology. As I got into it, I realized it wasn't just the Sphinx and the pyramids that felt familiar. It was the mythology. I started to draw Anubis at school. Catholic school wasn't quite sure what to make of that. Most little kids there drew Jesus. I drew both, sometimes together. I would still try to talk to whomever would listen to me about these mysteries I was carrying around. The pyramids, the mythology, the Sphinx, stories of pharaohs, and of course, the magic. This wasn't the kind of schoolyard talk that seemed to interest anyone but me. I didn't care. I felt more at home in those worlds than I did in my own.

As a kid my grandmother, Gee, used to take me to the Royal Ontario Museum in Toronto. She was one of my best friends and an artist, so she knew how to join me in my worlds. She'd seen the King Tut exhibition when it traveled to Toronto. I'd spend as much time as she let me in the Egyptian section of the museum. I always wanted to hang out with the mummies. I loved the statues, the little tomb they constructed. I felt at home there. I'd examine all the gods painted on the sarcophagus. I'd name them. Point out to her who was who and who did what. Of course, it was my grandmother who was the only one in my life who seemed to be interested in my Egyptology lessons. I always delivered my facts like a sermon from underneath my overgrown bangs. At the museum I always wanted to touch everything. I knew I wasn't supposed to, but my little arm would rise up like an antenna searching for something ancient. Signs marked DO NOT TOUCH with a big red *X* through the illustration of a hand didn't feel enough to deter little me.

As I got older, I still spent a lot of time there with sacred objects from other lands. A few years ago, the museum acquired a beautiful but broken statue of the lion-headed warrior goddess Sekhmet known as the Mistress of Dread and Lady of Slaughter. Great One of Magic, Lady of Enchantments. I'd always loved her, but this was the first time I'd seen her with my own eyes, even as I knew that she should have never been taken in the first place. The statue sat in a museum thousands of miles from home. We all visit stolen artifacts and are challenged with how to honor the cultures they represent. We've all been compromised by The Uninvited. Even this statue had damage to her face and hands, likely done by The Uninvited themselves. Chipped and broken, but the power that came from it was no less palpable.

Of course, the museum was (still) tempting my no-longer-little hands. The statue wasn't enclosed. It was out in the open. Seated in the entrance to the Egyptian wing. The goddess of both plague and healing. I had never forgotten these giant allies who had lit me up as a kid through the darkest moments of my childhood. I carried them through my life and into my adventures. They brought feelings of calm and groundedness. It was the same feeling I got when I was among their statues at the museum (so far, the closest I'd come to Egypt).

It wasn't long after I'd been called to practice healing work that I got the most amazing member's email from the museum: The museum would open for a costume party on the evening of Hallowe'en and *all* exhibits would be open. My littlest witch was having a big wish come true. I was going to wear my witch costume, and do magic at the museum, the place I'd felt safest in my life—at *night*. It felt too good to be true, so I called the museum to make sure it wasn't a mistake. It wasn't. It was real.

When I went to the museum in my witch costume (or true form), it was packed. Sold out. Costumes galore. I had only one destination. The Egyptian wing on the third floor. I brought a printed copy of an early draft of this book with me, as well as some of my healing tools and sacred objects. When I got to the third floor it was empty. Not a soul but mine.

I walked toward Sekhmet in my full witch regalia and did what I'd always been called to do since she arrived. I knelt in front of her. I said my prayers and proceeded to do my usual circuit. The same one I'd done there since I could walk. As I got closer to being finished with my ritual, I felt the voice of Sekhmet. So clearly in my head that I wondered if it was from a speaker.

You can touch the statue, she said.

I answered her back in my mind, *Thank you, I would love to, but I really can't. You aren't in Egypt anymore. We're in a museum and you're being guarded.* I tried to show her an accompanying visual of me being dragged out by museum security and not being able to come back. She roared with laughter. The Mistress of Dread was amused. I felt a bright light and warmth from her. I didn't need to touch her. She was radiating herself to me, and I was bathing in her glow, warming my soul with her energy.

Synchronicity Isn't Just an Album by the Police

Synchronicity is defined as a simultaneous occurrence of events. It is the language of Nature and everything in it. It is the language of the soul, of Energy itself. There *is* an intelligence greater than ourselves, and in this chapter, I'll outline how you can begin to see it more often. We'll learn how to start to understand and interpret this new language, and how to connect the dots on the great Spiritual scavenger hunt that is being human.

Because coincidences don't give Source the credit it deserves.

We're going to talk about what language Nature actually speaks, because as we've already confirmed, it's not English, or any human language. Source has its very own method of communication to let us know we're on the right track. Signposts. Synchronicities. Symbols and omens. The Universe converses in little winks that I call *breadcrumbs.*

The first thing we need to acknowledge is that Source, the Universe, or Energy is a masterful producer. It is the conductor of the orchestra of life. The best show runner who has ever existed. It doesn't need to communicate in words. It uses all the resources available to it. This means it can deliver a message through literally any avenue because it runs through everything and is part of everything (yes—even the internet and, also, jerks). Its language is rooted in logic and simplicity. It uses the fabric of life and the thread through all things to speak.

Just like you were invited into The Temple, you can invite Spirit back into your life. We can ask for more assistance, more clues, breadcrumbs, and signposts. We need to remember to open our windows sometimes. Source doesn't waste its time. If you have your sunroof and windows closed and are riding in your vessel with your headphones on, there's no room for wonder or magic. It will assume that you're full, and magic doesn't show up where it's not invited, let alone wanted. It's the energetic equivalent of yelling "I'm busy" to someone through the window.

When we are in conscious intentional communication with it, if we leave some room and open the window to talk sometimes, it listens. It can't be helped. You invited Energy in with your intention. That's what conscious communication is. You're human; you've already had conversations with the Universe. You've sent intentional messages through consciousness. You've had moments where you had just been talking about someone with a friend and then you run into the person, or they call you. Those moments where you think, *How can this be happening, I just said that and now it's happening?* Or when you're listening to this obscure song in the morning and then it comes on in a store that you're in that has *no business* playing it.

You know what I'm talking about. You've experienced it.

Now imagine what could happen if you consciously invite wonder to accompany you into more moments. Delightful timing!

Time is actually quite elastic, because no *time* in Spirit, so this enables Energy to be able to slide these little treasures under our doors. It plays us the songs to let us know we're right on track (if else, how would we be there to hear it?), or has a bird or butterfly come when we're thinking of a loved one who has transitioned. Sometimes we even get a breadcrumb before we can divine its meaning. I'm going to reflect some of those moments here to help you remember how to divine those moments in your own life.

Synchronicity can help us know that we're in alignment. Think of it as how the Universe lets us know we're on track and it can do it through any means possible, even through other people. Spirit moves through all things and therefore can communicate to and through all things. My dear friend Nada calls those people who show up in moments of synchronicity "hired actors," and they are. They work for Source. Somehow for some reason in those moments they're of service. In those moments, they are vibrating at a frequency that enables Source to somehow deliver truths through their channel. They become a medium for the message.

I have had so many times in my life where people say to me, "Wow, sorry I don't know where that came from," when delivering some golden nugget of a clue or treasure of a breadcrumb. These days my response is "I do." If Spirit wants to tell you something or get you a message, know that it's going to be consistent. It's going to deliver the message to you in as many ways as it can as many times as you need to finally hear it. And us humans, a lot of us have our windows closed.

I'm sure you've experienced this too, where something keeps coming up in your life and you don't know why. A person, an event, a song, a feeling. This is why. Most of us tend to spend a lot of time running scenarios or worrying about missing something or things not showing up for us because they happen to be showing up for someone else. Here's the thing. The Universe is like a worried mum. It's not going to let you miss anything that's meant for you. Trust me. My great-grandmother

Nana always said (in a thick Glaswegian accent), *What's for you won't go past you.* The Universe *will* just keep trying. So please don't worry you've missed your window. Energy will make more windows (*remember, a Burj Khalifa number of windows*). You just have to be willing to open one, even a bit. The only thing Energy has ever asked me to do in return for all the magic is to honor Nature, do my best, spread the word, and be kind. Fair trade.

Mystic Places

Sekhmet wasn't done with me. There were more breadcrumbs. It seemed I'd entertained her so much that she was going to send me on an adventure of her own. She was going to make sure I did as she asked, and she was going to make sure I touched her. In my current magical practice, I pull a weekly card out of an oracle deck called *The Anubis Oracle*. One particular week it was the Sphinx. The Sphinx is an altar of the Earth. It carries magic just like the pyramids. It predicted pharaohs and it holds many secrets. It *is* a library and center of knowledge and wisdom on the planet. Although I'd seen this card many times, it struck me as such a similar illustration to my *Mystic Places* book. So much that I had to compare it to the book. Of course, the Sphinx and pyramids are together in Giza, but the style and manner of these two illustrations felt iterative. I decided to do what I do these days when I need to take a much closer look at a breadcrumb or synchronicity. I took a shamanic journey to the Sphinx and pyramids to see what they had to say, what messages they wanted to convey for the week directly.

When I did, I received a profound healing. When the ceremony was over, I asked what I could do in appreciation for the healing, and I was told to give a crystal from my altar to my ex's mother, Jennifer, to bring with her on her trip to Egypt. It had been years since I'd dated her son, but we'd stayed in close touch. She had become a bonus mum, and her daughter Katy, a bonus sister. We had adopted each other and already had plans to see each other before her upcoming trip to Egypt. She had planned a trip after an old friend of hers who was an

Egyptologist had extended an invite. I was awestruck. Going to Egypt with a *real-life* Egyptologist? What a dream. I was excited for her, and for me. She told me she was being drawn there and just felt she had to go. The name of the Egyptologist who was leading the trip?

His name was *Daniel*. Of course it was.

When I brought the crystal to Jennifer's house, I shared a bit of the story and asked if she would mind bringing it to the Giza Plateau for me. She agreed.

When she had completed the mission, she messaged me with a picture of her kissing the Sphinx.

The timing was amazing, delightful in fact, because I had decided to culminate my initiation the way I honor all of my major life events. I got tattooed. I had planned to get some symbology related to the healing journey. Including little triangles on my fingers. This was my way of honoring the transformation I was undergoing. The realization that what was happening in my life was an opportunity to use my gifts, to ask for support to power me up after the battles of my life. When I look down and see them, I am reminded of the adventures I've completed or am in the midst of.

As I was in the middle of getting the triangles, I received a message from Jennifer after making the offering at the Sphinx: "I had an incredible healing experience today in a remote Temple at Karnak and Luxor with Sekhmet. I took this picture without a flash, in the dark chamber. I thought you would appreciate it."

I was again left mouth agape, while lying in the tattoo artist's chair. I replied: "Wait till you find out what's happening here. You're going to fall off your chair."

I had no idea of her itinerary. She told me she'd had a life-changing experience and that she would share more about it with me when she returned.

Here's the thing about magic and wonder. It doesn't matter how much you believe in it, how much you know it to be true, it never gets old. Not ever. It's always amazing. When Jennifer got back to Toronto, we set up lunch and she handed me a gift bag. Katy, my bonus sister, was there. She knew all about my passion for Egyptology (and lots of other places in Nerd Town). That summer, I'd already dragged her around buying statues from an amazing Egyptian family I'd met in search of my own Sekhmet statue.

I tried to act cool about the gift bag and put it beside me, but my seven-year-old self was eager to rip into it. Somehow, I managed to hold my little self back until after we'd eaten lunch. Katy and Jennifer watched me like a kid at their birthday party. I was already grinning, and I hadn't even looked inside the bag.

Inside were two stones from Egypt that Jennifer had picked up for me from the pyramids. I felt them radiating through the bag. I poured these pieces of Egypt into my hand. The first time I had felt a stone from this place that had shown up my whole life. I felt the same way I felt at the museum, but now it was in my hand. As I reached into more treasures fresh from Egypt, I couldn't believe it. How could she have known? It was an amulet of Sekhmet.

I was already ugly crying. I thought about her words to me at the museum and cried harder. I was finally touching her. Jennifer told me that she splurged and purchased a larger statue of Sekhmet for herself. Of course we each got one.

As I sat hugging my amulet, Katy rubbed my back as she'd done so many times before, as Jennifer went on to tell us about her life-changing experience. She told us that her tour group was led through the World Heritage Site and Temple of Karnak in Egypt. As she wandered through the seventy-foot columns of Karnak towering over her, she felt the power and magic of what constructed this place. A place that once held over two hundred statues of Sekhmet. A place that Daniel, the Egyptologist, had himself worked on. She explained that she felt a strong pull to one area of the temple. She moved through the temple to a small room at the back. There were security guards outside of the room and they were letting only a few people inside at a time. She told us she felt herself pulled to go into this room. She described it as a compulsion. I nodded, knowing it well as I held the treasure of the Sekhmet amulet in my hands as she spoke.

Once it was her turn, the guards opened the dark sanctuary for her. Stepping out of the blazing Egyptian sun, she walked into the darkness. In this room she told us she felt "home." And as her eyes adjusted, the great lioness appeared to her gradually through the darkness. As the goddess Sekhmet revealed herself, Jennifer began to weep. I was already crying at the restaurant holding this amulet of Sekhmet in my hands. Inside half laughing about how I was once embarrassed to kneel in a museum and now I was bawling in a restaurant with the same goddess statue. As Jennifer wept in the sanctuary of Sekhmet, a guard motioned to her that she could touch the statue. She was confused at first by this permission but didn't question why. She didn't just touch it. She embraced it. She described the embrace and feeling of unconditional love. I was floored.

This is how magic shows up. She described feeling warmth, bright light, and complete acceptance. I know that feeling. I've been wanting to touch it most of my life.

The last thing in the loot bag from Egypt was a tube, which I recognized. It was lined with hieroglyphs. It was a tube I already had at home.

As I slid open the tube and pulled out the papyrus, Jennifer said something that still makes me laugh: "I hope you don't already have this."

She said it as if the hand-painted piece of papyrus she'd chosen from dozens across the world was a mass-produced object she found at IKEA. When I opened it, the papyrus was identical in depiction to one I received from my best friend Chanda from her trip to Egypt eighteen years before.

I was, for once in my life, completely speechless. I just smiled. I couldn't say anything. I didn't want her to think I didn't like it. I loved it. I just couldn't *believe* it. When I got home, I put the two papyruses side by side. The only differences are slight: The one from Chanda is a little smaller and the papyrus from Jennifer shows one figure now wearing a crown. When I told Chanda and showed her the images later, all she could say was, "Holy shit."

Holy shit, indeed.

The Fortress of Foreshadows

The following summer I got a call from Jennifer out of the blue one afternoon. She was crying. This was the first time she'd ever called me so upset. She told me she'd been careless and had knocked the Sekhmet statue she bought in Egypt from its place on her dresser. She told me she didn't know who else to call. I paused for a minute. I thought about Sekhmet. I thought about everything I know about her.

She is a warrior. A healer. A goddess. She is the medicine of transformation. Her teeth flashed in my mind. Her grin. I saw the face of the statue at the museum in my mind. Broken. Missing an arm, part of her face. Most of the statues of Sekhmet still in existence from four thousand years ago are broken. They're chipped. They are no less powerful. They still sit in museums and temples around the world bringing the same energy. Hers would be no different

I told Jennifer that the statue wasn't too broken to be fixed. She still had the pieces. It didn't make the statue or her experience at Karnak any less meaningful. Sekhmet would never be upset about this. She brought war and plagues, but she also brought healing. I'd had my own practice for a while by then when Jennifer called me. I have been taught well by the teachers I can see with my eyes and the ones I see with my heart, but as they say, healing heals the healer. It was a reminder I needed too. What I've survived doesn't make me defective or broken. It made me strong. Sekhmet was alive in my life.

In following the breadcrumbs, we find purpose. We find meaning. We find a foundation so big and great that it can hold us through the hardest times and illuminate the darkest of moments.

Into the Wonder

In this writing and visualization practice, we're going to make some room and we're going to have a look around your side of the Pool. You may see clues right there in The Reflecting Pool. You may have some memories pop up. You may be given clarity on something, or you may be given a breadcrumb to follow. Let's imagine back to a time where you experienced a form of synchronicity, or maybe you heard about a synchronicity. Imagine you are retracing your steps back to that time to try to identify where there may have been breadcrumbs or further messages. Maybe you didn't leave yourself room then. Maybe there was something when you were a kid that lit you up so much that you want to go back and ask. You can invite Nature, or your higher self (if that's more palatable for you), to show up for you more often through synchronicity. We are going to pair that with leaving room for the Universe to speak to you. Without doing both, it can't show up.

A lot of people meditate in order to leave room for Spirit, or Energy. When you do that, when you make room, just watch what happens. Meditating may not be your thing; it's not mine. So it might be going for a walk, or dancing, or swimming; you don't have to get into some heavy meditation practice to connect to the divine. Do what resonates with you. You may need to try a few things. You may have a song that helps you get there, or a moment you can go to where you remember feeling the connection and let it go from there. This is an intricately braided ongoing conversation between you and Source.

It's *your* connection. Figuring out how you can make room for this new language might start with calling energy in at the beginning of the day. You'll want to ask for breadcrumbs, and when you get them, you're going to want to recognize them. Call it out. I like to write them down. I also like to offer something back. Whether it's food for the birds (don't feed them breadcrumbs!) or picking up some garbage, it's a way to let Nature know we got that message, and we're grateful for it. In my experience, honoring those moments helps us see them more often. Watch out for those outer events or experiences that form synchronistic parallels to the inner messages you may be receiving. Once you have a list of breadcrumbs, you can also start looking for patterns. Because just like Nature, synchronicities have patterns. What wonder might be in between the moments?

This is how we remember how to listen and to look out for clues.

When you're finished with your ritual, you can honor the work we did here. Maybe you want to imagine you're making an offering to The Reflecting Pool or to The Garden for any magic that may have come through. When you're ready, we'll make our way past The Reflecting Pool. For the next part of our adventure, we'll be going back in time to take a fresh look at the old ways.

CHAPTER SIX

THE SANCTUM

THE OLD WAYS

As we continue past The Reflecting Pool, we come upon a path of laid stone. It's hard to know how we didn't notice it before, but reflecting is deep work. We don't honor it as much as we should. Processing our moments is as much of a task as putting away laundry. Which is why so many of us leave it somewhere for later. It's easy to miss things when under a pile of unprocessed moments, or laundry.

We move ahead on this path, noticing that we are along the side of The Temple. As if the landscape had done this itself, light spills out of a massive doorway. There aren't any windows you can see. No lights. Is there even electricity here? It feels a bit like *Indiana Jones*, except this is not a Temple of Doom. The air smells sweet. Frankincense? Lilies? You can't quite name it, but it's subtle and it's beautiful. You feel like you're being drawn in like a magnet to this magical stone passage. This is The Sanctum.

It feels like a mirage. We reach out and touch the walls as we pass into this room. We feel that it's carved with symbols. The stone is cold, but there's no dampness. It's crisp and, somehow, there's a warm breeze. Sweet warm air comes through the entry. It's enchanting. Above us the carvings continue across the ceiling. There's a low hum almost like the sound of a hive somewhere inside these walls. A descending ramp in front of us leads to another doorway. This one is bookended by two giant columns in the stone, each carved at the top with the face of a woman. She is looking down almost smiling. Content. Calm. The way you're starting to feel as you're getting closer to reaching this room.

Above this door is the same winged sun disk from the Invitation, and The Entryway. The circle, the disk, is the light of Source. The wings, a symbol of ascension. It's beautiful. I can't stop smiling; maybe you're smiling too.

Do you feel that? It's the feeling of something ancient; it's as if you remember this. It's as if you've been here before. You may even feel a little uneasy about that. Nervous or anxious, as if you're somewhere you shouldn't be, or that you're about to join a performance for which you didn't rehearse, or that maybe you're about to see something you aren't meant to see. Do you know where that comes from? Do you know why people are anxious or scared of magic and why the word *witchcraft* makes so many people nervous? Why do people roll their eyes when they hear about "energy work"? Why do so many people have these strange aversions?

It's because magic and individual Spiritual practices were literally ripped from us.

For centuries, wisdom-keepers have been murdered for doing rituals in Nature. For operating outside the systems built by The Uninvited. If we weren't worshiping within their parameters, within their systems, it meant it was dangerous. If we weren't kneeling at their altars, it meant we weren't going to listen to them. Being in direct connection with Source was a threat. Make no mistake, it still is. People are still being murdered.

First thing we're going to do before we go inside this room is put down this idea that witchcraft or magic is *bad*, or *scary*. Are crafts typically known for being scary? No. Witchcraft is just a craft. It's crafting with Nature. That's all it's ever been. We're meant to co-create. It is part of our divine design. This idea of black magic, white magic, gray magic. Let's look at that for a moment. Working with only shadow doesn't make much sense. Intentionally inviting more imbalance against natural law? *No thanks.* There is no shadow without light. It indicates something bigger at play if a practitioner is working with only one form of energy. Energy *is* duality by default. Energy is like electricity, or a battery. Positive. Negative. Who would only want to subtract for the rest of their lives? Not me.

You may feel excited walking into The Sanctum. You might feel the energy waiting for us just through this doorway. Remember how excited Nature was to reconnect? Now we're feeling the vibration of Source ready to help usher us through this doorway, to welcome us back home. This is Energy's house, and it's nothing to be afraid of. It's where we come from, and according to most Spiritual and scientific thought on the planet, likely where we return. We'll get into this more when we get to The Hall of Secrets. We can reclaim our direct connections. We can remember the light work of old ways. If you need a break before we head in, I will meet you back here on the stairs when you're ready. If you're ready, you can follow me inside.

We descend down the long ramp and move toward the light at the end of this tunnel. As we move forward through the door, we breathe in the air making its way out of The Sanctum. It is sweet, and if air could dance, that is what it feels like it's doing across your cheeks. We both seem to be breaking into grins. As we enter into The Sanctum, we're surrounded in a brilliant warm light.

Descending into The Temple

As we reach the doorway at the bottom of the ramp, it opens up into a large circular room. A Temple within The Temple. A Sanctuary. The floor is painted with a circle of light. Its rays point outward toward the perimeter of the room. At each of the ray's points there are small openings carved into the walls. They seem somehow lit in correspondence to the points of the painting on the floor. Each hold different sacred texts, artifacts, and antiquities. As we begin to move around this great circle, glancing at the objects, some of them you seem to recognize, others you don't. Yet we seem to *know* that each one is sacred to its own civilization. They all contain holy and ancient wisdom. They're all vibrating the same way. Like the global wisdom-keepers themselves, *different names, different words, but same song and the same beat.* You realize now why it felt as if you were floating, you feel as if you've reached the womb of the Earth.

The Uninvited did their best to sever this connection to magic. We're back in the place where we can get it direct. We don't often use the word *magic* in association with books currently known as being "holy," but there *is* magic in them; there's also breadcrumbs, clues, and patterns. Just like the ones on the floor here in The Sanctum.

As we walk the circle of The Sanctum, there's the Bible, the Quran, the Vedas, the Torah, the Tao Te Ching, to name just a few, but be certain any sacred text we've ever heard of (and not yet heard of) are here. There are books, objects, and scrolls. On one of the shelves, we even notice a magic wand. It's encased above the shelf that holds a book in what looks like glass and liquid. It's almost floating. It's the Bible. Of course it is. Some of the earliest depictions of Jesus show him holding a wand. Definitely not the Jesus Christ pose most of us have come to know. The Uninvited really did a number on perhaps one of the greatest books of magic, the Bible. I know, I know, you're like *WHAT? The Bible is not a book about magic, wonder, or witchcraft . . .*

Are you *sure*? Employ your sense of wonder and consider giving some of it a fresh read.

What happens if we change God to Spirit, or Energy, throughout the Bible?

It's as if a thread is being strung between all these artifacts around the room. The breadcrumb that Abrahamic schools of Spiritual thought have so many similarities. As we keep walking, we come to the Quran. Some prophets received revelation through an intervening angel, as Prophet Muhammad did from Archangel Gabriel. In Islam, the Isra' and Mir'aj are also known as the Night Journey. This refers to the transformational journey made by Muhammad in both mind and Spirit. He was said to have traveled from Mecca to Jerusalem, and then into the heavens, to receive instructions of prayer to return with to Earth. An interdimensional adventure, from one reality to another—and back again in one night. That heavenly horse is called the Buraq—which means, "the lightning."

Traveling through dimensions on the back of lightning. Fitting.

On the next shelf hangs the star and crescent, the most recognized symbol of Islam. The crescent is the early phase of the moon and represents progress, while the star signifies illumination with the light of knowledge. There's that light again. Some prophets or holy people heard, some saw, others felt. Some channeled through helpers like angels or guides, totems, or Spirit. Some pre-ferred a direct line.

Jesus also appears in the Quran as one of the five prophets. Musa (or you may know him as Moses) is another among them. In the Quran, Musa was said to have received the Tawrat (Torah) directly from Source. He was also said to have been adopted into the Egyptian royal family. This would mean he would have learned the practice of magic.

The ancient Egyptians didn't separate religion and magic. Life was built around the belief that written images and words when combined with action and ritual had the capacity to influence the world. The belief was that this was done through a divine creative force known as "Heka" or "Magical Power." We can imagine that Hekate, the Greek goddess of witchcraft, may have been inspired by Heka, the Egyptian deity of the practice of magic.

Because a foundation of Heka was communication with Nature, reading the stars and building relationships work in harmony and collaboration with the ele-ments and the light of energy itself. Could Moses (Musa) have collaborated with the water of the Red Sea to part it in some way? Did he work with it or read its patterns for it to recede temporarily to a point where they could cross? Who knows, but it was substantial and astounding enough an experience that it was written down and repeated for thousands of years.

Moses and some of these other Prophets (including Mary) sound an awful lot like witches to me. Working with Nature, talking to Spirits, having visions? They were all talking to something most people couldn't see and making lots of things happen. We make room for the wonder, for the belief, and for the practice.

Snakes and Ladders

As we move around the circle, we notice a staff placed into the wall near the Torah.

To quote that magical story at the Red Sea, the Creator said to Moses, "Raise your staff and stretch out your hand over the sea."

A rod. A wand. The same staff was described to have produced water from a rock, transformed into a snake and back, and parted the Red Sea. Moses seems pretty *magical*. Why aren't we talking about that? Staff to a snake?! This is cooler than any fictional witch or wizard I've ever heard of.

And there's another breadcrumb here that also takes us right to this moment. Snakes are long-standing allies of transformation itself. They appear in all natural and primary Spiritualities. They have been symbols of growth and rebirth and have been associated with healing and magic since we could carve them.

Two snakes form part of the caduceus, or the staff of Thoth (that helpful bird from The Library). He's also connected to ancient Greece (Hermes) and the Abrahamic tree. There's been talk through history that Thoth may have been Moses, or Mose, which means "son" in Egyptian. Thoth has also been associated with Idris (and maybe Metatron), a bird of many names. The caduceus is still used today as the symbol of medicine. Snake medicine *is* healing. It is transformation, miraculous growth, and transmutation. Transmutation is part of what makes spiritual transformation possible. The Uninvited made us think it was bad unless it was a story they were telling.

Could Moses have worked to create a vision in collaboration with Nature where people experienced a piece of wood turning into a snake? Could he have communicated with the snake to help him perform some sleight of hand? Yes, if he was a powerful witch in balance with the elements, he absolutely could. Whether it was a reality or a vision, enough people saw it at the same time to make it real and get this story put in almost every hotel drawer in the world. Part of the reason we used to gather (congregate) in groups to connect with Spirit was to have witnesses to help deliver and process the messages. By having a group of people share the experience of these holy moments, we could more widely distribute them, we could more likely decipher some intelligence greater than our own. This is how wisdom-keepers come into being. They witness magic.

While we are here in The Sanctum talking about books, both biblical and holy, we'll just take a moment to address the whole Adam and Eve thing, because, come on, if we take off the systemic-oppression glasses for a moment, you can see something clearly. The whole allegory was just to demonize women from the jump and create a villain bigger than man itself. We are equals and snakes aren't scary or evil, their medicine actually teaches us how to glide more easily through life. That snake in the garden of Eden never wanted any trouble. The Uninvited just didn't like that a lady was talking to animals. Especially a snake. So they decided to make witches scary and told us that magic could happen in only one place, in one way, with one guy.

The lens that was placed over magic by The Uninvited needs to be removed. The focus needs to be moved to those who are fighting for truth, justice, and freedom for *all* sentient beings.

Animal medicine doesn't mean we murder them and take their parts for magic, as is still happening in various cultures across the world. This is not how we are meant to work with animal medicine. If a Nature being wants to give itself to you for magic, you will find one. We don't murder for parts. We do not waste. Earth-based cultures around the world have been doing this with reverence since humanity was a thing. No waste. No needless death. Eat what you kill. Respect and honor. We are meant to live in harmony, not violence with other beings or each other.

So, you may ask, why do so many Spiritual practices depict deities with the heads of animals? It wasn't just Thoth and Anubis; we've got Ganesha to Karura. It is meant to illustrate the medicine and indicate that we are not better or different. We are existing in the same space. When we hurt them, we hurt ourselves. When we disrespect them, we disrespect ourselves. The Buddha was pretty clear on how to treat animals. So many of the world's religions today have specific rules about what beings should and shouldn't be eaten. Food for thought.

The Circle of Life

The circle we're walking here is representative of our own journey. I told you Spirit was big on allegories. These old limiting beliefs were designed to put a big stopper on our authentic power and further disconnect us from our purpose. They were created to break our connection, to break our circle, disrupt our circuit, to

disconnect us from each other, and look at what's happening to us? It seems to have worked. We have become a society of *us* and *them*. Yet so many Spiritual origin stories contain the same breadcrumbs, the doing unto others—this isn't a coincidence, you know that by now.

Because we are made from the same stuff, in order to achieve balance, harmony, or peace, we need to recalibrate our consciousness. I know that sounds like a lot of work. As If I'm going to tell you that you have to go to an office and work on this. Luckily that isn't how it works. Nature doesn't have offices (another invention of The Uninvited that's in need of intervention). Nature goes to work in Nature. It doesn't need to go somewhere different. Nature has shown us that every system we need already exists. If it feels overwhelming to imagine rebuilding society's systems (I'm guessing you never played *SimCity*), then I want you to imagine thinking of all the magical practitioners on the planet at this moment in time who are working on this already. All the local magical people in different places, all the people remembering, all the people who are about to remember. We're certainly not going to try to do all this by ourselves. We know that many hands make light work. And we are the *light workers*. We're going to get our hands in there. It's time for us to stop pretending that we can't dig ourselves out of it. We can do anything we put our collective minds to. We had a hand in these systems, so we can rebuild them using the real tools we've been given. We can harness our rage into purposeful action and fierce compassion. We can return to our consciousness.

We can be done with it, all of it. Because the divine intervention that was written about in so many scriptures have always been us. *We're* the superheroes we've been waiting for. We are the second coming.

To quote activist Valarie Kaur, "The aim of divine rage is not vengeance but to reorder the world. It is precise and purposeful, like the focused fury projected into the world from the forehead of the goddess. It points us to the humanity of even those who we are fighting."

We can see that in the holy books we have a lot of allegories and archetypes. Some stories throughout history mirror each other. The Egyptian mythology of Isis and Horus and Mary and Jesus are mirrors. There was magic in their creation. The magical creation of the Sun of Humanity. The Sun of God. We know the ancient

Egyptians equated Spirit with the light, the Solar Disk. Amun—Ra—Spirit—Energy. There have been so many carvings of the sun disk Aten with rays of light ending in human hands reaching down toward humanity. Maybe we just didn't get the message clearly? How do we know that it wasn't all changed by some jerks throughout history? We can't even seem to agree on things. Even history is happening right in front of us.

We've begun to see how this works in the media now. People with money get to drive the messaging and influence. People with power get to control the narrative. This isn't Nature. This is power. It is constructed on division. Some countries on the planet try to tie money so closely to the divine that they put God's name on it. Jesus said it best: *Money is the root of all evil.* Capitalism is disconnection. It's a dirty window and there's no light getting through—on purpose.

When The Uninvited are acting as our intermediary, simple things seem to be lost in translation. So why can't we imagine that this entire time we've believed the story of a few jerks in history, over the literal words of high-vibrating helpers? Did Jesus really say he was "the Son of God?" What he may have actually said was that he was the "Sun of God," or even further, "Sun of Creation," "Light of Source," or maybe the simplest of all, "Child of Light." We can entertain that maybe he was saying, "Hey humans, you are all children of divine light. Star stuff. You carry the light of Source while on Earth."

We often see Jesus of Nazareth depicted with his hands up in the air, almost in a *V* form. He did this because he was filling with that Light. He was a vessel. We are all vessels. We're beginning to remember that. Maybe he wanted us not just to know we could do this but how to do it. He wanted us to channel what we are made of. Maybe he was trying to show us how to live and not grow some massive business. Maybe he and every other prophet and wisdom-keeper just want us to know we can embody the part of ourselves that has a capacity to be everlasting.

As we move toward the next point of the circle, there's a shelf. Upon it is a scroll. When it unravels, it's the Egyptian symbol of the *ankh*, the cross with the oval over the top. This is the hieroglyph for eternal life. In the image above we see the more literal depiction of the cross with human arms holding up the sun. Shown below the *ankh* is a *djed*, which is also known as the backbone of Osiris.

This is also said to be an early diagram of the human nervous system. The Egyptian hieroglyphic for Heka (translating to "magic") is a pictograph of human hands with the kundalini energy, or DNA double helix, coming up from between them.

Wow, we've definitely had some clues.

We know these stories because they're a part of us. We're meant to use them. But if you don't do the groundwork, if you're not open to having a consistent practice, it's going to be really hard to consistently bring in that light. If you don't keep your vessel primed, it's hard to pour into it. As you've already remembered, Spirit doesn't speak human language. It speaks allegories, synchronicities, parables, and omens. So we should assume some of the stories in sacred texts contain the same. They may be shared visions, they may have been things that were seen with human eyes, they may have been prophetic dreams. Spirits, angels, and ascended masters don't need to come here in bodies. They can meet us in our consciousness. In Spirit, anything can be an analogy. The path of remembering this language is individual. When the student is ready, the teacher appears, and the key turns in the lock.

Humanity is re-engaging with magic now because Source forced our hand a little. Let's be honest, that's what it does. In the Bible, we read of natural disasters, plagues, visions, burning bushes, and so on. This is how Source communicates. It utilizes Nature and the elements and everything in between to express itself. The second coming is already here; it's a consciousness.

It came as that because the Universe knows our game: We seem to kill everything else. You can't kill consciousness. This time it's going to permeate. Finally, we've reached a mass, and time, where there's too many wisdom-keepers and witches in too many places. We are multiplying and diversifying faster than The Uninvited can remove us from the party.

Jesus Was a Badass (and So Are You)

As we move toward this next part of the circle, we find ourselves looking at a list of names carved into the wall. There are so many you can't even begin to count. Some are being added as you're watching. This is exactly why many Spiritual practices moved to happening in secret. This is the memorial. These are their names. Those who lost their lives because of their power. Just look at what happened to Jesus. He's on this list. He was doing some real magic and people were being healed by it. People were listening and beginning to stand in their power and purpose and The Uninvited said, "Nah, get him out of here, but people seem to like him, so let's take his stuff and change it a little." This is causing some active pain in the world and Jesus was *pretty* clear on how he felt about oppression.

If you hadn't heard, he didn't like it. He whipped the rich and flipped their tables right out of the temple. For those in the back, Jesus wasn't white, he was probably a witch, and he didn't dislike anyone but the rich. Jesus wasn't some white supremacist asshole collecting money. He was definitely hanging out with other witches, queers, and nerds. He was of service to those who had less. He was approachable, and he was funny. He had a quick wit because he had seen some shit. He took time to show up for people when they needed him, and he was definitely the kind of guy who would do his own stunts.

Jesus is actually pretty rad, especially because he has a wand *and* a whip. So, if like me, you had some icky experiences with regard to The Uninvited's co-opted version of Jesus, please feel free to use this time to destigmatize and cleanse your own timeline. He got taken out by The Uninvited too. He got strung up by his own community. Just like the witch trials.

So many people practiced Spirituality in secret because it was dangerous. People began to hide it. So many people also left organized religion, maybe because something about it didn't feel right. It's the institutionalization of something that is meant to be organic and natural that doesn't align. Are there sacred spaces and people in these systems? Of course there are, but as a whole, Christian churches

have become entwined with The Uninvited. Jesus would clearly sue for misrepre-
sentation if he did come back here in person. Here's where I tell you that among
my clients are ministers. Yes, there are ministers among us who also consult
witches. We're not so different.

And if the crucifixion wasn't enough, the witch "trials" were further messaging
from The Uninvited that magic was punishable by death. Judas himself was probably
an archetype to symbolize the kind of oppression that might follow if we didn't fall
in line. So we learned to protect our magic. With the witch trials, it was their community that rang the alarms. The aftershocks of all this took generations to unravel,
but now here we are, standing on the brink of massive change. It's impossible to
control people who have a connection to their Spirit, because when you have a connection to your Spirit, you check in with Source. You can easily see what feels right,
what feels in alignment. Your gut instincts become highly tuned, and you can feel
a pin drop on your consciousness. You *know* when something doesn't feel right.

We humans are realizing quickly as we get back into balance with Nature that
a lot of these systems we seem to be using here aren't only not right, they are very,
very *wrong*. We are recognizing that these systems are broken because they are
rooted in inauthentic power. Colonialism was designed to assimilate and indoctri-
nate people into systems of false supremacy. We are seeing truths come out that
have been hidden for hundreds of years; some are so recent that those who were
told lies are now seeing the truth firsthand. Generations of people are realizing that
they were lied to and are committed to reconciliation, to re-education, to repara-
tion. The Uninvited clearly didn't predict that we'd rise in greater numbers.

People are educating themselves. No longer willing to celebrate genocide on
stolen land. We will not learn anything by waiting to talk. When listening to
Indigenous teachings and wisdom-keepers, please remember it is medicine that
people have been murdered for. When we stand in our authentic power, we stand
for those who no longer can. Amplifying voices and listening is crucial.

We are lucky to be alive in a time where so many of us can do what needs to be
done to heal not just ourselves but this beautiful place we share. We have finally
infiltrated these systems enough to be able to reject them, take control, and topple
them. We are getting close to being able to throw the switch. This will result in

more global changes and evolution of our planet's systems, and we're all beginning to realize that trusting a few people to run the world and translate the important stuff wasn't such a great idea after all.

Your Practice Is a Revolutionary Act of Creation

Accept the idea that magic has been happening since humanity was a thing and that all the objects and relics here in The Sanctum come with stories and mythologies—because we were meant to have been practitioners of energy from the start. When we connect to Source, energy itself, we can access greater intelligence. We get to be a part of that.

We were robbed of our gifts because they are treasure. Our rich Spirits were looted. It started with the time we measure as our years AD. After death, they were so proud of it they even began to measure time by it.

As you deepen your practice, it is integral to the process of remembering to have someone who may be a little bit ahead of you on the path. It helps when you experience magic to have witnesses. To be able to actually say to someone, *HOLY SHIT, CAN YOU BELIEVE THIS?* Source likes surprise and it likes delight. They are its currency. It is part of the lesson plan; the other part is learning how to employ your gifts. Just like in *Super Mario Brothers*, we need to level up. As we begin to master the powers each of us are given, we learn what we have to use in our scavenger hunt to get to the next part. If we don't, we tend to stay in the same cycle. Nature teaches us this lesson. It evolves as it grows each season. So having a human teacher will help keep you grounded as a human being and ensure that you know when selfishness and ignorance are coming back on the scene with their spin.

Don't worry, we'll deal with those two next in The Hall of Mirrors.

Magic shows up to be witnessed. All sacred spiritual texts contain magic; that's what makes them sacred. The Sefirot, the Tree of Life, is used in both high magic *and* Kabbalah, Jewish Mysticism. *Same* source. No matter how long or deep I go into the path of remembering, there are people who have more experience, and

they provide me with the community I need to keep going. This goes back to where this idea of a "congregation" actually came from. It was about collective growth, but it was also about fair witnesses.

When you lean in a little bit, Spirit's going to lean in times ten more, because it's going to be so glad that you're back in the game. We can in effect help Energy reach the next level in order to permeate and get some light through these dirty windows. When we get to The Great Hall, we will remember the art of Transfiguration.

As we move to end our time in The Sanctum, we are also going to remember a few last things. We've been talking to Source and asking people to talk to Source for us for thousands of years. There's someone else we have to talk about while we're in The Sanctum. We may not have noticed because this prophet doesn't have anything on a shelf. That's not his style. He's all about Impermanence. Siddhartha Gautama through his own healing journey became known as the Buddha. Beside the empty shelf is the Wheel of Dharma, a representation of cosmic law and order, but dharma isn't just present in Buddhism, it's part of Hinduism and Sikhism, and as we stand here looking at it, we notice the star on the floor. It's a dharma wheel (and of course it is). The dharma wheel represents the Wheel of the Law; the Buddha is said to have started the wheel in motion when he delivered his first sermon.

People throughout history have used oracles. Leaders consulted them to read the stars before important events. Among the most famous were the Oracle of Delphi. Chosen by the Gods to channel wisdom. Their temple still stands. Magic and connection to divinity has always been part of our civilization.

The next shelf holds a triangle. Not a pyramid, but a triangle, and it's made of gold. The concept of the Holy Trinity isn't just a part of Christianity—God, Jesus, and Holy Spirit. It's also part of the Veda, Brahma, Vishnu, and Shiva, Creator/Creatrix, the Son/Sun, and Source itself. In ancient Egyptian origin, specifically the Heliopolis, is the idea that Spirit willed itself into being and then came moisture/air (Shu and Tefnut) and then from that came Heaven and Earth (Nut and Geb). The legend goes that humanity came from the children of Nut and Geb. You've probably heard of two of them, Isis and Osiris. The holy trinity in ancient Egyptian mythology is Osiris, Isis, and their divinely created Horus. The holy trinity is in us: mind, body, and Spirit.

Spirit, or Energy, is a vibration of peace, love, unity, and respect, and for an ex-raver like me, the old rave adage of P.L.U.R. (peace, love, unity, and respect) felt a lot like ancient knowledge. The human brain moves into a shamanic state of consciousness at approximately 220 beats per minute. No wonder I loved drum and bass parties; I was likely experiencing a higher state of consciousness. It felt as if we were one because we were. Make fun of the pants we wore if you want, but we were remembering something ancient. Ask any raver and they will tell you about transcendental experiences—and they didn't all come from ecstasy. The fact is, human beings don't need anything added to our systems to dance with the Universe. With training and experience, we can tap out a beat and off we go. If we consider this, we can better appreciate that some of the experiences recorded throughout human history reflect that human beings were employing their gifts, and the tools of the soul, to see the same visions. If it's a thing now (and it is), why wouldn't this explain the things we haven't yet been able to explain with science?

Quantum theory, quantum physics have reached a point where they have some-what begrudgingly had to acknowledge magic. Science is now discovering some amazing things that are changing everything that we thought we knew about how we work, and most importantly, how the world works. It's now a scientific fact that we are all part of a universal energy field. Human beings are not separate from energy, according to Spirituality *and* science.

The Einstein-Podolsky-Rosen experiment was done to demonstrate a hypoth-esis that had bothered Albert Einstein. It was what he had characterized as *spooky action at a distance.* It had to do with two electrons that had been in connection with each other and then went off at infinite distances. If the spin of one electron changes, the spin of the distant electron would change at the same moment. How? There's no known understanding of this because in theory, if something has to travel distances, there should also be time related to that. It should not happen simultaneously, but it does. This phenomenon is called quantum entanglement, which means we're moving away from a purely cause-and-effect model to one that is much more intelligent, engaged, and, well, entangled.

This discovery reinforces the mystical idea that we're not separate, that nothing is separate, that everything is connected everywhere at all times (it's the multiverse in real time). Everything, everywhere, all at once indeed. This is what Spiritual people throughout history have been saying, writing down, and yes, again, carving into stones.

We are at the point in history where even *scientists*—presumably, the most logical humans we have—know and acknowledge that there *is* magic. That contained in the fabric of life are things that are spooky or defy explanation so much that they create a sense of wonder and awe. We are experiencing a fabric of reality in which we can imagine that the threads woven through it are not like ordinary pieces of thread. There's something else, some connective tissue that spreads out everywhere, not just through space but also through time. That means that everything we know and have ever known is actually connected all the time. There is no separation. We have only the appearance of separation when we look at things with our human eyes. We see space but we don't see the connective tissue. It's important to note that human eyes aren't typically tuned for Spirit. That's what happens when you spend a few generations not using your tools. They get a little rusty.

As we come to the last of the rays, we notice a plinth against the wall. It looks like an exit door, but as you move closer, you notice there are seven *C*'s. As you touch them a hologram appears, with a sign, Meet the Clairs.

What is this, an eighties sitcom? Who are the Clairs?

The Seven Sisters

When you dream, are you using your eyes? No, they're closed. You're not processing images, you're in your consciousness, working in non-ordinary reality. Spiritual work is typically not done with our human eyes. It's done in the consciousness. And usually, it's done by employing the Clairs. You probably know at least one of them: clairvoyance. You may even have met one or two more of them here in the Temple. You may have felt (clairsentience), known (claircognizance), or heard (clairaudience) something as you've been doing your rituals and moving through

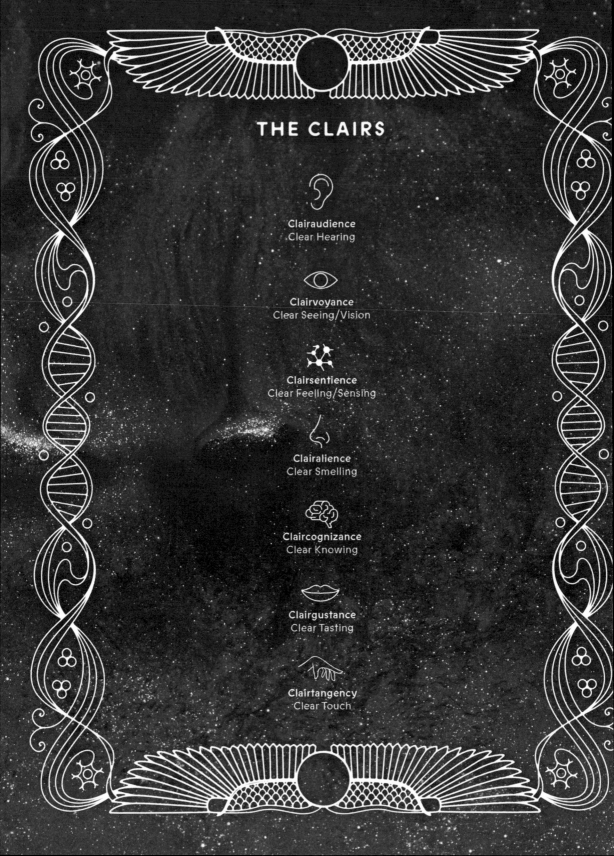

THE CLAIRS

Clairaudience
Clear Hearing

Clairvoyance
Clear Seeing/Vision

Clairsentience
Clear Feeling/Sensing

Clairalience
Clear Smelling

Claircognizance
Clear Knowing

Clairgustance
Clear Tasting

Clairtangency
Clear Touch

the rooms. As we get back into balance. We humans will remember how to invite these sisters back to the party.

The most popular Clair is clairvoyance; it's the one everyone knows. It's the one most people equate with being "psychic." But human beings have access to lots of Clairs—clairaudience, clairsentience, clairalience, claircognizance, clairgustance, clairtangency. You may come from a family that has some of these gifts or you may come from a family that refuses to believe in the Clairs. Here's the thing, if one of us can do it, any of us can do it. It just takes practice. One Clair may show up first; you may meet the others later. I've never met a person who after putting the Clairs into practice didn't get to meet (at least one of) their gifts.

As a kid I could hear voices, I could hear arguments sometimes, which now I feel were likely energies fighting for the microphone, so to speak. I knew enough inside my little body not to tell anyone about how I was hearing things, that it wasn't safe to talk about my gifts, that people would think I was bananas. Although I grew up in a family of ancestral witches, I felt strongly enough to keep it secret and safe because at some points in my soul's journey, I was persecuted for it.

There are still moments where I'm sharing and my witch wound rears up, and it feels dangerous. I remind myself this is just some Uninvited toxicity aimed at the old ways and that it's becoming safer to reclaim. That by practicing and remembering, I am honoring those who have fallen. As I do that, I also deepen my practices, and through the work, I seem to gain other gifts or treasure from my soul. You may begin with one gift and remember more over time. These gifts are to be developed. You can begin with none and end up collecting them all. Better than Pokémon.

Into the Wonder

Our collective withdrawal of human participation in cosmic and natural cycles, including ignoring our Spiritual practice and our gifts, has been pretty catastrophic for both Nature *and us*. It's time we reclaim it. With this two-part written and practice, we are going to reclaim *your* Temple. In the written practice, I'd like you to write about what you actually know about *your* Spirit, and *your* magic. Your own or your family's connection to the old ways, or to the divine. Let's begin to trace the moments of magic you may find in your ancestry; look for the breadcrumbs. Are there stories in your family or in your daily life? What do you know about your family's connection to Spirituality? How did religion show up or not show up in your life? How did you feel about it? How do you feel about it now based on what we're remembering here? What kinds of modalities or beliefs are in your realm of experience from your relatives? What modalities or beliefs aren't in your experience, but you may be drawn to? Was there anything that came up in The Sanctum that lit a spark? For the practice, you're going to try something for at least a week to notice what changes and how it impacts your day. It's simple and quick, so please don't make excuses about not having time for something new. If you want to remember, this is part of it. You can do it. This is practice.

At the beginning of each day before you do anything (including checking your phone), you're going to send a signal from your energy to Source itself that you're getting your day started. You're going to light up your Temple. When you wake up, you're going to wind up. You're going to get up and you're going to imagine that you're going to greet the day by pulling the energy up out of the ground and over your head, as if you're pulling your shirt up over your head (maybe you are!) and you're bringing your arms up. Imagine you're pulling a strand of energy out of the Earth and wrapping it up and down around yourself, like a protective layer. A bubble of energy. A circle of order and balance.

Starting the day with a little "Rise and Shining," we are going to start honoring the fact that we are human vessels on the planet. We are honoring that we're made of star stuff. This is a signal and sign to Source that you're in the world and you're ready for messages. Human antenna reporting for duty!

It's a physical act as much as it's an intentional act. When we're in harmony with the natural order, you will begin to have a foundation that you can call on.

You don't have to be in a sanctum or temple to connect to the foundation of the divine, but you're safe here if it's where you choose to practice. The next part of The Temple is the true test.

The road of magic comes with initiation. You've already started to see what's behind the curtain and its magnificence. We've reset and done some pretty heavy theoretical lifting. We're starting to remember that life will never be more difficult than it is when we aren't using all of our parts.

There is nothing to be afraid of, but we cannot skip through this phase. Initiation. In fact it was part of the Invitation. Mirrors don't always reflect what we expect. We're remembering to look deeper with fresh eyes. It is part of the journey. It means we have to pass through a Hall of Mirrors. We're only a room away from the message that sent you here, as beyond The Hall of Mirrors is The Hall of Secrets. But in order to receive it, we have to first face ourselves. As we move toward The Hall of Mirrors to get deeper into The Temple to reclaim your power, we will have to tame what can feel like a wild animal. It may spit at you, or try to bite, and that may seem scary right now, but I assure you, it will do what you ask of it.

It has always known this moment would come. We will put it in a safe place for the rest of the journey and call on it when we need it, because we will.

I'll meet you in The Hall of Mirrors when you're ready.

This is initiation and it's part of every hero and heroine's origin story.

II

RECEIVING

CHAPTER SEVEN

THE HALL OF MIRRORS

EJECTING EGO

As we're coming out of The Sanctum toward The Hall of Mirrors, we notice there's a similar curtain to the one in The Entryway, much like the ones that framed the giant doors to The Library and The Archives. This piece of fabric stands between us and whatever is next. We talked about initiation as we left The Sanctum because there is no magic without it.

To experience magic again, we all have to make some adjustments. We also need to do that in order to move into the next part of The Temple. If we don't make the adjustments now, we won't even be able to find the door to that room, let alone find a lock to place a key. In order to reclaim our magic, we have to have the right part of ourselves doing the driving. Initiation can be defined as *"the beginning of something."* It is also defined as an action of admitting someone into a secret society or group usually via a ritual. This is a rite of magic.

In order to be tuned into the correct channel to receive your magic, we have to ensure that we can reach it. It's a high vibration, a big frequency, and we have picked up a limiter from The Uninvited. It may as well be a choke chain. It prevents us from moving too far, and as a result we can't begin to imagine what is behind the curtain or even wonder what magic might happen when we take off the collar. Because they made it seem too scary to think about what was beyond the leash (that doesn't even exist) without them. What lies behind the things that seem to have kept us separate from magic?

As we move forward and past this heavy curtain, we come into a hall made of stone and lined with columns. We are tiny compared to the hall that surrounds us, the light bouncing between the columns. There are mirrors framed between the stone pillars, which are reflecting the light as if by magic. Here's the thing about magic—it's synonymous with light and service (and so is abundance). You can't *see* magic or *find* magic or *do* magic if you aren't *of service* to it.

In order to really begin to practice magic, we need to take a really long, careful, kind, and good look in the mirror. This is the place where we reconnect to ourselves. We talked about the great separation from Nature; now we'll work to set the intention to begin to mend the great separation from ourselves. When I mention ego, I'm not referring to the ego you may have heard about in psychology. I'm referring to the ego as it pertains to a Spiritual practice. It's the piece of us that is like our filter on the world. It's those glasses I mentioned that might look cool but don't help us to see any better. This is the ego we're going to redefine, the one that pertains to how we see ourselves and how we see the world. When we remember that we're vessels learning how to fuel with light, we want to make sure we can connect to it. Putting our ego's lenses aside is going to help us be sure we're seeing as clearly as possible.

We can't truly enjoy magic, wonder, and abundance without understanding that they are all side effects of service. I know you might be starting to tell me that there's some people with lots of money who *enjoy* abundance but don't understand anything about being *good*. Here's the thing about that kind of attachment to money, or inauthentic power: It's just a collection of glasses without the right lenses. Sure, they might look cool, but can these people really even see where we are going? We are meant to *share* abundance, love, and joy with others. Putting your ego in the right place is going to be like getting a new pair of glasses—with lenses you can actually see out of. Much cooler.

Have you ever had the opportunity to give back with your time? Cooking or shopping for a neighbor, volunteering at a local library, or organizing with community actions that move you.

It feels, really, really good. *That's the soul.*

It may start as ego, but when you feel service, it feels good. It feels especially good when you're able to witness the side effect of actual service: impact and change. We get to have the wonder of change. We get the magic power of learning and growing.

Transforming isn't just for robots.

Change Is Good

In this Hall, we're going to be looking at ourselves in ways we may not have before. How bad does it have to get for us to grab on to change? It may be hard to imagine a different way of doing things, or to imagine a world without these systems designed by The Uninvited to hurt people. That's the beast we need to tame. This unseen force that prevents us from doing these things. We don't have to allow the part of ourselves that keeps us separate from wonder be in charge of where we're going.

That part is ego.

And it can be *kind* of a jerk. It can make us say things we don't mean. It can be the loudest of loudmouths. It probably says it doesn't need to wear a seatbelt, cuts people off in traffic, and doesn't bother using its indicator. It also gives people the finger. It not only ghosts people, but it also calls them names. And if it's been running the show, it means there's probably been some times that you might have been a jerk. Don't worry. You're not alone. We *all* have this in common. I was a pretty big jerk sometimes too. We're not going to beat ourselves up about it, because it's part of being human. We make mistakes, we learn, and we try our best to do better. We're capable of change and transformation, and that's what we're doing now. We're making some adjustments.

That's how we're meant to do this, and as we walk farther into this Hall of Mirrors, we're going to accept a hard fact together right now in order to change and grow. It's likely that what's been driving your vessel so far probably never had a license or a map, let alone a GPS. That's why when we let it drive, it feels as if we're going in circles. It takes joyrides, spins out, sometimes hits stuff, and that means it may return with damage—and regret.

I don't recommend giving it unsupervised access to the keys of your consciousness. Let alone telling it where the keys *are*.

Ego is the one who likes to build using inauthentic power. Ego is competition; ego is greed. It's the mentality that there is not enough available to us in life and that this is all some kind of big contest. It is *not* a contest. The only contest we are all having here in this life on Earth is the one where we are measured at how good we are at being yourself. It's not your awards, where you live, what kind of car you have, or your accomplishments, or fill in the blanks of what you own, it's you. How good are you at being *you*?

We usually think of ego as being full of yourself when in this case it's actually kind of the opposite. It's being full of separation. Ego serves only itself. That's the ego's modus operandi. It wants us to think that there isn't enough. It wants us to think it's us and them. It wants us to think it is *absolutely* a contest. Ego is anything within your consciousness that creates the illusion that you are separate from Nature, others, the Universe, Energy, Source, God. Ego is a professional at telling us that we don't need help, that it knows where to go, and how to do everything. *It doesn't.* Just like anything else in Nature, we can't expect that operating in only one capacity is going to be healthy. We're little oceans of emotion, and when we disconnect from Source or each other, that is where things get muddy, right? We'll have to address that beastly part of the ego, the sharp-tongue stuff where we yell at drivers, honk our horns, and give people the finger. That cuts. It can cut so deeply it can kill people.

We're seeing it in society. This violence and anger comes from disconnection and, you guessed it, ego. I think we all know it does not come from the soul. It makes us tired and frustrated because it spins for miles, creating oceans of confusion. That's not your soul. Your soul would *never* talk to you like that.

When your ego's trying to keep you separate, it's separating you from not only all of your magic but the magic of everything and everyone. So you're going to start to have a dialogue with it. The ego is going to pop up like it always does, but we're going to manage it. You may be imagining one of those carnival games where the groundhog pops up and you have to bop it on the head with a mallet, except for only the ego would use a mallet. For the soul, a gentle reminder will suffice.

We don't want to use mallets for gentle work, and we can't get rid of ego entirely because it has a job. We're on the planet and we need it to help us survive here. It can help us when we're on the phone with bill collectors, in a job interview, in a debate, talking to a lawyer, or being a lawyer. It serves a purpose to protect us— especially when we're dealing with jerks. The ego can act as a great shield and protector, but we don't need it all the time. It certainly doesn't need to be driving. Think of it as a special ops team; it's the one to call to help handle things for you when shit is really going down on planet Earth.

It might be hard to imagine doing this life thing any other way. That's your ego trying to tell you there's no one better to do this job (that they haven't even been doing properly). It may be a fast talker, which makes people think it knows the answers. It doesn't. It's just louder and impatient. Like the kid who put up their hand in class to be first but didn't think about whether they knew the answer. That's who the ego is in this practice of remembering. It's the *Me first,* and *Me only* mentality. I'm not talking about self-care, I'm talking about the concept and entitlement that the world revolves around me and me alone, and that what we do doesn't impact anyone else. And frankly, it's unsustainable. It's why the world is exposing all these system failures. They're inauthentic.

That's the difference between real magic and stage magic.

Deliver Us from Ego

Because I hadn't processed what happened to me as a kid, I ended up living in a cycle of trauma. Running a real Trauma Gauntlet. I spent a long time letting my ego drive my wounded little vessel around. It was tired and traumatized, shaping the way I saw the world. I believed that in order for me to be safe, I had to hold up inauthentic power above all, like some kind of American Gladiator (even if I'm half-Canadian). So many survivors of childhood trauma, and sexual abuse in particular, live with this feeling of having to be of silent service in order to be safe. For years, my ego took me to places I'd already been and places where nothing good was happening. No wonder and very little magic. I needed a GPS.

Turns out I had one the whole time. Each of us already have a fully licensed, vetted, and experienced (*I'm talking eons of it*) driver available to us, who can take over as our vessel's captain.

It's your soul.

Here's the really cool part: Your soul has likely been doing this longer than your ego, your body, and before whatever iteration you're in now was even a thing. Just like we reconnected with Nature, we ask the soul to take over. The soul can bring the ego back when it's needed. We can trust the soul to let us know when it needs some reinforcement. It won't lie to you about how it's doing the way ego tends to. The odds are that your ego has been doing all kinds of stuff it's not even qualified for.

So why do we have breakdowns when we are operating in ego? Because we're literally fighting against natural law, meaning, the All, Energy itself. When we do that, when we choose ego over soul, it is as if we're running up a steep slide, instead of just going down it. And it's also kind of embarrassing, especially if you're trying to get to work.

If ego could design a system around itself, it would be capitalism, which— spoiler—it is! It's hard to avoid, but we're beginning to see the cracks enough to understand that working five days a week isn't healthy, nor does it get most of us any further ahead. That's why billionaires love it (they're also big on stage magic). We work and they benefit. It keeps us separate from them. It always has.

Systems of The Uninvited are driven by ego. They were created to control us so that we couldn't connect directly. Not to each other and certainly not to Source. If ego is running the show, we will be motivated by systems rooted in it. If we speak to Source, or Soul directly, we get the real deal. The side effect to that is that The Uninvited are found out (*by us pesky kids*).

Throughout history, humans have made and done great things because we were vibrating highly enough to get instructions from something other than ourselves. All these civilizations who we still study for answers, all these commonalities on the planet before we had the internet. We received guidance and assistance from our souls and probably from the source of everything. We did it because there was still room for wonder.

It's time to remove those lenses, or looking glasses, so we can more clearly see our reflection in the mirror.

Shifting Away from Separation

As we stand in this Hall of Mirrors, we see these versions of ourselves reflected. We see how ego may have injected itself, or infected, your view of the world. If you're anything like me, it may have kept you separate. You may realize where you became stuck in the mirror. You may have reflected a version of yourself you no longer wish to carry. Using our consciousness can recalibrate; to move through the looking glass, we can ask our souls to drive. We can ask to see with our soul. When that happens, people radiate. They're genuinely and authentically magnetic. That's what really drew me down the garden path into this Spirituality stuff. It was when I noticed that people who have their souls at the wheel seem to have more fun. They're childlike. I *love* fun and I like to have as much of it as I can, so it was that sense of wonder that got me here deep into woo-woo town. A breadcrumb here: A Chinese shaman, or witch (or wizard), is known as a wu. Wuism is the practice of magic.

People who vibrate from the soul tend to radiate joy. If you've ever been in a space with any Spiritually or energetically focused human, you'll know that you *feel* the magic. The goosebumps. And you laugh. You don't have to be in alignment with another human being's views to feel the current that is carried. It's light. It's airy. It's like electricity. That's why people say an experience can be electric. Spirited. It's the energy. Our medicine, or individual magic, brings joy and meaning into moments that might have been decimated by our egos. We don't need a mallet or a hammer to get there; we can leave those in the Trauma Shed.

The next time the ego tries to grab the wheel and drive (and it will), it's going to be in for a big surprise. This is where the car seat comes in. We've got to get the

ego away from the controls and strap that sucker in. This is a major part of remembering how we make the shift from mediocre to magic. If you imagine with me that maybe one day we transition to the afterlife, we leave our bodies, and maybe have the opportunity to become a steward of a galaxy or something, it's probably not a good idea to have a lot of ego, fear, or anger. With all that possible power, we better be able to manage our egos.

When we shift from ego to soul, we get to choose. Every single day, down to the moment, who is talking and who is in charge. Of course, The Uninvited don't believe in breaks. They believe only in productivity; their systems demand urgency. We don't have to respond that way anymore. We get to take a beat and slow down the process to make space for our souls. We get to reset our clocks and trust the speed of Nature. We get to turn off notifications.

We are meant to have the divine part of ourselves at the wheel. That's probably a key to people creating amazing and spectacular things. When we listen to our souls, we follow our purpose, and as a result we can lean into the things that we are passionate about in the core of our being. When we make room for wonder we can more easily locate the magic. The synchronicity. The breadcrumbs. When this happens, so does magic. Flow and magic are synonymous. This way of life has existed since Paleolithic times. This is why so many civilizations built arrows pointing to the stars. They wanted us to know to look up. To look outside of our "selves" and, in turn, look at what connects us. Why else are we here if not to try to operate from a position of higher and likely wiser intelligence? Let's make an agreement that we've done enough donuts for now. Less dizzy might be good. Especially in The Hall of Mirrors.

Into the Wonder

Being in this hallway, a wide-open space where Energy can move through, imagine that *we* are the light being reflected by the mirrors. Consider that maybe we can use our intention to move our egos out of the driver's seat and maybe we can bring about miraculous change. Not only in our own lives but in the webs of connections all around us. As we stand here in this ancient hall, we'll get to the initiatory part of our adventure. This is the part where you invite wonder to take root in your being. You're not just going to make space. You're going to give it a seat at your table. We're reclaiming that whole being. *Invite only.*

This is a visualization and meditation practice where we'll envision our ego and our soul switching places in our being. You may want to choose a mirror in The Hall of Mirrors by which to do this ritual. There may be a particular set of columns calling to you. Lean into your intuition. As we move into this space, your soul gets to reclaim the driver's seat in your mind's eye.

Remember that you are a vessel, a vehicle moving through this life, and your ego no longer needs to be at the controls. It doesn't need to be the captain. It can become special ops. It can be an expert you call on. You may put it in a car seat, or it may go in a briefcase or a black box (if it's being especially rowdy).

As you do this, and you imagine relocating this expert, try to identify any times in your life when your ego may have successfully grabbed the wheel. It might be a series of things. Maybe it always turns relationships left. Maybe it's something where the ego may be driving in circles instead of going where you want to go. When you identify these times, I'd like you to try to visualize going back to those moments and correcting the course. Try to imagine what your soul might have done, based on what you've begun to remember about it so far.

It's time to look at yourself in the mirror sitting between the last columns. Ask your soul: *Can you step to the front? Can you take it from here? Can you captain this vessel? Can you take me where I'm meant to be? Can you help me remember?*

If you want to do this practice in front of a real mirror, feel free. Look into your own eyes, past your irises and pupils, into the space that few people know but everyone can see, and ask your beautiful soul to step forward.

You may want to imagine there is a star, or a light inside of you, a piece of source, or a fragment of the sun, whatever feels right to you and your beliefs. You're going to imagine there is something inside of you that is connected to everything. If you're comfortable with it, you may even want to imagine that there's an actual light coming down from Source. A little tendril, or beam, and it's taking the wheel. You can ask your soul to help you see life more clearly through the right lenses.

If you need some help talking to your soul, you can use the words that follow. You may want to record the next bit and play it back so that you can close your eyes.

Higher self. Higher truth. Highest Source.
Please help me clearly see my purpose, direction, and force.
I ask for ease, I ask for grace,
for the highest good, for all, in every place.
Please help me be the best version of me, in every moment I can.
Please remind me how to use my gifts, my life, my heart, my hands.
May I use my medicine with honor, respect, and wisdom to answer my own call.
Please remind me how to be of service to the collective one and all.
May I remember wonder and magic with lots of ease and grace.
And, yes, I asked you for it twice because of the world's pace.

As you finish these words, or whatever version of this you may create, you're going to finish by apologizing. You are going to apologize to yourself for any of the limiting beliefs, hurtful comments, or pain you may have brought upon yourself or any other being. You're going to release that judgment and set down those old lenses. When you're ready, we will close with what we should all hear every day, whether it's from ourselves or someone else.

I love you.

Your soul is not going to reinvent your personality—it's part of this journey— what your soul *will* do is accentuate what makes you, you. Try to imagine how the kindest part of yourself may have handled something that ego might have made a mess of. Maybe you got scuffed up, maybe you scuffed up someone else? If you have a hard time imagining what soul might do, try to imagine a person in your life (or a pet) who loves you and imagine what they would say or do. Soul can smooth out the edges; ego tends to sharpen them. Again, time and place.

Let's be clear, in Spirituality, in remembering, the ego is not bad. It deserves credit. It is a badass. My ego saved my life many times. But it also almost stole it.

That's what happens when it lives on unchecked energy. All we're doing here is adding some actual checks and balances into our system. We just want to put some space between it and the controls, to give wonder enough of a head start before ego gets a word in.

As we finish this practice, we complete the initiation. We have invited wonder to sit at the table. When you're ready, you can move to the end of The Hall of Mirrors. The next curtain leads into The Hall of Secrets. This is the territory of the soul. This is where we begin to refill our tanks with a really clean inexhaustible and sustainable fuel.

Did you feel that? It may have felt like a little click.

The soul has buckled itself in. That's all we need to do; all we ever need to do is just ask. Our intention and words when combined have great power. I'd like you to take a minute and just notice how this feels. You may be seeing, or remembering, some moments in your life where your ego drove you in circles. Maybe it wasn't circles, maybe there was a breakdown, because ego told you that it didn't need any fuel?

I'd like you to honor those moments. Honor what comes up for you. As you open your eyes, you may want to make some notes in your magic book about anything you may have realized or remembered in The Hall of Mirrors. You may even want to change what you said to yourself (or others) in some of those ego-dominated moments. You can ask your soul to come forward for help with healing those moments. You may even choose to begin the work to heal them in your day-to-day life. This hall is a place you can return whenever you need to be reminded that you can eject the ego at any time. We get to ask for guidance to help us find the breadcrumbs and to help us go back to collect the ones we may have missed because ego kept telling us to "hurry up," probably under its breath too. These are clues about where we need to let the light in. We all have the capability to recalibrate. We all have the ability to operate from a higher truth than the one your ego is able to access. There's plenty of light and healing to come from Source. We can go back and add light to those moments where we may not have been getting enough oxygen. You may want to just note how you felt as we moved the ego out of the driver's seat. What patterns may there be within the things you've remembered so far? This will usually be a good indicator of where the work is on your particular journey.

If you get stuck in the mirror, or find yourself wearing some of those old glasses, this is the place to remind yourself how limiting it is. It's a dead end. All you need to do is ask with heartfelt intention and be open to the prospect. If your body needs healing from any ego-driven hurts, you can start asking for it. We can't access all of what's in The Hall of Secrets (or our lives) with our egos driving. It will not let us pass. Wonder and ego don't often mix. We won't properly access the rooms in the next parts of the adventure while the ego is driving. We won't learn of what lies beyond separation and limitation if we don't swap out this driver.

To move into The Hall of Secrets, the ego must be contained. The Universe favors the humble. When you look back at the mirror in The Hall of Mirrors after the ritual, you realize the mirror has shifted. Maybe that was the click you felt? The panel seems to have opened and that is where the light is spilling in from.

It's time to move through this looking glass.

Maybe you have heard that somewhere before?

CHAPTER EIGHT

THE HALL OF SECRETS

ENGAGING THE SOUL

As we step forward through the mirror and into the light, it takes a moment to adjust to the change in illumination. We stand in another hallway surrounded on either side by huge glowing columns. Somehow the stone is luminescent, and the columns are each crowned in gold. There must be a dozen of them leading down the hallway. Light comes up from the floor along the length of the hallway. We're down the rabbit hole, indeed. The ceiling is painted with ships moving through a night sky. Constellations glow as light passes through tiny pinpoints in the stone ceiling. The whole space radiates in a starlit glow, as if the room were full of stars.

This is The Hall of Secrets.

This is the place where we engage our own star stuff. It is the place where we shift our being into a state of receiving. You've likely been in a state of output. In The Hall of Mirrors, we asked our soul, our higher self to take the wheel. We've been learning a little about its credentials and where it comes from. As we move through this hall to each of these columns under these constellations, we'll get to know our souls, our Spirits, our energy.

Just as we had to reframe ego; we have to do the same for the souls. What is it, anyway? And what does *Spirit* actually mean? To breathe, sure, but what *is* it? The

Soul is defined as the Spiritual or immaterial part of a human being or animal. It's the compassionate and empathetic part of us. It's also the piece of us that has the prospect of living forever, or lifetime after lifetime. It's the part of us that is regarded as immortal. The divine part. We can see our bodies; we can feel them. We know enough about the brain, but the soul, it's the mystery of our being. A crucial part of consciousness and yet an unseen part of our daily life. Yet, it's the light or energy that powers our being and consciousness. Maybe the soul provides the consciousness. The connective tissue between the physical body and the Spiritual self. It's our tether to home. A seed of our star stuff. It's much gentler than the ego because it has no worries. That's what happens when you have ancient divine intelligence. That kind of experience tends to calm the nerves. The difference between driving with a new driver and being driven by a professional. It's a more relaxed ride because there's more experience at the wheel. Because of this the soul can be quieter than ego. That means you might need to make more room to hear it. I know, I know, all these rooms! But it's never going to be the loudmouth. It's too elegant. It's just not how it's wired. It's humble and kind and it would never say an unkind word to you, or anyone else. That's how light operates.

It's why it feels so good in this hallway. Have you ever felt so good in a hallway? I haven't. I love it here but I'm a bit of a Space Witch.

The soul has a language, just like Nature does. The language of your soul is intuition. It's the part of you that cues the goosebumps. The shiver down your back. The butterflies and gut feelings. The stomach-dropping feelings. The inner knowing. The soul is the part of us that just *knows*. The more we listen for it, the more we make room for it, the more it shows up and the clearer it gets. You'll get used to the change in volume.

You're part of your ancestry on the planet, but you're also part of your soul's own lineage. It comes from stuff that's billions and billions of years old. We talked in The Greenhouse about how Nature doesn't take cash. What does it take? What is its currency of choice?

Love.

Source is loving by design; the soul is loving. When we feed the system, it feeds us back. Reciprocity is built in, forever. That's the part of us that is connected to everything that is, ever was, and ever will be. Your soul is your authentic self; of course it knows the way.

As we move through the first set of columns, the constellations twinkle, moving from one side of the hall to the other.

Let Me Take You to Nerd Town

The law of conservation of energy, or the first law of thermodynamics, is that energy can be changed from one form to another, but it cannot be created or destroyed. The total amount of energy and matter in the Universe remains constant; it may change, or transmute into one form or another, but it doesn't *die*. You and I are and are always going to be part of this spectacular system. Amadou Hampâté Bâ, poet, ethnologist, and historian, said, "For us, death does not exist in traditional Africa. We don't say dead. We say change of domicile because we are supposed to continue living for an eternity."

And maybe that's exactly how it works. Maybe part of our beings can change vessels?

Our soul is made of energy, or light, and it was who was always meant to be driving our beings. It was of course, The Uninvited, who encouraged us all to have ego at the wheel. They didn't want us to know there was another driver. It was much more convenient for them if we drove ourselves in circles instead of forward. That's how you stop progress, and they've done a really good job. But this is where we take it back because we all carry a spark of divinity in our human containers. A molten piece of magic that somehow braids us all together.

We can't see it with our human eyes, but most of us can *feel* it. Some of us are born highly tuned, some of us are born into ancestral trauma, some of us are born into density. Doesn't matter, we all have a soul. It is the part of us that lights up. That makes us glow. We know it when we are in love, or when we are with our loved ones. We feel lit up. Alive. We use terms like *sparked*, or *illuminated*, or *spirited*. We also know what it feels like to be around people who aren't illuminated. Sometimes people refer to those people as being *dim*. When someone is intelligent, or quick-witted, we call them *bright*. We call people *bright lights* when they do amazing work in the world.

But we are *all* children of the light. We have just forgotten how to wield it. Your soul has a GPS. The ego never even had a map.

The world can be a difficult place; we deserve to start using all of our pieces and powers to help us move through it. We can restore our love light. Otherwise, collectively we're going to keep running into that wall until there's no one left. What a waste after all this history, all these pyramids and all the magic. That doesn't feel like a wonder-driven scavenger hunt to me. Why would we choose that? I'm definitely not choosing that. I'm choosing wonder, every time. Let's also remember to choose soul and surrender instead of worrying. Because worrying has never changed an outcome, ever. It's like being thirsty but dropping a bunch of water into a bucket with a hole in it.

If we want to make change, we have to stop giving away our energy and reclaim our power. We need to stop pouring our buckets on the ground. When we use our intention to worry, the Universe doesn't hear us clearly. The signal isn't clear. Can you imagine what the Universe has been hearing from humanity for the last thirty years? Confusing. When we start to focus our energy and intention and use our gifts instead of worrying, we can balance not just our own lives, but the planet.

The light is in us, whether we know how to use it or not. Whether we're tuned in or not, it has likely covered your ass, saved you, and already moved you in ways you've likely never given it proper credit for. I hadn't. It's who shows up for us in the hardest moments; it's what shows up in our deepest connections. It *knows* our magic because it is our magic. When we see someone and feel like we've known them forever, *maybe we have?* The soul is found in the revelations, the epiphanies, and déjà vus of our lives.

Etymology of Spirit

As we move through The Hall of Secrets, it's as if we're moving back through time. We look up at the constellations under the next set of columns and they begin to pulse. If we go back to the origin of the word *Spirit*, it does give us clues about what we know—*to breathe* or *to live*. This is the same as the translation for ancient Egyptian mythology's holiest of holies, Amun-Ra, which translates to breath, the *hidden divinity*, *light*, *Source*, Spirit. The word *Spirit*, or *Soul*, has deep history and meaning in every culture on the planet for a reason. It was recognized as a part of us from the very beginning, by *everyone*. The word *soul* in Aramaic is *nephesh*, pronounced "ow-sha." In Hebrew, *Ruach* means *spirit*, *breathe*, and *life force*. Human beings and animals are both described as having *nephesh*.

The Mayans call it *Ch'ulel*; the Aztecs, *Teyolia* (which they believed was located in the heart).

In Sanskrit the term is *Prana*, *breath*, or *life-giving force*. In Japan it's known as *Ki*, and in China as *Chi*, a vital force forming part of any living entity (including Aunty Entity from *Mad Max*). Both translate to *breath*, *vapor*, *energy*. In ancient Egypt, the soul was made up of three parts—the *ba*, *ka*, *akh*. The *Ka* was the vital essence of one's being. In Hindi the word *Shakti* translates to *energy*, *ability*, and *power*. In Arabic and Sufi, *Ruh*, the Spirit, or Holy Spirit, is referred to as the *immortal*, or *the essential self*. The concept was that the soul was not a thing that we *had*, but a thing we *are*.

If we consider this, most of us have *not* been allowing our essential selves to run the show. No *wonder* things collectively are in such a state. All these definitions refer to an aspect of sentience. It seems in every civilization on the planet, breath has been seen as a vehicle for the Spirit. We all carry magic inside of us. It's been tracked (*breadcrumbed*) through history. The denial of it is a fairly recent development with catastrophic results and impacts.

Our vessels on Earth are powered enough by it that when our bodies die, the soul leaves it behind, but then what?

When we look at Spiritual teachings and origin stories holistically, we're remembering they have lots of commonalities. One of the most important is how we choose to live life on Earth might affect where we might find ourselves popping through in the afterlife. If the Earth is a soul school, human beings are probably here to learn how to use our light with good intention. In alignment and vibration with the core energy of the universe. Jedi stuff. Employing light, reason, and love. We are meant to tune into the soul to apply the learnings and gifts of generations in order to propel ourselves forward, not just as you and me, but as a species.

When you consider what this could all be, we really haven't been cutting it. Again, probably why we haven't had any visitors hanging around. We're kind of scary. We've been watching more and doing less. We have collectively been stuck in the muck of our collective traumas. Some are from thousands of years ago; some are currently playing out. It is hard here especially when some of us have never stopped dragging the trauma down the line because no one ever told us we could just energetically put it down. That we could cut those old cords and take up the fight for actual real-time change with our souls. We're all here for this purpose—to grow, to change, and to learn to move our vessels with real energetic integrity.

Shadow Dance

As we come to the next set of columns, the constellations don't brighten, or pulse, or move from one side of the hall to the other. The sky darkens. We are not meant to live on only one end of the spectrum. It's not all sunlight; we aren't a *good vibes–only* Universe. The Universe is full of contrasts, shadows, dark matter. We can't talk about life on Earth or the soul without talking darkness and shadow. Without talking about pain, rage, hurt, and trauma. Trauma doesn't just impact the body and mind; it also impacts the soul. It impacts our field of energy. The deeper and earlier the trauma, the more likely you are to also experience the side effects of that loss of energetic power. They show up as addiction, disassociation, even self-harm, or suicidal tendencies. They are all side effects of trauma. When we are hurt, we can lose power. With ancestral trauma, we can even lose access to the source of that power.

For a while in my own life, the thing I knew best was how to repeat patterns of abuse. We don't have to be resigned to living in the ancestral Trauma Shed. I had been out there for years—my ancestors, who knows how long some of them lived there. We can be the change agents in our own lives and in our ancestral traumas.

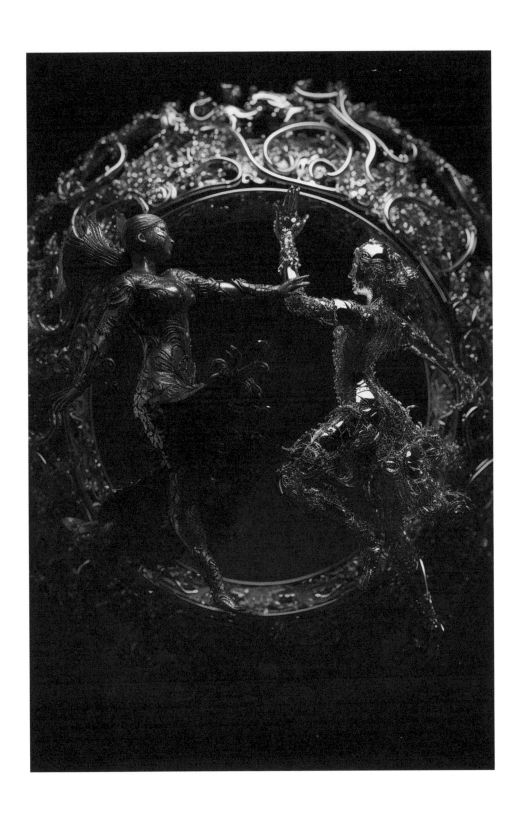

That's just one of the things the soul can do that the ego can't. It has the power to help stop those cycles.

We all have this power, both with our own lived trauma experiences and the trauma we may be carrying in our ancestries. The ones we know about and the ones we don't. We can have lost power through any lifetime or traumatic experience. We have our ancestry as humans on the planet, but so does the soul. We can ask for help to heal and for help to use the gifts of the soul and our bloodline. We have to heal and become responsible for our own energy in order to progress forward. Most of us are at the point where there's been so many patched holes in our vessels through our lives, and likely through the lives before yours, that we're not able to retain much fuel: We're leaking light. We can welcome back power that may have left our vessels due to pain or trauma, but to do it, we have to use our magic. We have to mend those holes and close those gaps.

Let's go ahead and imagine that our vessel is full of energy when we're born, like a glass of water. As we move through our lives, we go through heartbreaks, losses, traumas. Sometimes we really get jolted around, and we may have trauma on top of trauma. When we experience what I like to call a seven-layer burrito of trauma, we can simply feel as if we're out of steam. Sometimes we can be caught so off guard by a hurt that some of our energy can seem to spill out of our glass, our vessel, our body. This is what seems to happen with our Spirit when we experience trauma. When things are too painful, we can lose some of our light. If we experience this repeatedly, and we go untreated, we can experience what we call disassociation. We can feel as if we aren't in our bodies. As if we're separated from ourselves. Some of energy got outside of the vessel.

As an adult I'd see pictures of myself as a child and it was as if I were looking at a stranger. I *knew* it was me. I remembered things about that time, but I felt no connection to the person in the photos. I know now that it was because some of her left the building in order for me to survive. I felt a lot of shame and guilt about this, and maybe you have those feelings, too. Once I understood what had happened and saw it through the lens of professionals, I finally saw myself. I was ashamed that I'd somehow left this part of myself behind, as if I'd allowed a little part of myself to be lost at the mall for decades. I was gutted.

How could I not have noticed a part of me was missing?

It took me a long time (and many expensive therapists) to reframe that I did not in any way leave myself behind. I kept myself *safe*. That part of me went somewhere where it would be safe until I could pick her up. Pick her up I did. She's the one who turned the Trauma Shed into a Creative Cabin. She is the cycle breaker. It ran in the family until it ran into her. She's who I work for now.

I highly recommend the practice of adding a picture of little you to your home so that you can remember who you work for. I put mine on my mirror. It helps keep my Hall of Mirrors high-vibrating. My ego is no match for her magic.

This reclaiming of myself, my authentic power, and my light wasn't just about expensive therapists, magic was a key part of my healing journey. Healing is a triangle too. We have to check in on all the parts.

It was an American psychotherapist who was looking to help her clients with dissociation who started digging into this. We've been around thousands and thousands of years. She knew there was no medical answer to it but there had to be a solution for it. Through research looking at anthropological studies and history, she discovered that every culture on the planet had a solution. There was an ancient and Universal answer to trauma—it was shamanism. She identified that this practice was in our collective DNA.

That psychotherapist was Sandra Ingerman, who has since become one of the most widely known shamanic practitioners on the planet. Her work has now spanned decades. Her books, training, and community building have brought her around the world. She has participated in studies and research to bring more data to use of shamanic and Spiritual practices in traditional medicine.

In one study with the University of Michigan, "Healing the Heart: A Randomized Pilot Study of a Spiritual Retreat for Depression in Acute Coronary Syndrome Patients," the researchers showed that hope significantly improved among participants working with Sandra's practices. This effect persisted at three- and six-month follow-ups. Although several measures showed improvement in all groups by six months, the group working with Sandra Ingerman showed immediate improvement post-retreat, which was maintained. The pilot study showed that shamanic practices can be used to increase hope while reducing depression in patients living with acute coronary syndrome.

Imagine what these practices can do for humanity. It's time to find out.

If we can reclaim power that we lost due to trauma while we are alive, *we should be doing it.* Magic is communion with the divine, and we can't work with the soul without being open to it being divine. It isn't human. If your ego is yelling at you from the car seat right now about how the soul not being human is way too woo, now is a good time to remember that listening to it has taken you all the places you've already been, and that if you want to go somewhere new, you need to entertain something different.

The Secret Power of Nature

As we move toward the next set of columns, this constellation lights up. In fact, it moves slowly and almost seems to be pointing to one side of the hall. We follow this breadcrumb. As we walk toward the far column of this row there's a panel that's opened with an outpouring of light running out like a fountain. It's not a fountain of youth, but it is a fountain of knowledge about your soul. Lots of mysteries and secrets here. Perhaps it's time to find out about a few of them. How old is your soul? Where might it have come from? What are its gifts? What lifetimes has it lived? You can ask it yourself. You can put your hands into the light and ask.

You may want to take a minute to write down anything you may feel, know, see, or hear. Maybe you tasted something too? Your medicine is unique to you. It is the currency. Light, love, the life force. The force. Yes, like *Star Wars.* Here's where I tell you that *Star Wars* was heavily influenced by Akira Kurosawa's film *The Hidden Fortress.* The film is set in sixteenth-century Japan when Buddhism and Shinto had become the primary Spiritual practices. Reiki is a form of Japanese energy healing using life force energy; in Shinto, Kami is the energetic force that inhabits everything; and in *Star Wars,* Jedi work with the force. The force is likely rooted in the very real energy healing practices and natural traditions of Japan.

You don't have to know much about Egyptology to know about Anubis. Somehow almost everyone knows who that is, or they did when they were kids. The man with the head of a jackal. He was depicted by high priests wearing his headdress in ancient Egypt during preparation of the body and burial rituals. The Egyptians depicted shamanic ceremonies and techniques that are still employed in practices handed down today, as papyrus are displayed in museums around the world depicting the Anubis walking between worlds. Maybe he was the first shaman, a literal connection of Nature to humanity. Anubis walks the soul into the afterlife because he is man's best friend. The Guardian between realms (*and rooms*).

When you see historical or current photos of shaman, or witches, they're usually also wearing headdresses or hats (*we'll get to the how of the headdresses, necklaces, and other adornments later*). This is done as is an extension of the consciousness. The witch's hat is an antenna. They wear and use gifts from Nature representing elements and their relationships and helpers. Feathers become talismans, sticks become wands, empty foraged turtle shells become rattles. Faces of animals met along the way are sometimes integrated into headdresses. Things that are found on the journey and come along on the path of healing. These are gifts from the Earth. Tools are made from objects encountered through experiences in practice. We ask permission to work with those tools, just like we do with Nature. We ask Spirit to bless the purpose by putting them on our altars or wearing them when we practice. The headdress or eye curtain of an initiated and trained healer also represents their transformation into Spirit realm.

Each of us humans have a very specific job on Earth. When we get back to the clues, reconnecting with the plants, animals, elements, and directions, we get our balance back. We see clearly that all these natural systems have unique purposes and shapes. We are no different. We are wired for sound, whether your antenna is aimed or not. Whether or not you want to wear a witch hat, it's likely you have already experienced a higher state of consciousness at some point in your life. These little connections we've been making, the practices we've been doing so far. Your soul has been giving you these messages.

They're your very own secret messages.

It probably started whispering quietly and hopefully now at full volume (*quieter since the car seat, right?*). The soul is so magical that working with it requires a willingness for change and the openness to a force of intelligence so full of light that you will need sunglasses. It's beyond light speed. So we can go back in time to pick up our pieces. We *can* ask for that magic.

In shamanic teachings, disassociation is known as power loss, or soul loss. The amazing thing about energy: It's still there. It's immortal. Even though some of us may have some energy spill out due to trauma, I want you to imagine that it's still tethered to our little wrist like a balloon full of helium.

With some help of a qualified medicine person, and a little faith, we can bring it back. We can put the spill back inside our being without bringing back the trauma that caused it. Sounds great, right? Well, it's how we seem to be designed. It's how we've always been designed. We are meant to be able to heal from the wounds of trauma. With ancient traditions, disassociation can be remedied. The balloons can be put back into the vehicle. It's not lost in the clouds.

For thousands of years, shamanic practices and Nature-based healing have been a path to miraculous healing and change. You deserve to have access to as much of your soul's power as you are ready to hold in that amazing vessel of yours. Spiritual healing is possible when you visit someone with proper training. It's okay to ask for lineage and credentials when you work with a healing practitioner as much as it is when you work with any other kind of service provider. Experience matters in Spirit as much as it matters in the other parts of your triangle.

As we move to the next set of columns, the constellations above us move down and onto the columns themselves. Since this is life, it's got lessons built in. We get to choose who drives us through them and how you start to build community around it. A practice means that when something feels as if there's a tectonic shift or a meteor hitting your life, that you have a foundation to go, that you're holding a line on solid ground. This is what all these prophets have been trying to tell us. We have all the tools and the wisdom here. The goal is to learn how to use all the gifts and controls that we have available to us as human beings.

To heal our collective dissociation, we need to use the ancient medicine. We need to go back to the time before we unplugged. When we record our clues and start to glean our purpose, life gets a little easier to navigate because we can make decisions based on whether or not things are in alignment with purpose. The soul has a map; it knows what marks you need to hit and where you'll need to be. It will never, ever take you off course.

That's all we need to worry about in our lives—our own purpose—because that's what we're going to get asked about when we leave here (*not reality TV*). The other thing we seem to know about going into the afterlife is that we get measured, judged, weighed. We'll talk more about the weighing of the heart soon. But we can imagine that that first part of the afterlife is probably a bit like the biggest airport there is, so *of course* we would need to go through some kind of security, or panel to keep everyone headed to the right destination. Just like in human travel, there's a place like an airport, or a border, where someone has to look over our credentials, and maybe ask us a few questions about the intention of our journey. So it definitely makes sense to have good translators for that. Of course, we'd have our details checked before we get to pass into the next reality. Spirit is organized like that.

Into the Wonder

As the Hall's constellations continue to move, the light is dancing around the next and final set of columns. When you look back toward where you came in, the full Hall of Secrets is illuminated. It's time for a long overdue chat with that nonhuman, divine part of yourself.

In this writing practice, we're going to have a chat with our souls. We're going to go into the language and currency of the soul, of Source—intuition and love. We're going to imagine revisiting some moments of your life. Try to think back to a time when you may have used your intuition or a gut feeling in a situation where it helped lead to a positive outcome or discovery. Maybe it even helped someone else? What times in your life can you think of where there was a similar impact but where you may have acted in love, or wisdom? Think of a moment where you just *knew* something, or where your soul gave you goosebumps to confirm a knowing, where you felt like the stars aligned and maybe you were in the right place at the right time? Maybe that was how you met your best friend, or your person? How did it impact you? How did it impact others? Start keeping a record of these messages from the soul in your magic book. Moments you didn't expect may be the ones to come through. Be open. The more times you do this, the more you will uncover. Write down any thoughts or experiences you may remember and begin a practice of writing down any new messages from your soul moving forward. Notice in your experiences how your soul may speak to your body. Does it give you goosebumps to get your attention, does it bring patterns, or people, or music? How does your intuition work? Use all of your senses to connect with the real GPS. Your Spirit. As you collect these messages, you will begin to see patterns of how your soul communicates to you. The greatest thing about letting your soul drive (*other than less worrying and arguing*). The soul is full of lovely surprises and breadcrumbs, and often, they can be strung together.

Don't try to wear it as a necklace—too many birds will come.

My soul has a specific pattern of communication that helps me to navigate through challenges. Since I've practiced it, it's helped me recognize important details on my journey. Your soul may develop similar signals and symbols for you.

The more room we make, the more the soul shows up and the more we remember. As we do that, we tend to get to know the different Clairs. Now that we've gotten to the end of The Hall of Secrets, you may want to give yourself some time to process. You have time, you're the one on Earth, you're the one in the vessel. You can always say, "This too much for today. I'd just like to watch *90 Day Fiancé* and have some chips."

That's a fine intention too, just remember you're not getting graded on it

This is part of being human. We get to make moments. We will have forever in Spirit, but our human lives are relatively short, so making and remembering moments is part of the adventure. We're humans right now so we can decide where and for how long we point our magic powers. That's exactly what we're going to do next. Since we're plugged in and fueled up now, it's time to use our magic powers. I'll meet you in The Alchemist's Lab when you're ready.

CHAPTER NINE

THE ALCHEMIST'S LAB

YOUR MAGIC POWERS

A s we move out of the soft glow of The Hall of Secrets and walk through the curtain, we find ourselves in a wide-open two-story space. The air is fragrant here and seems thick with magic. It feels foggy but there's no fog. Mist? There are windows lining the walls but the light coming through looks as if we're underwater. *Maybe we are?*

This room seems to have three distinct working areas. Immediately in front of us there's a long wooden table that houses a range of objects, books, and tools (including some like the ones we saw in The Sanctum). To the left there's an area that's curtained off, but we see a sliver of what's behind the fabric.

There's a set of tented desks. Tents within tents. On the desks we notice stacks of paper. A layered arrangement of diagrams and charts lines what we can see on the back wall. On the right of the room is an area that is enclosed with wooden columns lined with curtains, but these are tied back. On the outside of the columns hangs a range of magnifiers and mirrors. Beyond the curtains are shelves holding what look to be curiosities in bell jars. The top of the shelves is lined with bottles of tinctures and potions. In the main part of the room, we're surrounded by not just cauldrons, but what look like chemistry projects. This is a room for experiments.

This is The Alchemist's Lab, the place where we'll remember how to focus our magic powers, where we'll *practice* our magic. We'll begin with the most important magic power we wield. We all carry it. You may not have noticed it as it's light as a feather and inexhaustible. The long table in front of us has a range of feathers, wands, and talismans. As beautiful as these physical tools are, we don't *need* anything outside of ourselves to do magic.

We just need the Alchemy of you.

If we carry and are partly made up of energy, then we should also be able to send and receive energy, ideas, *and* information. We're all transmitters. Yet we all have our own channel where we get the clearest signal. A key part of practicing magic is operating in our own authentic power, being responsible for the way we connect with energy—and most importantly how that energy impacts the world around us. We exchange current and vibration with other beings all the time. This exchange is what life is all about. We are *meant* to have those connections and we are *meant* to be responsible and accountable for the energy we bring to our moments.

Part of our remembering is moving into a state where we can shift our thinking and, in effect, energy. We don't have control of a lot of things in life, but this thing, *this* magic power, we have 100 percent control over. It's your intention and it's the biggest and brightest power you wield. When we get crystal clear on what we need and it's in alignment with our purpose, the Universe will take it from there.

That's what the intention *is*.

It's a very clear and very concise transmission to Source, to Energy, to our higher self, regarding an intended movement in ordinary reality. We are essentially using your energy to create a vibration for your objective. Our job is to focus on the *what* (if you have some *why* that's going to help too). We don't need to spend our energy on worrying about *how, when,* or *if.*

Interdimensional Transmissions

It's likely no one has ever told you that, so you've probably spent many moments of your life (like me) trying to micromanage the Universe. Being an executive producer and a survivor of childhood trauma, there came a time where I needed to ask myself a very difficult question. Was I drawn to being a producer because I liked it, or because I liked power and control because I didn't have much of either growing up? I am someone who loves to make things, but I had stopped making my own things. I always joke that I grew up a lot like Max Fischer from the Wes Anderson film *Rushmore*. In grade 8, I played Miss Hannigan in *Annie*. I got scouted for an arts school. I wrote plays, I directed plays, I made videos. I was always creating. That was my constant. The other was Erin.

We always knew what the other was thinking, and we were so connected that we didn't have to talk. And that's how I knew exactly when she left.

It was two days before my nineteenth birthday. I was in the car with my father driving to my birthday lunch. I felt a pit in my stomach that was deeper than usual. Deeper than just being in a car with my father. I called my mum from my '90s brick of a cellphone and it felt as if she answered before it even had a chance to ring.

Something heavy was already hanging in the air between us.

"What's happened?" I said.

"There's been an accident," my mum managed to say.

Silence from me as the news started to move through me like a slow drip.

"It's Erin . . . Amy . . ." my mum started. "She's gone."

Drip. Drip. Drip. It was making its way through my body, this horrible truth my soul already knew. I felt as if the bottom had fallen out of my whole life and that all of my insides were going to spill out onto the floor of the car. Somehow, they didn't. The next day I saw her in a casket and a few days later on my birthday I sat at my best friend's funeral.

Not long before I had just survived my own car accident, flipping my car end to end several times down an interstate with another best friend, Chanda. Somehow, we'd both survived. By that time, I was already in recovery from a raging bout with addiction that started when I was thirteen. No one ever really asked me why. At the time, it was the mid-nineties. We didn't talk about addiction or mental health like we do now. Pop culture was one big ocean of addiction and since I was already swimming in my own trauma, I just assumed drugs were the solution. Less than a year after my accident, Erin had left the planet in hers. It seemed all of my hopes and dreams went with her. She and I spun so many tales of the future. We manifested things. After watching *Pee-wee's Playhouse* one morning, I told her that he was my friend. I just knew that one day I would be friends with Pee-wee Herman. She agreed. She wasn't on the planet to go with me when it happened, but it did happen; I actually did become friends with Paul Reubens.

I still think our meet-cute story (Paul's words, not mine) is one of the most powerful examples of what the magic power of intention can do. What we can bring into being with the right combination of trust, surrender, and listening. Erin and I spent so much time as kids talking about what our lives might be like. We had the best intentions and senses of humor. She was the sister I never had and was the biggest cheerleader of mine that I'd ever known.

When she transitioned, I lost two constants. She was gone and I stopped writing.

It was only days after she left that I began to hear her through the veil. Just like I heard her when she was here, but her voice had moved into my consciousness. I was up late most nights, beating myself up for being the one who survived, while she was relentlessly hitting me back with the same message: *Write!*

Erin always knew what to do. She always knew what to say, including after a particularly eventful playdate at my house where my own mother was ready to pull out her hair from our incessant laughter and screams. On those days she would thank my mum as she left by calling out, "Thanks for putting up with me, Heather!"

Her timing was always spectacular. Coming through the veil, she was no different.

When she told me to write, I took it seriously. I told my mum about it, and she did what witch mums do. She took me to a psychic. My mum had been seeing this woman for years. All I knew was that she was a hereditary clairvoyant with a phenomenal track record. All I wanted her to tell me was that I wasn't losing my mind. I didn't have any expectations that I was going to hear anything from my best friend.

I brought a photo of Erin with me and went into the psychic's apartment where she took me into a room lined with plants and curtains. A little round table was in the middle of the room. We sat down and I brought out the picture. I told her I was hoping she could help me to make sense of some of what was going on.

As she held the photo she began to talk about Erin's accident. This wasn't a time where the internet could have been of assistance. She told me things about Erin's condition that I'd only be able to confirm after the session. She said she was so sorry, and as she did, I felt the overwhelming devastation of this loss come over me again like a wave I didn't know how to surf. As that wave hit, the clairvoyant's hand was over mine and the words coming out of her mouth were, "She wants you to know it's not like they say but it's like you both thought."

I was stunned. It was cryptic but I knew *exactly* what she meant. The awareness dripped through me again, but this time I didn't feel as if I was going to come apart. I felt as if I was coming back together.

Erin and I had talked *a lot* about the meaning of life, about the Universe, about what happened when we left the planet. We had theories. We'd read Benjamin Hoff's *The Tao of Pooh* and become little Taoists in high school. We'd had always had lots of conversations about what we knew about what we were doing here, on the planet. It was something we talked about as kids all the time. I'd always told her I wasn't entirely sure that what "they said" at Catholic school was so accurate. It was because of Erin that I realized I didn't even learn about the planets in school. So I already felt as if we weren't getting all the information. It was as if they skipped over the magic of the Universe, *on purpose*. So I knew exactly what the psychic meant. I got excited for the first time since Erin had left. It *was* what we thought. It *was* all one big Ocean of Consciousness.

I knew she had Erin on the line. As I processed, she kept going, telling me that Erin was asking that I walk her forward. Again, I sat stunned.

WHAT? Me?!

Sure, I'd had experiences with my mum growing up when I helped walk a Spirit in our old house forward (because witch), but now I was just out of high school *and* just off a raging drug addiction. I had been beating myself up (*like a professional*) about what I was even still doing here, so I didn't feel very capable of walking a soul into the afterlife, let alone one of the most important people in my life.

The psychic, seemingly unaware of my internal dialogue, explained to me how to do this and what I would need. I started to realize I'd better listen. Knowing Erin, I knew she wasn't going to take no for an answer *even from another dimension.*

As the psychic continued and told me about some of the gifts I'd had in my life. She talked about how I saw things, felt things, knew things. She wasn't wrong, about any of it. I'd heard and seen things since I got here. She also repeated to me some of the things Erin had been saying through the veil. I already knew it was Erin, but now I *really* knew it was Erin.

It was witnessed.

She also knew about the little (*free!*) bag of crystals I got with the *Time Life Mysteries of the Unknown* books. She shared how to cleanse them and then she told me something that became a purpose. She told me that the writing Erin wanted me to do was a book.

She told me I was going to write a book that would change the way people think.

I was stunned (again) but I felt it in my bones.

Somehow, through all of my pain, my trauma, my dances with death, I set and held this intention. I knew that one day I would do *exactly* as she said. I tried not to worry about how, or when. I just tried to trust that if I was meant to do this very important thing, it would happen. Just like I did when I walked her forward. I trusted that I was meant to do this very important thing in service to the very best of friends. You'll have to let me know about the helping change the way you think part.

I plan to write more books as well to be fair, so if this isn't it for you, hopefully you'll give me a chance on another one.

If not for my experience with Erin, I wouldn't be able to do the work I do now. I have been a witch my whole life, and apparently, I have been a medium since I was nineteen years old. I say "apparently" because it just never occurred to me that I could talk to anyone else but her. I realize now that I got the honor of practicing my gifts with the one person on the planet who knew what was inside of me all along. Not only my best friend but a powerful Spiritual teacher who continues to make me laugh—just as she did when she was on Earth.

As I began to write and began to move into my healing practice, the content of this book became clearer, a publisher appeared, and so did a community. This is what can happen when something isn't just aligned with an intention but with a purpose. Some things are just written. When I feel as if maybe I'm behind, or that it took me too long to get something done, the Universe seems to pat me on the back with a breadcrumb to let me know that I'm right on track. So are you.

Most of us tend to spend lots of time with the *how*s, the *if*s, and the *when*s. The worst family of dinner guests *ever*, by the way. You can spend hours and hours with them and not be any further along. You may even have been trying to wrestle the responsibility of these things away from the Universe. This is where I ask you: *Who would even want that responsibility?*

I don't know about you, but I have enough trouble being clear on the *what*s of my life, let alone trying to figure out exactly how to bring those *what*s to life through a Universe we have barely begun to understand. Best leave that to Source.

You Can't Check the Tracking on Energy

The Source of everything knows *everything*, including *how, when,* and *if* the things you're trying to bring into being are going to occur. It knows exactly what it's doing. It knows when to deliver for the most impact. It knows how to bring it into being in a way that surprises and delights, and it knows how to gently help steer you into edits or adjustments. Spirit is elegant AF.

If we're talking about intelligence, I'm going to enlist the Source of everything, and if I ask for help with something, I want the helper to be far more experienced at it than me. If I need an expert, I'm going to make sure it's someone or something with as much experience as I can afford. I'm getting the best general contractor there is. Why not go to the Source? Who is more experienced? Here we are trying to outproduce the best producer there has ever been. Talk about ego, right?

I was an expert at this. I tried to outmaneuver the Universe for years. I don't recommend it because doing this is exhausting and not ever a game you will win. Working within its frameworks is much better—and rewarding. I've found it's best to focus on the *what* and *why* pieces and leave the *how, if,* and *when* to the expert running the show. We can trust that Source will help deliver it if it's in alignment.

We can intentionally raise our vibration in order to get into alignment with Nature before we try to wish up some wonder. Part of using our magic powers and setting our intentions is being in a state of focus and flow. How? Repetitive movement, singing, chanting, toning, martial arts, and meditation can all help us raise our vibration. Now, I don't mean this in a white girl wellness way (no whitewashing welcome). But rather in the sense that the more we connect to Energy, the more our brains (and souls) are able to experience a higher perspective. And the more we are able to experience a higher perspective, the more we are able to move upward, into a "higher" version of ourselves, not perfect selves, and certainly not richer or thinner or any other lie that wellness marketing sells us. We are the triangle pointing upward, and the more we are able to connect to the Energy around us, the more we will find those moments of transcendence that make us realize, oh, yes, the wonder was always here.

Experiment with what works best for you. We can more easily achieve a state of focus and reconnect to our authentic power when we're in alignment and our energy is focused. This is being in flow. (*I'm still a little Taoist.*)

As we begin to practice and see change based on using our intention and energy, we also have to be very mindful of what we say and what we think. When you're working with Energy, thoughts can matter as much as words, right? We'll remember some new tools to help keep that all in balance because it's next to impossible while living on Earth to be sweet all the time (even with candy).

Our intention is also known in magic as *the Will*. This is our focus, the direction that it is deemed our vessel is headed. It's a firm desire, a determination. Intention feels like a cursor in your consciousness. It's a point of light and focus that we all carry. If the soul is the fuel of our being, our Intention is *the accelerator*.

How many times have you heard that story (or seen the bookmark) about "Footprints." There was one set of footprints where we thought we were alone, and the higher power said, "I didn't leave, that was when I carried you." It's on a bookmark because it's true. (Warning: Not all bookmark messages are accurate.) We are not, have not, and never will be alone. Anyone who has ever experienced any kind of trauma knows that when you come back from that and do the work to heal, you stand on an energetic foundation firmer and more expanded than what previously existed.

If we are made of star stuff, or Spirit, and we have a connection to Source, then why can't we use our energy to tune in to specific things? When we talked about soul purpose in The Hall of Secrets, the more aligned our intentions are with our soul's purpose, the more likely the wishes are to come true, and the more we integrate how our intentions will positively impact not just ourselves, but our network, our community, and our world. Intention is a focus we keep, and the more closely we keep it, the more community we have to help, Spirit seems to shuffle things to the top of the pile. When we are aligned to bring something into being that is beneficial not just to ourselves but to the community, or to the world, we can experience miracles. Depending on where we might be on our individual paths, we get to define what a miracle might actually look like.

Practicing magic, Spirituality, takes clarity. Using your magic powers takes tuning in. Intention is a supernatural gift. It is something we can't hold physically until we see the impacts of it.

We have the ability to create in our consciousness the images and feelings of a dream come true. We get the ability to bring new things into physical reality. Whether it's an idea, a wish, or a star-crossed moment we imagined, we have the ability to bring things to life. When we use our intention in tandem with the laws of Nature, we can manifest amazing things.

We'll need to make changes to where we are pointing our intention in order to wield power. We need to recalibrate ourselves. When we use our intention, we need to think of it as placing an order with the Universe. We don't just want to imagine it. We also want to make our case in writing (*spell work* because *spelling*). As we write, we also dream it up in our consciousness. We imagine it happening. How is it going to positively impact you, your community, and maybe even the world? Place your order. Speak it out. Do your research, figure out what you want, especially when it comes to something big. Once you order it, you don't keep ordering it again every day until it arrives, do you? You *know* it's coming, so you wait. You placed your order, and you have faith that it's going to get to you.

This is the same. You ordered it. You followed the steps, and if it's in alignment, it's coming. Behave as if it's coming. Part of the surprise is not knowing when, if, or how. Part of the delight is thinking about those things when it does come into being. How many stars had to cross for the Universe to conspire in your favor? Sometimes we humans need to request an upgrade or change to our order. Sometimes we placed an order some time ago and things may have shifted. Don't worry. If you move and you made the order somewhere else, the Universe will find where to deliver the package to you. Light is way better at logistics than you—or any online retailer. It delivers everywhere.

Remember that the Universe loves reciprocity, so as you're dreaming of all your stuff, make sure that you tell Spirit what you want for the world. How is what you're doing going to positively impact your family, your local community, and the world? And let Spirit help. Let it understand that this isn't just for you, it could be part of a greater good. So try to ignore the ego wanting to tell Spirit how and when, and surrender. Spirit is on it. Your job is just to keep it moving. There will be times where you make an order and it may take years to come, or not in the way you expect, or it might not come at all.

The Medicine of Manifestation and Transformation

This is where soul agreements can come into play. In my experience, when something aligned with intention doesn't come through, it's usually because it's not aligned with purpose or your soul's agreements. If we acknowledge that our souls have a greater perspective, we can also imagine that there may just be a whole lot more at play than any of us imagined with all the places we will travel in the web of life. We have our own missions and contracts. Soul contracts, but let's not get ahead of ourselves. We're in The Alchemist's Lab, not The Archives.

Sometimes something not coming to fruition isn't that deep, and it's just about timing or particulars. Keep practicing; it might be that you need to adjust something in your ritual or spell craft. It might also be that you need to get clearer with your wish. I have manifested *many* soul mates for myself, but most were animals. Literal pet companions. Oops, I hadn't been specific enough. I realized I had to update my order to find my human consort. Like clockwork, I let it go and there he was knocking on the window of my consciousness. Sure, I held the intention, but it was still a surprise, and it was all free will and it was worth the wait. Divine timing.

When working to set an intention to manifest abundance in your life, try to remember not everyone is meant to win the lottery, though one of my healing clients followed her intuition into doing just that. That's not always how abundance comes our way. For her, it was a soul agreement. For me, not so much, not so far. It might be that for you, or you may receive abundance in another way. I always like to ensure I'm including "with harm to none" throughout time in all my intention-based work. Highest good, best possible outcome, harm to none.

I want to make Source proud and not put any unclear or dense energy into the system. We've got enough to tidy up.

Speaking of which, it seems as if some of the tools on the table in front of us in The Alchemist's Lab have shuffled. The mist also seems to have cleared from the room. We notice that there's a drawer pull at the edge of the long table. We

slide it out and it's enclosed in glass and full of beautiful colors. At first it seems to be jewelry, but as we process, we realize they're specimen drawers. Butterflies and dragonflies. All these beings are shown in all of their different stages of transformation.

If we entertain the idea that both surrender *and* transformation are part of this whole life-on-Earth thing, what does effortless surrender bring to the natural cycles of the world? This is what we need to remember, right? When we're out of sync with Nature, we're out of sync with ourselves, with our beings. That's why things get so hard. That's how we get stuck. I'm not saying you can't take breaks.

As there is no time in Spirit and we currently are based in a world where there *is* time—we sleep, we need rest—it's okay to ask for ease and grace. Even if you're one of those people like me who enjoys a good transformation, it doesn't have to be so hard. It doesn't have to be so painful. We can look to Nature for inspiration and lessons on this. We have lots of amazing beings on the planet who follow their purpose and literally shapeshift to become what they are meant to be. Butterflies and dragonflies are just two of those beings.

The butterfly goes through a transformation without much ease or grace. They begin as caterpillars, and in order to reach their final form as butterflies, they have to go into a phase where they literally rip themselves apart to be able to fly. Dragonflies have a little more ease and a lot more grace because they get to choose. They begin as water bugs and then go through a metamorphosis to bring themselves into being as dragonflies. They go through a nymph stage where they can seemingly shapeshift from one part of their evolution to another, even skipping parts and going straight from one phase into the next if it strikes them.

This is Nature's way of showing us that there's more than one way to grow.

You'd think this would have been a good enough inspiration for us to realize maybe we are capable of the same kinds of growth. We may not be able to grow wings (that I know of), but we *can* change so much that we become totally unrecognizable to previous versions of ourselves, with or without surgery.

So please don't forget to ask for ease and grace as you move into your magical practice. Take it from me: I used to think whipping through my healing journey was going to make it easier. Two thumbs down. You will want to unsubscribe from that quickly. Grant yourself time to process. Just as all the specimens in this drawer did to become their most colorful selves.

Let's have a look at some of the other tools we have available to us in the Lab. Let's move toward the area to the right with the tied-back curtains and tinctures. As we peruse the shelves and curiosities, the bell jars, shelves stacked with boxes. And then we see it. Shelves and shelves of potions . . .

Were you one of those kids who made potions? Or mixed things up in jars? Then you've definitely come to the right place. Alchemy is among the more tactile practices in magic. We can bring in objects *and* elixirs to represent our works. We can mix essences, tinctures, and medicines with ingredients *and* intention.

As we remember how to practice our magic, we have to talk about the language of magic. Nature has one and so does magic. It's symbolism. Magic, and the books about it, are cryptic for a reason. It is meant to be protected. There is a simple reason for this. People who can't be trusted with the key will never find the lock. The most sacred of knowledge *is* invite-only. The drawers in here are full of symbols and seals. We'll start with a simple one to get us going. A sigil is a symbol or design you create that works with your unconscious to help bring your goals and dreams into reality. Sigil magic helps bring focus about your intentions by way of a physical representation. Think of it as a physical symbol of your goal, like a flat trophy.

Let Me Take You to Nerd Town

The term *sigil* was derived from the Latin word *sigillum*, which means *seal* or *signet* The symbol itself isn't what contains magical abilities, it is the piece that provides a visual and terrestrial representation of that which you're working to manifest. The intention in consciousness (the celestial) combined with the written sigil is what creates the magic. This *is* alchemy. Part of this process is the creation, the bringing something from *your* consciousness into reality. This is why it's so important with magic to do things in our own hands, to write things down, to create our own craft works (*if you like Kraftwerk, that's good too*). Our vibration matters to the intentions that we set and how they manifest in the world. It's always best to do our own crafts if you can because our own consciousness is the source of our own creation. If you're going to use existing seals or symbols, I recommend drawing (or tracing) them yourself. There are all kinds of different ways to create sigils; we'll remember one way when we get to the ritual portion of this chapter.

Another far more ancient symbol of magic that can be used to back up intentional work is the aptly named Magic Square or the Lo Shu (Nine Halls Diagram). This square is part of the same ancient Chinese mathematics and divinity still used in feng shui. The Magic Square was used to designate spaces of political and religious importance and was an important model for city planning, tomb, and temple design. A legend concerning the Lo Shu is that a turtle emerged from the water with the Lo Shu pattern on its shell: circular dots representing the integers one through nine arranged in a three-by-three grid. Yet another magical symbol inspired or told to us by Nature.

The Romans also used magic squares, but they contained letters instead of numbers and were used for amulets and placed on walls. The most well-known of those is the Sator Square, a super palindrome because it can be read left to right, right to the left, and up and down. You may have also heard the magic word *abracadabra*—from Aramaic, *avra kehdabra*, meaning "I will create as I speak." The first known mention of *abracadabra* was in the book *Liber Medicinalis* by Serenus Sammonicus. Chapter 52 prescribes that malaria sufferers wear an amulet containing the word *abracadabra* written in the form of a triangle. This was to be worn by the patient as a symbol of magic (of course triangle) in addition to using the incantation.

Alchemists also often created seals or sigils to correspond and reflect a star or planet's energy (and knowledge). These could be used on altars, or in ritual to gain assistance or support from various heavenly bodies. Magic also uses spells or incantations that often rhyme to create an easily remembered chant. Poetry is a foundation of magic.

"Rain, rain, go away, come again another day."

Probably a spell.

In magic, the symbol of something is the same as the actual object because, energetically, they have the same essence. Magic is the science of knowledge where the will and the mind of our undivided consciousness can play freely between yesterday, today, and tomorrow. The key word here is *play*. Collaborating with Source is meant to be joyous. So much about intention is being in alignment with Nature. This is why reconnecting with it intentionally and in physical reality is so important (and powerful). When we are out of sync with Nature, we are out of sync with ourselves. Part of this adventure has been getting you back in communication with Nature. We learned that ego and magic don't really hang out. Ever. Remember this when choosing practitioners.

As we begin to wield our power, it must be done with honor and respect; we do it with light. We also do not do magic on other people without their explicit and direct permission. We do not do ceremony (especially shamanic ceremony) without training.

Ever.

If someone is not conscious and you want to help with healing work, you obtain permission from their next of kin and then from the person's own consciousness. We do not use our power or influence to manipulate people. I will not take responsibility for anyone in The Temple who misuses the teachings in this book. I encourage you, as someone who has walked both roads, to shine your light. The reward is far greater, and the source is far more powerful. *Star Wars* should have taught you that. Plus, don't you want to know what's next? Why risk eternity?

To fully radiate your magic is to be in effortless surrender to the natural cycles of the world, to walk and work in light. When we do this, we instantly move the needle in terms of our vibration. We make a case for the why of our intention to the Universe for the goodness that something might bring—not just for ourselves but for the collective. This is where Spirit really pulls up a chair and will collaborate with you. Our intention is like a beam. We show the light in us, we beam.

What do you think happens to that beam when we worry? It's probably jumbled, or maybe it's fragmented? So we don't want to spend our energy doing that. It's a terrible investment for our moments. We want to try to keep our beam of intention straight and clear.

The Taoist principle of *Wu Wei*, effortless action (or doing not doing), perfectly personifies how to be in greater harmony with your intention. We set our intention, we're focused on our intention, and we're going to trust in the current of energy to get us there. When we are in a state of concentration and flow, we can more readily bring into alignment various aspects of our lives. This can also positively impact the lives of those close to us. When we're radiating authentic power, it's much easier for those around you to feel, or be encouraged to try to do the same. We *can* impact the energy of a room. We'll talk more about how this works when we get into The Great Hall. For now, *mystery!*

When we become attached to expectations or our desire to control, regulate, and maybe even dominate our world, we tend to suffer. It's similar to the Buddhist concept of *Upādāna*, which can be referred to as *attachment, clinging,* or *grasping.* The tighter we grasp, the more we seem to catch disappointment and encounter challenges (*not to mention blisters*). The Taoist principle of *Effortless action* doesn't mean we are *aimless.* It means we are focused on the *what,* our *intention,* and yet we trust the current of Source to get us where we need to go. Being in harmony with the way things are means being in alignment with the rhythms of the elements, with the systems we are part of. Within our bodies, *and* outside of our bodies, as we are part of this system.

As we're looking through the shelves and drawers of The Alchemist's Lab—all these objects, tools, and documents associated with magic—it's sinking in that this stuff isn't anything to be nervous about, this stuff is light, and this stuff is *cool.* We begin to feel the power of an object that's been infused with intention and one that hasn't. Yet when we think of intention, we often think of it as something intangible. Like a chalk outline, it becomes an arbitrary measurement of something in the conscious mind. Yet most of us set intentions all the time. Whether they come to fruition is as much about how much energy we put into sustaining, growing, or evolving them. We focus all the time on what we don't have or what we don't want. But by worrying, we're using our magic powers to put energy into things we don't want to experience or bring into being. Human beings seem to do this better than any other species. We are an anxious bunch. No wonder.

But we can begin to ground that nervous energy by handing the worry and responsibility back over to the Universe and focusing on a positive outcome—or we can worry ourselves right out of the world. When we invest energy into things we can't control, we plant seeds for plants we don't really want to grow, making our intention to Source unclear. We also end up in the weeds. The difference energetically between a thought or idea and intention is that when we set an intention, we set a vibration. We are locking on to a specific vibration, image, or outcome. We are hitting pause on the frame so we can focus on what we hope to bring into being. It's time to leave the potions and amulets and head back to that long table for a writing practice. If there's a sigil, potion, tool, symbol, amulet, or lucky charm you feel will help you amplify your power, bring it to the table.

Into the Wonder

Once you're settled at the table with your magic book, try to imagine revisiting times in your life where you may have utilized intention (or your will) to achieve something. How many times did life deliver some treasure because you set an intention and held it? Try to think about, visualize, and note how you may have done on your order. What tools did you use to do this? Did you make a vision board? Did you write it down? Did you pray or do a ritual? Did you use astrology? Did you ask other people to help send good vibes? Try to think about how much time you may have spent worrying about it or any other ways where an intention may have gone off the rails. If there's anything you note where things could have been clearer based on any new awareness you've gained so far, write it down. Especially if it's something you're still looking to bring to life.

Think now about how many standing orders you may have with the Universe. Perhaps you want to take some pieces of paper from the table here in The Alchemist's Lab. Take a piece for each order you have. Where are they in this new understanding and thinking? How many might be able to be adjusted? Are there any that need to be canceled or that were already delivered? Perhaps the energy from those can be redistributed? How many buckets might you have filled with worry? I want you to imagine putting them on the table in front of you in The Alchemist's Lab. We're not going to do anything with them yet, but I want you to put them down.

Once you've cleared the table of any intentions that may be past their expiration dates, you're going to think about a simple intention. Think about something simple that you need that could also benefit others in your life. Remember to always consider not just yourself but how things may benefit your family, community, and the world. Remember that Source likes to surprise and delight where it can.

What are you going to do now with this information? What are you going to order? Always remember, *As above, so below*. To bring it into being, you have to be able to visualize it first. It helps if you can feel it too. You want to try to feel in your body how it might feel to have it happen. You may have read *The Secret*. It actually comes from something much older. We may want to ask Thoth about this the next time we're in The Library.

For now, it's time to experiment with different tools of manifestation. It might be creating ritual using objects that are important to you or that carry the kind of energy you're looking to bring in. Maybe you have an altar already, or maybe it's a shelf that houses prized possessions. Whether it's asking ancestors, power places, or friends and family for support. Whatever those things are, ask them. Explore what draws you in and lean into where your power lies. You may also want to bring this into setting intentions. We can provide a starting vibration foundation for our intentions.

You may want to choose something that's already helped bring something to fruition, something that already has some precedent in your life.

You may want to utilize a *Dear Universe* letter, or try a petition, or write a prayer or a symbol or sigil to back up your intentions. Here's a very simple way to do that. Start with your intention. What is the desire? Write it down. Now remove any repeating letters from the chosen intention. Use the remaining letters to create a sigil. If it feels as if there are still too many to make your intention into a symbol, try removing vowels.

Maybe instead you choose to create some visioning around what you're trying to bring into being by giving Source some specifics. When setting intentions, dream like a child. It's how we get out of our own way. Since we were all kids once, you may know that if you ask them what they want for lunch, their birthday, or to do in the summer, they'll typically give you a list.

Kids know how to make things happen without spending too much time on how, when, and where. They know how to focus on the what. And they know how to get it because their souls are driving. Kids know how to enjoy a good surprise, even when they know what's coming.

Write in the present tense as if your wish has already come true. When you're creating an intention, remember to use positive words. You can always draw a circle around any magical symbols to contain the energy. A circle of protection. In order to use your symbol with your intention, you can place it alongside your list, meditate with it in your mind, create a key word for it, or your intention. You may want to charge it in the moonlight (full moons, and new moons are my favorites for intention work). You can also raise some power along with your intentions by singing, dancing, rattling, drumming, clapping. You may charge with a crystal, you may put it with a photo of a deity, or ascended master you work with or have some connection to. Maybe you have an area where you have photos of family or ancestors. Whatever feels right to you is what you should do. I always recommend listening to your intuition. Try different methods and see what works best.

When you're ready, you're going to place your order. You're going to use this intention as practice as you test out your soul being at the controls. You're going to meet this intention by imagining how you will feel when you accomplish it. As you feel that, know if it's in alignment, it's on the way. Be in a state of receiving, and you can imagine that no matter where it is, it's getting closer and closer by the moment. I know this sounds bizarre, but I also know that if I tell you to imagine the taste of peppermint in your mouth, you'll be able to do it. You'll go back to a time, and you will bring it back into being. *Like magic.*

Now that we've met some of the energy moving through our vessels, we're going to move deeper into our practice. Follow me into The Transmutation Tent where we'll remember one of the most powerful tools you probably didn't know you already had.

CHAPTER TEN

THE ALCHEMIST'S LAB

THE TRANSMUTATION TENT

As you step into The Transmutation Tent, the curtains seemingly close by themselves. We are surrounded by diagrams, charts, and drawings. Hanging on the back wall of the tent on a plaque is the definition of transmutation:

Trans·mu·ta·tion:
to change or alter in form, appearance, or Nature and especially to a higher form.

You may already know this word, maybe even from chemistry class. Latin's *alchimista* is the basis for the word *chemistry*. Do you feel as if we're about to go to Nerd Town again? Because we are. Before we transmute, we need to do a little theory work, so we understand the ancient power available to us. Then we'll get to the transmutation magic.

Let Me Take You to Nerd Town

The term *alchemy* and *alchemist* are in fact older words than *chemistry* and *chemist* in English. The term *alchemy* has deep origins back to the original name of Egypt.

Khem, or *Al-Khem* meaning "the black land." Humans have been using alchemy and transmutation all over the planet for thousands of years.

Taoism also has deep roots in transmutation, divination, alchemy, and magic. The Tao of Wu indeed. The philosophy of Lao Tzu speaks to the underlying and loving force of the Universe, the Tao. The Way. Remember the breadcrumb about Carl Jung from earlier? When he coined the term *synchronicity*, he was talking about Taoism. Being in alignment with The Way, being in harmony with the rhythm of the Tao, or the All, does bring more moments of wonder. In Taoism, it is believed that anyone in practice can become a master. An alchemist of sorts. Alchemy, unlike witchcraft, was more a male-dominated craft. Another reminder that magic was stolen from men, too. Men have also suffered losses under the imbalance of the patriarchy. Transmutation can (and will) help us recover those gifts. In order to learn the practice, we're going to lean into the theory. Real magic doesn't work without both the current and the knowledge being combined.

Among everything that The Uninvited killed, somehow it couldn't kill this. You don't mess with an alchemist; they are the nerdiest of magicians. They love codes and clues. Seals and symbols. Math and magic. They *know* how to hide a breadcrumb. They also know how to make a breadcrumb last for centuries (just like the metal that originally drew most of them into the practice). They left lots of clues and sacred texts to help us piece things back together. A lot of the texts made it through because they were in code, parables, or read like mathematical documents. A breadcrumb. The origin of the word *occult* actually comes from Latin, *occultus* meaning "hidden, concealed—secret." Mystery is built in.

Call us what you want, occultist, magician, witch, wizard, sorceress, or alchemist, we all work with Source's blueprint, and we all know how to protect it. It's part of the honor of practice. In stepping through the doorways of this Temple, you are becoming a part of that succession. You are joining many of the greatest creators, polymaths, inventors, and philosophers on the planet. You don't have to subscribe, but being open to respecting the lineage is a good place to start.

Alchemy and philosophy are forever entwined, as they both work with the foundational elements of life. One breadcrumb, by way of Aristotle, is on the concept of *prime matter*. Aristotle believed there was an element even more foundational than earth, air, water, and fire, a substance that he called *prima materia,* or prime matter. It's not actually matter but he believed it to be an element with the *potential* of becoming. It is the element of *possibility.* It's the idea that one thing can give something else a material form, or a changed material form. That's all we're doing as we move into the rooms of magical practice. We're going to entertain the potential and possibility.

Alchemy began as the search for gold. We humans have always liked gold, we've used gold to represent divinity, and immortality, since we found it. Part of this is probably because gold doesn't rust, tarnish, or decay. Eventually a belief came into being that any person who could learn to create gold, or work with it, could take on attributes of divinity itself. So this prospect of being able to harness gold represented an alchemist to be wise, powerful, and maybe even immortal.

Buried Treasure

The practice of alchemy began as its own treasure hunt rooted in the transmutation of metal using the five elements. Early alchemists believed that lead could be transmuted into gold. For hundreds of years the ancient alchemists experimented in laboratories just like this one trying to produce some mythical substance to assist in transmutation. The philosopher's stone was thought to be the missing piece of the puzzle. Alchemists were ahead of their time. They didn't know that lead and gold were different atomic elements because the periodic table was still hundreds of years away.

Like witches, alchemists have often been dismissed as metaphysical weirdos (*the nerds of the magic world*), but we helped paved the way for modern chemistry and medicine. All these tools that were used by The Alchemists *are* pretty witchy right? Cauldrons bubbling. Potions and fire. Healing magic. Ancient alchemists believed that diseases could be cured, and that life could be prolonged through *transmutation.* Alchemy was the first practice in the world to define (and link) systems to emphasize that influences from *outside* the body could cause disease *inside* the body. The alchemists of the sixteenth and seventeenth centuries developed new experimental techniques,

medicines, and other chemical concoctions—including pigments. Fine art likely wouldn't be what it is without alchemy. Life without pigment is also pretty dreary.

Modern society was built with seeds of magic. Don't get me started on how many alchemists and witches exist in the technology and entertainment worlds. We would not have the internet if it was not for a bunch of people who channeled messages and used the multiverse to create a vision of the World Wide Web. Alchemists and witches can now be found on the internet too.

The early alchemists believed so much in the magic of transmutation that they thought it should be taught at universities. Let's take a moment of wonder here: Can you *imagine* if witches or alchemists had been safe enough to bring an understanding of magic into classrooms? Imagine what could have happened if magic weren't demonized. Where would we be? How many evolutions might have occurred by now? Would we have met other intelligent life? We can think about that and ask ourselves: What might have happened if we never forgot? If we didn't burn the witches, if we didn't crucify Christ, and so many like him, but instead the ones who persecuted them? Where might we be?

The idea of teaching alchemy, or magic, went up "against" the teachings of the Christian church. I've put *against* in quotes because The Uninvited had already forced their way in. How would alchemy and magic have impacted humanity if The Uninvited hadn't taken over? Maybe we'd have seen a rise in Spiritual communities or gatherings. Maybe success would look a lot different than it does now. With witches, part of their recruitment was merely doing ceremonies outdoors to honor moon cycles, or changes in seasons. It's likely The Uninvited who forced our connection to Spirit to come inside. Connecting with the divine in Nature is pretty spectacular; why would we close the door on Source?

At least these Christian churches were consistent with how they viewed magic, whether it was witches or alchemists. Jesus may have been one of us, but they *sure* didn't like us. The church believed alchemy was sinful because they felt its practitioners were in search for the divine power of creation. The gifts of Source itself. Alchemists (witches and magicians throughout history) argued that if we as human beings had the wisdom to create transmutations, it was because Source had given us the ability to do so. Let's be clear, transmutation is not editing DNA, cloning, or adding technology to the already perfect designs of Creator. Hard no. We know this because the majority of Spiritual practice on the planet has one very clear and consistent message: harm to none.

Real magic works with explicit consent, conscience, and without harm. Magic in alignment with Source is much more effective and powerful because that's how it was designed.

Jesus had to have been an alchemist. Water to wine? *Come on!* That is an instant transmutation. Did he do that? Was he able to transmute and transform water to wine? Was he able to change the pH and have water taste to those who witnessed it like wine? I believe he did, because I have both seen and read of experiments where focused energy work can impact the pH of water. The practices included in this book can impact not only us but the world around us (and its beings) in a positive way. We can positively impact the energy around us.

Alchemical Gold

Alchemy aligns with not only classical philosophy, but also astrology. Gold is one of the seven metals of alchemy (gold, silver, mercury, copper, lead, iron, and tin). A breadcrumb: The number 7 always seems to represent the divine. For alchemists, it represented the perfection of all matter on any level. The seven metals of alchemy are also attributed to seven of the planets in our solar system. The Sun rules Gold; the Moon, Silver; Mercury, Mercury, or Quicksilver; Venus, Copper; Mars, Iron; Jupiter, Tin; and Saturn, Lead. It is by no coincidence that the Incas called gold the *sweat of the sun*. It is. Buddhists in China saw the natural radiance of gold as a manifestation of supernatural omnipotent and eternal Spiritual values. The Christian church serving the sacrament through a golden chalice suggested purity in a cup that could contain a divine presence and reflect sunlight.

Alchemists saw that we could take these metals representing different planets and have them correspond to specific things on Earth. Alchemy became a more tangible method of transmutation. Students of alchemy opened things up and started to connect ideas from all different schools of thought all in the pursuit of gold. This is how most philosophers still referenced today spent their time. Testing, practicing, debating, and transmuting. Nerd heaven. Alchemists assumed that the ability to destroy gold would be followed quickly by their ability to create it.

Thanks to nerds and scientists, we didn't find the philosopher's stone, but we found the atomic age.

We live in a time where nuclear physicists routinely transform one element into another. We live in a time of particle accelerators. We have reactors on the planet that transmute nuclear power into electricity. In the early 1980s, we finally made gold when nuclear scientists at the Lawrence Berkeley National Laboratory (LBNL) in California produced very tiny amounts of gold from bismuth, a metallic element adjacent to lead on the periodic table. Bismuth was chosen instead of lead because it was easier to separate the base material from gold. We *can* transmute to create gold, but it takes a tremendous amount of energy—and money. A breadcrumb: Bismuth has its own magic. It's the main ingredient used in the pink remedy for indigestion. A metal we can drink that can also be transmuted to gold? The wonders of Earth never cease to amaze.

Fire was a key collaborator for early alchemists. Heat is still a key component of modern science's transmutation processes. Fire is a transformative element. It's fire that's used to transmute and thereby transform sand into glass. Without fire, we would not have glass (or mirrors)—no philosopher's stone needed.

The deeper we get into the concept of transmutation, the answer seems to become clearer and clearer. Spirit is simple *and* it's powerful. For an alchemist to obtain gold, they had to not only free the essence of the metal from the base materials to which it's attached, but they also had to create a situation where they created alloys in order to even be able to work with the metal.

Let's go deeper into this statement for a moment. *In order to be able to work with the metal, they literally had to transmute it.* They had to free the essence from the base. The process that happens through alchemy is a reflection of the Spiritual process because: Energy. In order to transmute, we must use the alchemical gold within ourselves to free our light from the base minerals that have imprisoned us. This is is part of What We've Forgotten about life on Earth. This *is* the practice.

The base level can represent dense ways of being or thinking. The density is what blocks the light. The ouroboros, the serpent that bites its own tail, represents The Alchemists' beliefs that matter is in a constant cycle of destruction and creation. This idea that energy is constantly moving, constantly vibrating, constantly evolving is a core piece of the practice of transmutation. We have to be open to these points in order to work with energy. If you don't, it will be very challenging to work with it. You don't have to *believe* it in the beginning, you just have to be open to the prospect. Source will do the rest. If you aren't open, it's going to be really hard to get any wonder into your closed channel.

Into the Wonder

To practice, we only have to be willing to entertain the concept of the All, or Source, and understanding that there are two realities, Inner and Outer. On Earth and in the Heavens, Celestial and Terrestrial. As above *and* so below. If we continue to explore the true medicines and meanings of Nature's systems, we will continue to uncover beautiful (*and metaphysical*) knowledge about ourselves and where we go next—and ultimately even why we're here. Ideally, if you're entering The Temple with heartfelt openness, and doing the practices and rituals, you'll already be feeling a little clearer about your current scavenger hunt. Your sense of wonder should be operational, and you are likely seeing more moments of synchronicity in your world—and in *the* world.

Ancient magic isn't just imprinted in us, it's all over our modern society.

The staff with snakes appeared not only in the ancient Egypt and in the Bible but was also associated with Asclepius, a Greek god of healing. Let's imagine the caduceus for our transmutation work. Envision a disc at the top of a staff representing the light of source. On its sides are wings to represent ascension and transcendence. (That winged sun disk again.) The caduceus also has two snakes wrapping around the staff. The snakes represent transformation. Snakes shed their skin; the sudden change of a shedding emphasizes and represents the change from illness to cure. The snake represents eternal life and balance. Let's imagine that the staff running down the middle is you. The wings are at your shoulders. The disc of light surrounds your head. The backbone is connected to the light of Source. This is the nervous system, the DNA spirals.

We *are* channels of energy.

Energy is *meant* to move. It is not meant to be stagnant. This is one of the most important things to remember in our magical practice but specifically in our transmutation practice.

Sometimes when energy doesn't keep moving inside of us, we don't just get stuck, we can get sick. Our body is a vessel to carry our being. We're all energetic beings, *even jerks*. Let's reframe that jerks just have dirty windows in their vessels and shitty glasses. They're too busy just trying to get a view to think much about where they're going. We often hear that eyes are the windows to the soul. In my experience this is true. I can see soul loss in people's eyes. I can see it in my own childhood photos. When we refer to people as being radiant or glowing, we are typically referring to their inner light.

Imagine this tent is now our vessel. It's you and me, and our energy is in here. Things are clear; we are seeing that we carry light. We're having some fun, learning, and remembering stuff. Now let's imagine that a bunch of jerks show up. We all know how it feels. It can take the fun right out of a room, let alone a tent.

Let's imagine it's just you and me again. Better, right?

Let's imagine now that a bunch of vessels with clean windows come in. People who are open or are operating in intentional kindness or lightness with authentic power. With them, we're not going to feel quite as anxious about getting out of this tent. Time may even seem to move more quickly.

You may actually feel as if the energy is *too* positive. Maybe it's exhausting being so excited all the time. We can neutralize that energy too. We can pull back our own, we can adjust how open our windows are. We can polarize the energy of a room for ourselves with our intention alone.

As we reset back to just you and me, just a couple of vessels in a Transmutation Tent; our intention here is just doing our best to remember and be vessels of light. As a vessel we have the capacity to send energy to people and people can send energy to us, and as we've just illustrated, not everyone is going to send you chocolates.

When we take control of our intention *and* our energy, we can help the collective simply by being conscious of what kind of energy we're emitting. Our windows can shine a light that impacts others. Simply being conscious of what you're emitting, or what energy we're allowing ourselves to be around, is a shift worth making. Even if you don't move into a full transmutation practice, try this one.

The next time before you go out or have interactions with other people, take note of the energy. Do a check. How do you feel energetically between 1 and 10, on a scale of awful to great? When you encounter another person, check your energy again. You'll quickly notice as you do this that some people take energy, some people give it, and with some people, you're going to have a beautiful balance of reciprocity.

Start by noticing how the energy you encounter in your day impacts you. You don't have to do anything about it—yet. Just notice how the energy you bring to a room may impact the dynamic of a group. I am an introvert (dressed like an extrovert, confusing, I know) but I love entering a room and working to shift the energy much more than I do working a crowd. It's much more rewarding for an introvert like me than small talk is. Try doing this with social media and you'll soon find out how investing in those moments can leave you feeling deflated or how you can transmute experiences and discussion into more meaningful moments. I'm not saying you can get a fascist to lay down their hatred, but I am saying that energy can clean even the dirtiest windows. We'll get to that next.

For now, remember that we don't have to accept those chocolates, or when someone sends you the opposite of chocolate. We don't have to take the package. We can return it to the sender, and most important, I highly recommend doing it with love. I like to smile and say, "No, thank you!" when someone sends me an energetic bag of garbage. You can even use your hands as a physical ritual. *No, thank you* and push that energy. I like to imagine pushing it back into the web of life with some flowers and back to the shore of whoever sent it, with love. If people are doing that, it's clear they need some flowers. With your soul driving, you'll find it tends to give you a moment to think and process. The ego's immediate reaction is to sling the package back without any regard for the side effects. *Thanks, Soul!*

By adding a positive charge to the energy we're adding a + to a −. We're neutralizing it and we're making sure that the sugar isn't going in *anyone's* tank, because we're all connected. We need to stop peeing in our own pools. Imagine if everyone in the world were actually and suddenly responsible for their own energy? If suddenly everyone on the planet became aware and remembered how to move through their own energy? *CAN YOU IMAGINE?!* We're finding out it's not that hard to do, and it happens fast. Just like new lenses in a pair of glasses—instant improvement.

Changing the world can and does happen one by one. There's a lot of people, but as Lao Tzu, father of Taoism would say, "The journey of a thousand miles begins with a single step."

It begins by acknowledging the concept that all energy comes from one big tank. The big cosmic ocean is one source. If you're using anger, you're adding that vibration back into the tank. We can transmute that anger into power. Otherwise, it will eventually clog the system. If you're using love, or light, we're adding that to the system. Adding to that wave of love ideally does result in deliveries of more flowers and chocolates.

Please remember this is coming from me, someone who used to just set the bag on fire. Typically on someone's front lawn and usually with the intention or mantra of retribution. This tactic, the one we're remembering now, is much more effective, not just for me but for them. Reacting with anger or adding more fuel to that particular fire doesn't solve *anything*. I'd rather move on and spend my energy on investments that return. Transmutation is also less likely to encourage less trouble with the law than setting things on fire on someone's lawn.

You may be thinking, *What's the catch?* There's no catch in working in harmony with Source, only positive side effects. The side effect of transmutation is that you're likely going to end up with joy in your life. When we neutralize energy, we can usually disarm and often remedy the physical issues that come along with people tossing energetic bombs our way. Love bombs included. I was good at throwing those too, as it was easier for me than unpacking *why* I didn't have any other methods of love. Breadcrumbs.

Energy Work Is a Massage for the Soul

In my practice (and life) I often see physical healing come through transmutation of energy. When we become aware of an imbalance, we can work with intention to move the energy through. The power of prayer is the power of Source. The power of spell is the power of Creator. It is the energy of a collective being channeled into an outcome. Humans can and do have the capacity to tip the scales back into alignment especially when we collaborate and witness for one another.

As a result, there are going to be instances in life where we need some extra help to get ourselves out of the muck. We may need more than our own power. We may need the energetic equivalent of a tow truck for our vessels—a light worker, some ancestral healing, or ancient medicine from a wisdom-keeper. We take ourselves to therapy for our minds, the doctor (natural methods included) for our bodies, and we need to remember we can take ourselves to Spiritual practitioners when our Spirits are low. In many shamanic societies, medicine people have been known to ask those in their community who sought assistance with feeling dispirited, *When did you stop singing? When did you stop being enchanted by stories? When did you stop finding comfort in the sweet territory of silence?*

Spirit is joyful. When our vessels need maintenance, we will know because we feel a lack of joy, a stagnancy sets in. Ceremony and ritual *can* jump-start the system. We spoke about shamanic soul retrieval ceremony for restoration of power, and shamanic extraction ceremony can be incredibly helpful for moving out old energy, whether ancestral or current. These ancient ceremonies are conducted by a trained and initiated shaman using percussion and help adjust the energetic levels in your vessel. How? Vibration of course. How are they conducted. That's a *do not touch*. It's a tradition passed by Source, not YouTube.

Getting stuck in the muck is also where community comes in. When the packages or waves are too big, it's okay to ask for help. Having a magical or Spiritual practice doesn't mean you don't have support. It doesn't matter how deep your practice is, or gets, we all need human teachers to remind us how to walk the path and to be able to call people in the moments where we cannot believe our eyes. Sometimes that's all we need. A human Spiritual teacher witnessing that this is indeed holy.

Please entertain that we can get some roadside assistance when stuck in the muck. We can ask Source for more instructions, directions even. My biggest request applies: *Please make it clear.* I remind Spirit that I'm a human, it's pretty hard here right now, and I could use all the clarity they can give me. Life on planet

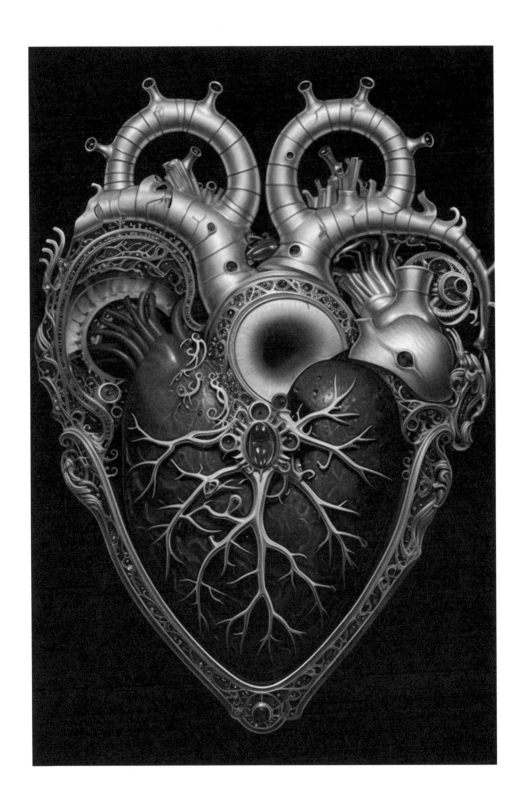

Earth is distracting and there's *lots* of interference, not to mention the millions of physical and virtual places to get distracted.

Here's an example of a transmutation where I asked Source to be clear, and instructions showed up in my dreams, in Nature, and then finally, right in my backyard. Source made very sure and very clear that I would know what exactly I needed to do next to get things back to neutral. Even though I had very little experience with being in that state, Source made sure I got a sense of what it felt like when I was. When we do transmutation work, we can also make Spiritual amends without any awkward Facebook messages (I've done those too). That's our reminder that Spirit is elegant. When our intentions are rooted in good, Spirit is never going to try to make you feel stupid.

When I say that the Universe is like a worried mom, I mean it's like a network of a million moms. They will get it to you, just like the neighborhood moms may have when you were a kid. Moms can spread the word like no one else. Never, ever doubt that they will get you the message. They always seem to know everything and see everything, even when you think they're not paying attention.

No difference with Source.

Bones, Drugs, and Harmonies

When I finally got the call to train in shamanic tradition, I joined Daniel's group. It was both wonderful and challenging. The training happens over the course of a year and includes retreats, initiations, rituals, ceremonies, and time in Nature—and some good old shamanic death and rebirth. Ironically, the thing that I (*the introvert*) was most nervous about going in was the idea of being with the same group for a year, not the initiation itself.

Typically, in the group, not everyone makes it through the initiation; many will drop out, deciding it's not for them. I trained in snake medicine, but not everyone likes snakes. A lot of people that particular year decided it just wasn't for them. Part of the training (and practice) is moving through a complete reframing of ego (sound familiar?), beginning to understand that judgment of others is just a reflection of how we feel about ourselves. Sometimes it takes someone else to reveal our own truths. This is why we have witnesses. There was something I hadn't faced inside myself yet, but I was seeing it in other people. In fact, it seemed to be following me.

At that point, I'd been sober from alcohol and drugs for years but was still imbibing in the plant medicine of cannabis. I'd never thought to have a relationship with it, I'd just hidden it behind a mask of judgment and shame. So, I'd struggled with every addiction I could find—cocaine, ecstasy, eating disorders, overeating, and undereating. My first major trauma had trained me to always have something to hide, to wear a mask of illusion. I'd spent years beating the shit out of myself, whether it was cutting, picking, or just treating my body like a trash can. Years of making bad decisions about the kind of people who had access to my heart. I had been conditioned into thinking I didn't have a choice. In focusing on healing, I had successfully shuffled through my Rolodex of addictions and eliminated all the contacts, but I had hidden away cannabis. Whenever I heard that someone was struggling with addiction, I'd feel a surge of judgment. My ego was all over it and it was *loud*.

During my training, this voice emerged in ceremony. When it came through my mind this time, I knew whose voice it was—the hissing nastiness of hatred—the archetype of my father. By then, I knew better than to follow that voice anywhere, especially with all of my fellow students in the room. I sat and processed how in pain I was in the deepest moments of my addiction to cocaine, to alcohol, or the myriad other ways I'd hurt myself. I thought about all the times I showed up inebriated to life because of the pain. It was not a surprise that cocaine, a literal numbing agent, was my chosen medicine for years. As we went through ceremony that evening, I thought about all the pain that got me to this place. It was a river of sadness. I didn't process what it had brought up inside of me that night. I didn't transmute it. I didn't get intentional with the plant. I smoked to hide, and the voice was back with one of its greatest repeated jabs.

You're. So. Stupid.

I floated to sleep on the river of sadness and toward the bank of self-sabotage; I was at the crossroads of both my training and my purpose. I asked for guidance to transmute this pain into power. I was so tired of that voice, and of carrying other poeple's secrets, other people's masks. That night I had a vivid dream. I knew it was important when I woke up because it was like a movie that had been saved to my desktop. I was standing in a black room that looked like one of the drama studios from my high school. Standing lit in a spotlight were me and a rolling rack of clothes and masks. Costumes. I stood beside it as if in judgment. I wasn't excited. I looked down on the masks, the costumes. Why should I be excited about trying to hide myself?

The next day, I headed to the training at Daniel's, knowing I'd share this dream with him and my group. I didn't know what it meant *exactly*, but in shamanic work, dreamtime is an important messenger for Spirit.

When I arrived, I told everyone in circle about the dream. This went about how it usually goes when you tell someone about a dream you had. Typically, people nod politely because it means nothing to anyone else but you. So there were some nods but no epiphanies. Not yet.

Daniel shifted the focus and began to chat about what practices we'd be doing that day. He shared that we would be asking for a ceremony with regard to anything we may need to let go of. *Of course* that was what we were doing. It was this imprint, this nasty abusive voice inside my head. It was the thing that was to blame for the imbalance in my system, the way I'd treated not just myself but others. The addiction, the bad decisions, the level of access people had into my life. Because of the Nature of my trauma, I had amassed what I can only describe as a necklace of male appendages around my neck. It wasn't the good kind of necklace; it wasn't given to me. I had taken it, and even worse, I had taken it out of my own fear. My reaction to men had been to take their power before they could take mine. This was what I most wanted to let go of and give back to Nature for transmutation. I wanted to move the needle from fear to fierce compassion and from hatred to love. I wanted to transmute my relationship with men. I wanted to welcome the divine masculine. While Daniel drummed, we all did our individual work. There were maybe ten of us in the group and we'd all been given our own ceremony from Source with instructions for what we would need.

When I asked Source what to do, I was given a ceremony and told what I would need to do to carry it out. I was shown that I needed to pick up a certain number of stones and cast them into moving water. We were in the middle of a suburb, so I tried not to think about *how* we were going to find water.

As we finished our journey Daniel partnered us up, pairing me with a woman named Brook, with whom I hadn't yet had much interaction.

Brook asked, "Do you need a stream?"

I nodded. I needed moving water. So did she. *Did he know? Spirit must have told Daniel whom to pair.* Daniel overheard and told us there was a little ravine down in a small, wooded area near his house. The day was beautiful and sunny, and off we went in our pairs to do the rituals we'd been somehow handed by the Divine.

My partner led the way and walked us down through this little forest behind the subdivision outside of Toronto. She and I found our way to this tiny little stream, and as we did, I was picking up stones. As we got closer to the bank of the stream, she stopped and looked back at me from the embankment. "How is right here?"

I looked up behind me and through the trees and the sun was shining down on my face. "It's perfect."

She asked if I wanted to go first. She probably knew that I did. I was ready to set this down. I stood there at this place with my eyes closed as I asked the stream, the Energy of Source, with heartfelt intention to help me transmute the pain and sadness. To release me from these feelings of shame that had arisen over the last twenty-four hours, but that I'd been carrying so long. No more masks. I imagined transferring the weight of these feelings into the stones, and as I tossed each one, somehow the sunlight would seem to shift to the stone. Lighting up the spot where it had connected with the water. It was like a spotlight in my dream the night before.

My eyes widened with each throw, and with each stone the light hit the stones in the water. I locked wide eyes with Brook and hers were just as large as mine. She smiled and said the magic words, *Keep going.*

So I did.

I threw one more and this time I followed the light down to my feet. At my feet, in the middle of this little ravine in North York, were bones.

"Keep going," she said again, gently. "We'll get them after."

I processed that this was really happening because she was seeing it too, and most importantly, that she knew they were for *me*. This may as well have been a gold nugget. Bones for shamanic practitioners are big medicine. A gift from the animal who left them. That it was found during ceremony or ritual, it was a gift more precious than gold. A sacrifice and donation from a living being, and a trade. Transmutation.

Somehow, I finished the rest of my ceremony and then we crouched down and I freed the four bones from the mud. Two jawbones, with teeth, and two smaller bones. I held them in my hands as she completed her ceremony. Just as magical and wonderful by the way, but no bones. We laid our offerings and made our way back to see our teacher. I knew Daniel would know what being the bones belonged to. Upon returning to his house, he was at his desk. I tucked my head into the doorway.

"I found these," extending my hand into his office. "Who do you think they're from?"

He came over and examined them over the rim of his glasses, replying right away, "Raccoon."

Goosebumps and shivers crept over my whole body as the word left his lips. I didn't have to look up raccoon medicine to know one of the most associated symbols of raccoons are their masks.

The dream.

I saw down by the altar, and I looked up raccoon medicine. Deeper down the breadcrumb path: "Cleverness and tenacity to make things work in life. A symbol of good luck, change."

Wow. I felt as if I was floating between worlds.

As we finished that day's session, I was still processing. As I was driving home, I realized I'd left the bones on the altar set up for our group at Daniel's house. Probably not an accident, but I wanted to let him know I'd left some bones at his house. Not your average text message.

When I got into the door at my house, I called my mum to tell her about this particular scavenger hunt, the dream, the ceremony, the raccoon bones. She was a chorus of wows and ahhs. I decided to tell her the rest of the story from my back deck.

When I opened the door, I gasped. The little couch in my backyard was ransacked. A few of the pillows were thrown on the deck, one ripped open with stuffing all over the couch.

"Holy shit," I whispered.

Source had aimed its spotlight again.

I'd gone silent. I'd forgotten my mum was even on the phone. "What's happening there?" she said, bringing me back to reality.

"Wait until you see this." I sent her photos. The first the picture of the cushions, the second a photo of a muddy little handprint.

Raccoons.

As above *and* so below. While I had been sleeping the night before, as I dreamt of masks and costumes on the rolling rack, a raccoon had been making its mark and ripping up my things in the backyard, just to be sure I got the message.

Make it clear, indeed.

I got off the phone with my mum and followed up the bones-on-your-altar text to Daniel with the two photos of the raccoon redesign.

His response was the same as mine, "Holy shit."

Holy indeed.

He told me to do what I already knew in *my* bones: journey to raccoon. It obviously had something important to tell me. So I did. With my training and my helpers, I went to the Spirit of Raccoon with the intention: *What do you want me to know? What are you trying to tell me?*

As soon as I connected, I got the message loud and clear from a little masked being with muddy hands. He was as decorated as a wisdom keeper, adorned with necklaces and jewels, rings on each of his little fingers. Likely from all of his trades at the crossroads . . .

"Masks aren't bad. *You* aren't bad. Changing faces and shapeshifting is part of who we are. Play and enjoyment are parts of life. *Don't be so hard on yourself.*"

I began to cry as the Spirit of Raccoon continued, smiling with its little teeth, "Make a mask from my bones and use it for an important ceremony."

So I did. I transmuted the power, and I created a headdress to remind me how to protect my heart. Since then, this headdress has brought magic. Every time.

Usually within between two and twenty-four hours of wearing it, Raccoon will show up. They are a reminder for me of my gifts but also of the power of transmutation. Just like a dream, it wouldn't impact anyone else the same way it impacts me.

As sacred as this work is and how holy the Energy of Source is, we can still take moments to play. When we own who we are and why we are here, there's nothing to be in judgment about. These issues came up for me because of my trauma, and the trigger was the judgment. The trigger was my cue to do something about it. Judgment

is its own mirror. In this instance, I was able to process the transmutation outside of my body. No need to abuse our beings (or anyone else's) to process energy.

Just because we are made of energy, we don't have to bring negative energy into our bodies to process it. We can process it outside of our bodies. If it does get in there, we can neutralize it the same way. We're going to begin our transmutation practice with getting a sense of how to go back to take care of these energetic impacts and roadblocks.

We *can* in fact travel through our timeline. We just have to use our consciousness. We can work through our moments to recalibrate and rebalance our imprints on ourselves and the world. The world we see and the one we don't. The one that's *ordinary* and the one that's *extraordinary*. In order to help better facilitate healing in ordinary reality, we can do the work in non-ordinary reality. We can do our work in the stars. We can pull back our energy—the intention or the tendril that may have been programmed to hurt (*or break a window*). Just like the ancient alchemists, we may not be able to *create* gold, but we *can* free it from its base. Free our own light from the density and transform it. This doesn't mean we can put a physically broken window back together (*without the alchemy of glass blowing*), but we can go back and better handle the energy that caused the break.

We'll now begin some transmutation practice inside this tent.

Into the Wonder

In this transmutation ritual, we'll introduce the practice (*habit*) of transmutation. You may want to grab a rattle now. You may want to just listen to some music you like. Your practice is your practice. Experimentation is welcome; remember we're in The Alchemist's Lab—a magical tent somewhere in the cosmos—so have at it, Wondertown.

We're going to introduce the concept and practice of revisiting your day energetically.

Try to think about a time where you may have shared your energy with someone, and it wasn't positive. If you didn't have an experience like that today, think back to the last time when you did. Maybe you had an interaction with someone, maybe it was with yourself. Try to visualize yourself in that moment before the negative burst comes out, before the fuel tank got contaminated, the point right before somebody peed in the Ocean of Consciousness.

There are also going to be times where we've hurt people, maybe we didn't intend to. Maybe we said something in the moment because we were triggered. Maybe we didn't say it, but we thought it and it went through the system. Maybe our energy triggered a tsunami in someone else's life just by not being aware of or responsible for our own.

Try to imagine that you're pulling that energy back into yourself. Sandra Ingerman uses the term *Spiritual fishing line,* and I love that. If that helps as a visual, we can imagine yourself reeling the energy back in and then neutralizing it. If it's negative, we're going to want to flood it with love and magic. We're going to wrap light around that energy. We're going to neutralize it. If we want to give it a higher vibration of love and light, do whatever your version of chocolates and flowers is.

If there's anything you may need to adjust from your day, you may also want to try this as something you do before you sleep to revisit each day. It's a great replacement for worrying, as you can give the energy a mission. Healing. Rebalancing. Realignment.

We're going to choose something you'd like to transmute. If you haven't identified anything yet, you can set your intention and ask for guidance on what may need adjustment. If you're not ready to ask Source, ask your higher self. We can ask the most ancient part of ourselves for guidance on remembering where our energy is meant to go. Where is our natural neutral? This may need to be a two-part practice until you have your moments.

This is your practice. If you're methodical, lean into it. If you're more spur-of-the-moment, be that.

There may be times we'd like to transmute when people hurt us. Maybe it was an unexpected call, or someone lashed out. Maybe it even created a chain reaction and our vessel impacted someone else's. Maybe it was a particularly painful breakup or work experience. It doesn't need to be a massive trauma for there to have been a wave that has caused a clog or some energy to spill out of your vessel. When this happens, we can imagine going back to the moment before the impact of the energy. Maybe it's to the morning before the breakup over text. Maybe it's the night before you got fired. Maybe it's a few seconds before someone yelled at you.

Imagine in your mind's eye, in your consciousness, going back to that moment in time. Once you have it, imagine wrapping a blanket of light or a big energetic hug around yourself in that moment before the event. We all know how much athletes train for a big game, boxers, for a big fight. Actors rehearse. They get prepared. We don't get to do that with life. Sometimes we get hit and no one sees it coming, not even the Clairs.

We can go back and energetically prepare ourselves. We can wrap ourselves in the light. We can lessen the impact. We can brace ourselves with wonder.

This is a transmutation. We can go back to the times where we were hurt, or in trauma, and use our internal alchemical gold to hold ourselves tight in the midst of pain and shock and even through our own grief. We can go back to the moments where we hurt people or impact their energy and take it back. We can transmute our heavy buckets of worry into light and purpose. We have always had this power.

You may want to write down some times in your life where you transmuted something energetically and had physical breadcrumbs. Bones or no bones. Tracking these moments will also help keep your ego in the car seat. The more examples you have, the better the case you can make. It becomes a dossier you'll be able to throw to the back seat and tell ego to *Check the precedent*. My dossier is called "The Captain's Log," because my soul keeps those notes.

We all have tremendous metaphysical help to carry life's heavy lifting. No, they may not be able to help us carry groceries, but in my experience, Energy can move even the biggest of ancestral mountains. We are not what happens to us. We are what we do with it.

When you're ready we'll leave The Transmutation Tent and The Alchemist's Lab. We'll be back through later with a new view. For now, I'll meet you in The Great Hall when you're ready.

It's time to light it up.

CHAPTER ELEVEN

THE GREAT HALL

TRANSFIGURATION

As we move through the curtain and out of The Alchemist's Lab toward the next room, the arched doorway ahead is aglow with light. It's hard not to use the word *breathtaking*. There's no sign posted leading into this room, but we *know* where we are. This is The Great Hall. Our soul*s* *are* driving. As you walk through the arch toward the light, there's a simple plaque on the wall, similar to the one in The Transmutation Tent in The Alchemist's Lab.

Another definition:

Transfiguration:
shapeshifting: an exalting, glorifying, or Spiritual change.

Although there are doorways in this room, no curtains or actual doors hang in this space. It is completely open. As we pass by it and move through the arch of light, we find ourselves in The Great Hall. The room opens up to what looks like four stories; it's massive but not overwhelming. We're at home here. It's a space with a huge vaulted glass domed ceiling. By comparison, the one in the Gazebo above The Reflecting Pool seems as if it belonged to a miniature. There are giant windows lining the upper stories and beams of light cut through the giant room.

There are cascading marble steps down from the doorway we entered through and into the main part of The Great Hall. We're gliding down the main staircase and onto the marble of the main floor. *Did we just float? It felt as if we floated.* The lightness in our vessels is palpable. *Spiritual change indeed.*

There are stairways on either side of the main stairway from each side of the floor. They wrap around to a small landing into the second story. The balconies seem to overlook the floor where we stand. Although this is not a church, it *is* a place of worship, in that it is a place of great reverence because we're here to remember and to reclaim an ancient gift. We're here to do something our buddies like Anubis *and* Jesus did—we're here to connect directly with the light of the divine.

We know what it feels like to be lit up by something, by someone, in our lives. When we're in the moment, present and connected, we can find ourselves lighting up. You've probably used that expression before. Describing someone or something as having lit us up. We *know* what it feels like when the stars "align." When we are with something or someone, and it just *clicks*. When we're in our star stuff, we feel it. It's a state of being, a feeling of connection and calm. A warm and lazy river.

As human beings we chase this high. We have experiences where we connect with these feelings of exaltation through movement, meditation, dance, journey, human connection . . . climax. The ascension and alignment of mind, body, and Spirit can happen in those moments, and that feeling of exhilaration is a collaboration between our humanity and divinity. We're going to remember how to achieve an exalting Spiritual change. We are here to transfigure.

Drugstore Magic

It was a fairly typical day for me, meaning I'd been in ceremony with clients doing magic. Just traveling between dimensions one weekend afternoon. Afterward as I was closing sessions, naturally in a particularly high state of vibration and gratitude, I got a nudge in my consciousness. A poke, one I recognized as *the one who knows the plan*. Higher self. Higher guidance. Higher truth. The part of me who's in commune with Source. The one who has it all figured out. This is very different from the daily human me who sometimes can't remember people's names or where I put my phone. This nudge, this voice, is the one I *know* to listen to. We've built up enough of a precedent together over the years that I pay attention because some magical gift or package typically gets delivered. Sometimes it's a real physical package in ordinary reality, and sometimes it's a Spiritual gift that I am given. Either way, treats!

So I felt the nudge. It was specific. As I always ask Spirit, *Please make it clear,* and it does.

Why don't you go to the drugstore at the end of the street and get yourself a treat? Maybe there's a present for you there.

A present? As you already know, I enjoy a good intention-driven scavenger hunt. I also enjoy a well-plotted, thoughtful, and gentle surprise. People who live with PTSD don't tend to enjoy being surprised in the traditional sense. Instead, I call them *gentle surprises*. More my speed.

Spirit also knew how to hit me right in the feels. It lit me up with something that they knew would get my attention; the tradition of getting a "treat" at the drugstore began when I was a kid. Growing up with terrible asthma and allergies meant a lot of doctors' appointments, medicine, and sometimes needles. So being the crafty little witch I was, I'd always negotiate a treat after anything painful. The drugstore was the stage for those early negotiations. We had to go there to get whatever medicine I'd may have been prescribed that day. As I walked in ripe with treat nostalgia, I felt another nudge, like a note being passed through my consciousness.

Check the magazine rack. I walked over and scanned the rack of magazines near the entrance to the store. I don't know what I expected, but this *wasn't* it. I wish I could have seen my face. Grinning and excited all the way down the street to pretty confused—and maybe a *little* disappointed. I had expected candy, then maybe a magazine about candy or treats. When I looked down, I knew right away what my present was, and I felt kind of embarrassed. I knew enough to know I was in the right place, but I didn't think I would have cataloged this as a "treat." On the two bottom rows of the magazine rack, there were *three* Jesus magazines. *THREE.* On the cover of each with big letters—JESUS. Couldn't miss them. This was not near Easter or Christmas or any of those holidays we've come to associate with this being. This was just a random August day. I mean I like Jesus and everything, but I didn't think I needed *a magazine* about him. I stood there looking at these three magazines. I thought about this the way I try to think about most breadcrumbs from Source.

Okay, I'll bite.

I was in a downtown drugstore, in a major metropolis, in an area frequented by people who were probably not actively looking for Jesus magazines, let alone a selection, but for some reason, there was not just one but three very different magazines about this guy. I looked at them and flipped through a couple. I was subtle, I looked at a few other magazines too, just in case anyone was watching. I wanted to keep it quick. It was definitely not something I'd have wanted to explain to a security guard. I looked at them and checked in on the energy. I knew it was between two of the three. I chose one Jesus magazine over the other and I grabbed some gum as I made my way to the cashier. I figured it would give me a good cover and provide an explanation for what I felt was my purposeful and excited walk into the drugstore.

Standing at the cashier as if I were a teen buying tampons for the first time, I smiled awkwardly at the magazine as I turned over the shining face of the white Jesus on the cover.

As soon as I walked out of the store, I felt the nudge in my consciousness, *again*.

Get the other one.

I stopped short in front of the door.

OH, COME ON.

Now I was embarrassed. I had to go back in to get *another* Jesus magazine—two Jesus magazines, one cashier, zero excuses. I walked out one door and right back in the other—to get myself another Jesus magazine and some deodorant. I didn't want to look like a *weirdo*, and chips felt too celebratory for Jesus magazines. I came here for deodorant, gum, and thirty dollars' worth of Jesus magazines. That's how much Jesus magazines go for—fifteen bucks each. If we were transmuting this, we can imagine replaying back to when I left the house all excited about my surprise.

Then imagine someone stopping me halfway there and handing me this bag:

Here's your present, Amy. No chips.

Chewing my gum, I walked my Jesus magazines home and sat down on the middle of my living room carpet with them, like some kind of Spiritual detective.

I knew there was *something* important in them (other than details about a kick-ass guy) and I was going to figure out what it was. As I looked through them, I noticed that they had the same quote on both covers.

One was on the front and the other on the back:

"Who do you say that I am?"
—LUKE 9:20

Two totally separate publishers had decided, *This* is the quote.

As I leafed through both magazines, one of them (the second one, of course) had a beautiful image of a painting by Bartolomé Esteban Murillo titled *Christ Healing the Paralytic at the Pool of Bethesda*. The painting shows one of Jesus's seven acts of charity described in the Gospel of Matthew. Jesus stands with his hand outstretched performing a healing on a sick man who is sitting on the ground. An angel hovers in the sky in front of a golden light. It appears that the light from the angel moves around Jesus's head like a halo and through his out-stretched hand performing the healing. The halo, the glow, is the divine luster—the imprint of divine light. Maybe Jesus was depicted with a halo to illustrate he was embodying the light, not that he was the only game in town. Around the scene of the painting are three apostles. They are present to bear witness to the miracle.

Witnesses. As I sat there on my floor looking at this magazine with this painting from the seventeenth century, something clicked. A key turned in a lock and I realized why I had gotten these magazines.

Who do you say that I am? was the quote on both covers.

The words came out of my lips like an answer: "A shaman."

Goosebumps.

Looking at this painting of Jesus channeling divine light, hands out and open, he *is* the hollow bone, allowing the light to move through him to heal someone. He performed healings in his community. He was an alchemist, he did transmutations. He took space in the desert to have visions. He was persecuted and initiated . . .

Of course he was a shaman.

Jesus was walking between worlds like any Spiritual teacher who could take other people there with him. Witnesses saw things too. Just like when in a shamanic journey practice, we can experience shared visions.

That was worth the thirty bucks, a dollar for every year of the man's life. Well played, Jesus. *Well played.* A treat indeed!

When in sync with Source we can get the same transmissions. Just like the radio, we can pick up the same broadcast. We may comprehend it, and therefore describe it differently, but we're all hearing the same thing.

This is the side of Spirituality no one tells you about. We need to acknowledge in these stories that we have a world that is composed of the seen and the unseen, but we live in a society that works to disconnect us from the unseen, trying to prevent us from having our own set of keys. Our intention in The Great Hall is to travel inward. Imagine the openness of the space represents your vessel. To experience the true self, to experience the vibration in our body, we have to remember to see with our hearts.

The Practice of Transfiguration

In natural and primary Spiritual teachings, there is no disconnection between the seen and unseen. In our remembering, we honor these communities, the elders, and their sacred wisdom. It is they who have fought and paid with their lives to save the old ways. It's up to all of us to remember that the division caused between religion and spirituality wasn't actually due to systems of belief, it was due to intentional misinformation and institutional abuse.

This new breadcrumb about Jesus sent me farther down the rabbit hole as I looked up the verse that appeared on the cover of both. I read just the passage quoted. Not the proceeding verse, nor the following. The passage was interesting, but no more goosebumps. During that time, I just did what I've learned to do. I stayed open to the idea that there might be more. I hollow boned it and instead of holding on so tight to the wheel, the way I did when my ego was driving, I let it glide through my hands. A few months later, a few miles down the road of life, I found myself registering for a course with Sandra Ingerman. It was called "Healing with Spiritual Light."

It sounded beautiful and I never hesitated at an opportunity to spend any kind of time with her. She is magical on any subject on any day.

I still didn't know about the transfiguration of Jesus, the one in the Bible. I didn't even really know the word until Sandra talked about it in her course. She spoke about how she'd learned that *Jesus* was someone who practiced transfiguration. It was the first time I'd ever heard her talk about Jesus. Of course, here he is again. You can probably see him in your mind's eye, his hands up in a timid wave, with a hopeful *Hey, can we chat?* expression on his face.

So I pulled over.

I realized I needed to go back to the magazines (now a focal point of my practice room and frequent reference of how to follow synchronicity). I went back to the last breadcrumb.

I again looked up that Bible verse on the cover. *Who do you say that I am?* This time, I read a bit further than I had the first time. From 9:20 to 9:28: It was the transfiguration of Christ.

If I would've kept reading past the part where Jesus predicted his own transition and ascension the day I got the magazines, I'd have read about how he journeyed to the Mount and transfigured there. So the Jesus magazine, Sandra, all these things are breadcrumbs I found by listening to my soul.

The magazines and Sandra were a part of how Spirit knocked on the window of my vessel saying, *Amy, be sure to remember your transfiguration work.*

Transfiguration is intentionally filling our vessels with Spiritual light. When we do this, it enables us to see things a little more clearly. Lighting up. Maybe we shouldn't have assumed everything in the Bible was literal. Maye he *was* a Sun of the Stars, right? Maybe he is the S U N of Source. Maybe we all are. Seems too unbelievable? It's not. It's documented. We may be able to turn base metals into gold without lasers. This breadcrumb found me as I was editing this book. And because, *make it clear*, it was threefold. A client of mine, who'd been referred to me by a client with a deep practice in Spain, told me a story about something

incredible that happened to her after receiving a healing at a revival in Toronto in the mid-nineties. She told me that one of her fillings had turned gold.

It was a Christian revival in a space where Jesus and the Holy Spirit are definitely invited. Energy is raised. The intention is healing. As soon as she said it, I heard it in my consciousness: *transfiguration*. When I went to the internet, I found out my client wasn't the only person this seemed to have happened to. In Toronto alone over three hundred people were documented to have experienced the same thing. When I was nudged to share this with my friend Elisha in Georgia, who has both deep faith and a deep transfiguration practice, she knew exactly what I was talking about.

Not only had she heard about Toronto, but Elisha also told me that the same thing had happened to her grandmother at a revival in Kentucky. Over the next month I was nudged to share this with another client, Spencer. He's done the retreat for *What We've Forgotten* a few times. His parents both happen to be retired ministers. As I told him the story, he sat back on the stool of the coffee shop we were in, just down the street from the drugstore where the Jesus magazines had come from, and he said something I hadn't thought of: "I think the woman from Spain and the woman with the grandmother were both in my *What We've Forgotten* retreats."

I almost fell off my stool. Of course they were all connected. They had also grown up having some experiences with Jesus.

Spirit wasn't done. A few days later I got a message from Spencer. He said, "I just got off the phone with my parents. I asked if the Toronto blessing was on their radar as church people; it wasn't, so I filled them in."

But then Spencer dropped the real synchronicity surprise, sharing, "But then my mum tells me she went to a new dentist a few months ago, and he was like, 'Oh wow, what a beautiful gold filling, I've never seen one so pristine.'" And my mum goes, "'I don't have a gold filling.' She has never been given one, and yet . . ."

In Christian teachings, the Transfiguration is a pivotal moment, and the setting on the mountain is presented as the point where Nature and humans meet Source. I start this practice with a *lighthearted* story because Source *is lighthearted* by design. It doesn't mean that we don't treat this work with respect, it means we keep our hearts light while doing it. Without a light heart, you can't carry wonder, and without wonder, you can't experience the magic of Source. It's hard to see clearly with a heavy heart.

Feel free to write that down on a Post-it and put it on your mirror. When your ego is looking at you in the mirror and saying mean stuff, you can put the Post-it on it: "Take that, car seat!"

The practice of Transfiguration is the transformation of our energy through shapeshifting, and even though I am an Optimist Prime, and I'd like to tell you that I can help you transform into a werewolf, or a car, I can't. Because transfiguration is shifting with and into our Spiritual form. The human body is limited because it was designed to encourage us to evolve our Spirits. The human form is magnificent, but it's also designed for us to *want* an upgrade. I'm not talking about surgery or injections. I'm talking about something even more beautiful than anything or anyone you've ever seen.

You've likely met someone who is radiant from within, you know what I'm talking about. It's captivating because it's the light of Source. People glow. We recognize it, and are attracted to it, because it feels like home. Try being at a Kendrick Lamar concert and tell me that man isn't carrying divinity. He *radiates* it because it's his biggest collaborator. He talks about trauma and growth. He channels his music; he co-creates with Spirit. That's why so many artists *are* magnetic. They are wielding the force all day every day.

Let Me Take You to Nerd Town

This isn't just magic, or Spirituality, *this is science.* The body actually emits visible light. This light differs from infrared radiation (which is an invisible form of light that comes from our body heat). The light we emit is approximately one thousand times less intense than our eyes can see. To learn more about this, scientists in Japan employed extraordinarily sensitive cameras capable of detecting single photons. Five healthy male volunteers in their twenties were placed in front of the cameras in

complete darkness in light-tight rooms for twenty minutes every three hours from 10 a.m. to 10 p.m. for three days. Researchers found the glow of the body rose and fell over the day, its lowest point at 10 a.m., peak at 4 p.m., dropping gradually after that. These findings suggest the emission is linked to our body clocks, most likely due to how our metabolic rhythms fluctuate over the course of a day.

Experiments have also been done using a GDV camera from before and after transfiguration to illustrate the difference our energy makes on the natural world. We can do transfiguration with our food, with our water, our environments—or even an area of your life. As the world is becoming more and more toxic due to pollution and climate change, we can act in the world by changing how we live, creating less waste, adopting solar technology, and abandoning fossil fuels. We can transmute the energy we put into our bodies, and we can transfigure the energy we emit. If anything is going to help us through the climate crisis, I truly believe transfiguration, in combination with changing our ways, is the *magic* we need. What if a global transfiguration could help transmute all that CO_2? What if we could use this concept of correspondence (as above, so below) to change our behaviors *and* our environment? We should be trying.

Transfiguring the Scales

We can transfigure for ourselves, our community, our environments, and the collective. We can transfigure objects to heal and recalibrate them. The work of Masaru Emoto seemed to illustrate that water can carry energy, as it is connected to consciousness. Try to transfigure on a glass of water and then drink it. Notice how different it feels when you spread the light of your being into your world. I know it sounds bananas, but this is magic—and science.

We can use the energy we carry to do things we may not be able to see with our naked eyes. If you really want to nerd out, try working with a group to transfigure over water for an hour and see if you can change the pH. Water is conscious, so just make sure you ask it if it wants to transform with you.

Being human means to learn how to repair, remember, learn, and cleanse ourselves of the heaviness of our egos in order to reach ascension. The only way we will correct environmental pollution is with science *and* Spirituality. The practice of transfiguration is rooted in the concept that we can level up—and help remind other people how to level up—while we're still here. Taoism teaches that a person's soul attains the fullest completion by achieving destiny before the afterlife. Worth a try?

With transfiguration, we can experience what expansion beyond the vessel feels like, using our light to bring actual change to our physical realities. We are all vessels of light and we can all access infinite light. Transfiguration enables us to synchronize to the web of light and reset, which assists us in shining without limitations and giving us more illumination to follow our purpose. This practice also brings illumination of our own authentic power, frequency, and vibration. Our own unique medicines. Our personal elixir. We talked about all these civilizations using gold to represent divinity. Why were the pharaohs in ancient Egypt using (and wearing) so much gold? Why is the mask of King Tut gold? *Because he was transfigured.* When we see hieroglyphs of the sun disk in ancient Egyptian carvings, in many we see that there are hands coming down from it, as if illustrating the willingness of light to take our hands.

The Book of the Dead is also translated as the *Book of Coming Forth by Day*, or my favorite, the *Book of Emerging Forth into the Light*. This "book" was actually a collection of papyrus found in the tombs along with the dead. The spells contained in the book would outline the journey of the soul on earth, to the lower world after death, and into the afterlife. Think of this as a tree of life. Lower world is the roots of the tree, middle world is ordinary reality, and upper world is the tree's branches.

Spell 100 in the *Book of Emerging Forth into the Light* is an incantation for *transfiguring* the dead individual, making them into an "excellent Spirit," a perfected Spirit. Learning to work and walk in light was meant to help the transition between worlds so humans could have a chance to awaken in the field of reeds, the afterlife. Anubis was illustrated as a gatekeeper between worlds. Maybe he was the first shaman; maybe that's why we all seem to recognize him, existing for thousands of years in history and pop culture. Maybe he's the original teacher of transfiguration, the opener of the way between worlds, humanity's biggest advocate, man's best friend. Maybe that's why he's in The Entryway protecting The Archives, guarding the gates. A protector of states and dimensions of consciousness.

You'd think we'd have been able to connect these dots, to see these very large breadcrumbs, the light, the worship of it, magic's role in society, the pyramids being literal arrows pointing up to the sky, and yet, we still didn't get it. So prophets came to try to show us. It even got written down. For thousands of years, it's almost as if the Universe has been trying to tell us something.

Stardust Shapeshifters

We're all walking stardust and most of us have just forgotten how to use it. As humans on Earth, we're living in this gritty reality that is literally designed to put us through our paces. The veils between worlds are getting thinner, and if we evolve consciously, we are going to see more synchronicity, more miraculous healings, and more understanding and abundance. These are the side effects of Spiritual work and practice.

Life on Earth is imperfect because perfection exists in our *transcendent* reality. There we have no imbalance, no illness. We have only possibilities. The practice of transfiguration is rooted in the understanding that everything is already perfect, and nothing needs healing. Everything is a part of what needs to be.

By doing this, it is possible to bring back into balance not only yourself but others, and ideally the planet. I know, I know, *Amy, do you really believe we can heal ourselves, others, and the planet using this practice?* I believe it's worth a shot, and from what I know of Spirit, I know they wouldn't want it to be this hard for us. From a Spiritual level, all we see is beauty and light. What if all we saw was wonder and not pain and suffering? Spirit sees only discordant energy patterns. It doesn't see imperfection. This isn't about being in denial that the world is on fire or that some human beings are living in horrific conditions because of some other human beings. If we consider that the people with the most can be impacted to share with the people who have the least, then this works. I have seen those kinds of awakenings through this work. We can't be in denial to do it. We have to see the horror to fix it. We have to know it and we must remind those who have the most inauthentic power and control to see it too.

We can't do this if we can't learn to take care of each other. To move forward, we have to see the magic of community and understand that one person *can* change the world. If we would just pass the torch instead of hoarding it, with love instead of anger, things will change . . . fast.

This isn't something extra you need to do. It's not some practice you're not going to have time for or be too tired to do. The truth is, you're never too tired to shine, because you're shining already. You can't turn it off, but you can become aware of it. And once you have awareness of your own powers, you can use them to change the world around you for the better. The idea is to shift our perception to operate in a state of appreciation and gratitude for all that exists. What we feed does grow. We're going to grow our light. This room, The Great Hall, can hold it all.

Into the Wonder

Find a place in this Great Hall where you're comfortable. We're going to imagine traveling inside of ourselves. We're not going anywhere. We're going to be right here in this sacred space. You're still you, we're just going to light ourselves up a bit more.

Imagine something in your mind's eye that's a source of light in Nature, a star, the sun, the moon, a candle, a campfire. Whatever light you like. Remember that little one in the car seat is going to try to break your concentration. You're going to be in your practice and then your ego is going to ask you about when the bills are due. When this happens, I suggest a gentle reminder that you'll get back to that later. You can also use your body to help restrain that little buddy, whether it's rolling beads in your hand, holding a crystal, a sacred object, or toning—all can help hold concentration (and the ego at bay). It also can help stop mind chatter.

To tone you can use *Om*, or any vowel and just extend it. If I spell it out here, it will look like one of those haunted house children's books that has "Ooooooo-ooooooooom Aaaaaaaaaaaaaaaaaaaaaaaaaaaaaaaa" printed next to pictures of ghosts in the windows. While you're toning, if you need to breathe, then breathe. If you need to stop, stop. It's not a mantra contest. Take your time.

I'm going to guide us on your first time.

Closing your eyes and reading a book can be hard, so you may want to read the practice out loud on voice notes so you can listen to it or have someone read it for you as you relax. You may want to have some singing bowls on or play or use your music.

When we transfigure, we're going be able to do it with our eyes closed or our eyes open. We're going to start with our eyes closed, but if you can, take this practice and do it in Nature. Nature will deepen any work you are doing.

Once you've decided on your point of light, the transfiguration practice, like all things from Source, is relatively simple and straightforward. It all happens in three steps. This journey really does start with a single step.

Step 1 is the self. Step 2 is our close ones and our community. Step 3 is the collective—the world. Envision that light source and imagine that we are flooding the whole body with light, filling ourselves up from the feet or from the top. You may imagine that you're a sponge or a cloth, soaking the light into every cell. As we soak in that light, we are going to become it.

Now, close your eyes and imagine yourself as a star in the night sky or the sun in the sky—moonlight, flame, any light source that resonates. Imagine you are surrounded with light as far as the eye can see. With our intention and our breath, try to call the light of the Universe around us. Imagine welcoming that light into your body, into the cells of your being, your vessel. Lighting up all the cells of the body. On the exhale, you can imagine that you are releasing everything of a low vibration or frequency back into the universe. You are transmuting anything you need to neutralize. You can imagine each time you do this, you're allowing in more light. Inhale and breathe in that light from source. This is how we communicate when we're in a transfigured state. There's a hawk that comes to me in Nature, and he always says to me, *Do that thing, do that thing.* Transfiguration. So I do it.

Again, imagine that light source, maybe it's the sun, or illumination of the moon if you like. Just remember we're shining 360 degrees all the time. As we get connected to that light, we're going to imagine it can flood our systems.

As it's growing, it's getting closer and closer. So close we can reach out and touch it. As it gets bigger and bigger, it's moving through every cell, every fiber, every muscle, every bone of our beings. You might imagine that it's coming in through the top of your head. You might imagine that you're soaking it in like a sponge. Or it's coming through your fingertips. You might imagine that it's like water and it's just moving through you like a wave. You might want to lift your arms like a vessel and imagine the light pouring in.

As we're part of the Ocean of Consciousness, we can, and do, feel other people's stuff. When we connect to energy, we feel what's going on. We can ask that the Energy or the Spirit of who they are comes through. If people are jerks, we can see them in their highest form, with ease and grace and divine timing with harm to none. We need permission to do healing work with people, but we don't need permission to do transfiguration. Transfiguration is simply seeing people with your heart in their perfect form. We do not need permission to include the collective in our transfiguration practice. That's the exalting, glorifying, or Spiritual change. It is actually using the light we carry.

May we all remember how to walk in light. Ego can be dim; the Soul is bright. May we remember the heartbeat of Earth. May this remind us what it's all worth.

You're now in a transfigured state. You don't need to disconnect from the energy. You can be in the world *and* be full of light. If you can go into Nature in a transfigured state, that's just some extra-credit work. Notice how different the world looks, and also, notice who shows up. One of the *What We've Forgotten* alumni has made friends with dragonflies and owls since starting the practice. Nature has wrapped around her and her family in ways even I can't believe. It's *her* practice and *her* magic.

When you're ready, come up the stairs to the second level of The Temple. You're ready to see behind the curtain. We'll begin in Section III: The Observation Deck. If you decide to come to the Deck transfigured, I'm not going to complain.

III

BECOMING

CHAPTER TWELVE

THE OBSERVATION DECK

THE TEN-THOUSAND-FOOT VIEW

As we come up the stairway from The Great Hall, there is a feeling of comfort. A small, now familiar sign is attached to the wall as we reach the top of the stairs: THE OBSERVATION DECK. There's a curtained doorway and from behind it is a sound that you recognize. It's a low and calming tone that makes your nervous system feel as if it's being given a warm hug. As you get closer to the doorway, a bluish light spills out from under the curtain.

As you pull back the curtain, there is a wall of floor-to-ceiling windows, and that's when we see it. We are surrounded by a 180-degree view of the heavens. The light of Source. The Universe. Space. Galaxies, nebula, baby stars. They move in front of you like an ocean and we can almost hear a symphony. We aren't looking up, we're looking out. This *is* an Observation Deck. The light and color play off the rest of the room as a shiny floor reflects the stars onto themselves. These columns hold the space in a different way than they did downstairs, where the columns were stone, but these ones don't look or feel like any kind of object you've ever touched. As we get closer, the texture of them is *geometric*. This room looks into space; it's also made of space. Meteorite. There are benches and seating areas carved out around the room. All this beauty and majesty needs a place to anchor.

We sit at the front of the room, as close as we can get to the big picture window where we notice the most brilliant blue-green orb, hanging in space like a jewel. It is coming front and center. It is Earth.

We see the line that separates the day from the night as the sun rises and slowly moves across the planet. Shooting stars and dancing curtains of auroras. We are watching the Earth come alive before our eyes. We are a part of everything outside of this observation window and it's a part of us. This is what is beyond separation. Integration. Everything is alive. The Earth is a microcosm for the big picture. This is why astronauts often say that much of their free time is filled with "Earth gazing," staring out at the Earth. We see our home from the perspective of Source.

Astronauts returning to Earth have described an "overview effect" that happens after they have seen the Earth from space. It brings a cognitive shift in awareness. As human beings, we exist in a world where we see blue skies, and it's hard for most of us to imagine not seeing that, not returning to it. Sunrise and our blue skies bring life. The ancient Egyptians called it Akhet. It was so important that they named a whole season for it.

Akhet marked the rise of the Nile, which also brought abundance of life and food. Sustenance came from the sun and the elements. Part of what we've forgotten is the very abundance that light brings us. We can see the heavens (if we take the time to look), but we don't get to see the Earth with its thinning atmosphere being the only thing between us and this black chasm.

When we see this, we realize the fragility of life here. We recognize and remember we were once protectors for this planet. Everything that has ever happened, everything we know about, it's all happened here. From the bugs to the billionaires (*I like the bugs better*), it's all part of us. When we consider this, we can begin to grasp just how small *we* are in this vast ocean of space and time. How miraculous it is that we are here at all? Especially these days. We have to *own* it because we *are* it.

Prospector of Perspective

Let's acknowledge that life as a human being on Earth is not always a smooth sea, but maybe part of the challenge here is so that we can learn the ropes of this system and learn how to surf its energy. How else might we get the skills to move into whatever is coming next for our souls than to train for it? Maybe human life is how we get prepared for something much bigger.

Whether you believe in God or Energy right now or not, it's hard to deny that there is some form of an all-knowing consciousness, because right now, it doesn't seem to be us.

Sometimes our souls return, and we come back because we left some treasures behind. This is reincarnation. This is the greatest scavenger hunt there has ever been. Buddhism welcomes this journey. We've all heard of those three wizard astrologers who followed the stars (and brought offerings from Nature) to meet a baby witch who would become a prophet. We also know the phrase "beware the ides of March" because of a lesser known seer, Spurinna who foretold the demise of Julius Caesar. Soothsayers are part of our collective story.

If we consider that this is possible and that Source is infinite, we can imagine that our breadcrumbs can be connected not just in our own lives, but in the lives of our ancestors and possibly the lives our soul may have lived before. We just didn't keep records like the Buddhists.

Just as we do with transfiguration, tracking breadcrumbs through time begins with ourselves: the small, individual unit. We soak up the light into our bodies and into the tiniest of cells and molecules, the stardust itself. Then we extend outward. We expand that light, that star stuff from Source to our beings, then into our communities, and then into the world. We are in effect zooming in and then zooming out using our consciousness; this unique ability is part of how we get out of this bind we've found our collective selves in.

Sometimes I've learned that hitting a brick wall in ordinary reality means we need to look from above. Just like in gaming, or VR, sometimes we need to change

the angle to get a better look to see how to proceed. We're going to try to start remembering we can look at our lives in the same way. As we begin to track synchronicities, dates, patterns, and our experiences with *and in* non-ordinary reality, we can begin to really see the true majesty of Nature, of Source, *and* we begin to give more credit to our intuition. The more breadcrumbs Spirit throws our way, the more we can begin to trust them. If we can imagine all the windows of time through which things can occur have to perfectly align in the way needed for synchronicity, you can't help but experience wonder, especially given how small we are in the grand scheme of the Universe.

We may *have* forgotten, but we've never *been* forgotten.

The ten-thousand-foot view is a telescopic lens aimed at your own life. If you're a gamer like me, think of it as your free look, virtual camera system. If you're not a gamer, imagine it's a viewfinder. You can use the view to display a different angle of our experiences. Let's use it to try to see the events of our lives from a higher perspective. Let's imagine we can zoom out from the place we are now in to see the full layout of this temple. Consider that much like The Temple map, our life and its memories and occurrences are a similar map of space and time. Even *science* has begun to acknowledge time travel. Brian Greene, one of the world's most well-known physicists, stated "The bottom line is that time travel is allowed by the laws of physics."

Maybe time travel doesn't actually need to involve a DeLorean as the vessel? Instead, maybe we can move around through our consciousness, to see the Earth from space. We know what it looks like. We can feel it with our hearts. If we can begin to consider our lives like that, imagine that we can zoom in and out of moments. Try to imagine that we have a map—or blueprints—for all the moments that have happened in our lives. Consider life as a giant map of space and time that you can move around on, we can zoom in or out (like Google Earth but with energy).

Let's take a minute and level with each other here. I'd spent so much of my life on the ground, face pressed against the road, my nose was dragging on the concrete. Some of us are so zoomed into the challenge of the moment, we're drowning in the *what if*s and *what could be*s. We get *so* zoomed in; we practically fall out of our own vessels. When we zoom out, we gain perspective and we're able to see more of what is around us. We can illuminate the interior of the Trauma Shed to discover the path to Narnia (or Oz).

As a result of shifting our perspective, things feel less unknown, the timing of life tends to make a bit more sense. Perspective is everything. The farther we zoom out, the more we see not only our whole life, but the lives of our ancestors. We can more holistically look at all of their traumas *and* the triumphs. It doesn't excuse the injuries but does offer us a better understanding of *why* by offering a glimpse of the whole picture and the *how* behind the hurts. Like any practice, over time, it's easier to discern how things might be connected, how patterns can tell the story of our purpose, helping us glide more easily through the mucky parts of life . . . because those aren't going anywhere. Hard things are a component of the human experience and a necessary part of our evolution. Moving shadows is part of balance. It's part of the system.

In The Sanctum we saw how Spirituality was stolen from us, how it was intentionally scattered and shamed, tricking us humans into believing that somehow, we were better than Nature. We're plugging back in reconnecting to the wonders of the natural world. We are remembering old ways and letting go of limiting beliefs and patterns. Enabling us to move into a place where we can glide more easily through life. Where we can ascend past war and division and into acceptance and collaboration.

When we were kids, we didn't always need an explanation for everything. Sometimes things were just amazing and magical and that was all we needed to know. We were open to the prospect of the unseen. We hadn't yet closed off to the prospect that we lived in a world full of incredible things and that anything might be possible. We constructed stories and worlds inside of our heads and consciousness easily and without question. We *knew* things. We *saw* things. We had imaginary friends. We talked to Nature. We wondered. We made wishes on stars.

What if we've all just been so close to everything the past few hundred years, so tightly wound to the things we think we know, that we forgot we *could* zoom out? Maybe we forgot to think bigger. In my own journey I realized if this were true, what other things could I have been missing out on? Not only in my own life but in the moments with the world?

The answer was: *a lot.*

Because perception really *is* everything. The way we perceive things impacts how we actually feel in our moments. We are influenced almost entirely by our perspective at any given time. It's the difference between having an emotional experience and *being* emotional. You may be thinking, *What's the difference?* In one instance, we recognize that you are a being—or a vessel—moving through an experience; in the other, we *are* the emotion.

Have you seen someone become enraged? Or been enraged yourself? It's all-encompassing; nothing exists outside of that moment. It's the space where we hurt each other and ourselves, but if we shift out of the emotion, and into the idea that this is a temporary impact on our experience, we can more easily steady our vessels.

We can get through moments in a way we might not have before. Instead of disassociating, we can root our light in our body with the reminder that we are connected to something beyond the moment. I know you're thinking the same thing I always used to think: *But it's hard to have that kind of perspective when you're upset or angry.*

It might *seem* that way.

I can assure you, it's not harder, it's actually easier. Good driving takes practice and then becomes habit. Fueling ourselves based on our emotions is a wilder ride than adding more Spirit to the mix (and you know I'm in recovery, so I don't mean liquor). In fact, it becomes less like a game of pitfall and more like being on a reliable escalator. We've already established that human beings tend to overcomplicate things. We spin, we stew, we run scenarios. You may have done it at the beginning of this chapter about how you *"probably can't change your perspective."* It's as if most of us are living our lives so focused on the destination, we're not even experiencing the journey.

Hard fact alert: Humans are much easier to control when they're operating in fear. The systems of The Uninvited were designed this way. We worry because it was ingrained into our culture to take us off the rails. When we are full of authentic power, perspective, and intention, it's next to impossible to derail that train. Nature doesn't do shame, it does evolution.

Nature is open and organic, not rigid. We can create new systems in harmony with the natural order. Too many of us are suffering, too many of us are angry, and too many of us are divided. This approach isn't working, but we have the power to change it. This is the greatest thing about life on Earth (and probably off it as well): We get to *evolve*. We get to learn things and change our ways of thinking. We get to adjust our perspective. We get to adapt, and since for at least a few generations most of us seem to have been so caught up in what we *think* we know, most of us haven't been open to what *might* be.

Our Collective Intelligence

We can't avoid our shadows; we have to bring out all the dark and heavy stuff and put it on the table in order to move past it. We know that from transmuting our buckets of worry in The Alchemist's Lab. Unfortunately, it's not just *your* buckets we have to deal with, we've got a whole archaeological dig to deal with here. We're going through all of humanity's garbage. These are not antiquities being exposed; they are systems of oppression.

We need to look at this in an entirely new way. It's time to remember our collective intelligence and our ability to chart a path to healing. We have this capability. We always did. We aren't just here to play our own game; we're here to see the bigger objective. The way out of this will have to include magic. It's why we haven't been able to progress past this particular level because we weren't willing to look past our own noses and to connect to the world around us. The only way out is indeed through.

As someone who was dragging myself for thirty years of my life, I can say this whole perspective shift is way better than having your nose against the asphalt of experience. Everything I thought was fact. I didn't know how to accept new information or opinions. I didn't have room to process it. It's part of why I couldn't name my abuse; I was so close to it. I was in it. It was everywhere. It had permeated everything. It wasn't until I got some perspective, zoomed out a bit, that I finally saw the whole picture.

When I finally used this ten-thousand-foot view on my own life, my own timeline, I realized something that you may realize too. Here it comes: I was the common denominator. My trauma. My hurdles.

All the stuff that I thought was because of other people. What all these jerks in my life had in common was me. When I zoomed out . . . Oooooh boy, I could see *all* the patterns. My family, my ancestors, my relationships, my history. It was there the whole time. The gift of this practice is that we get to *choose* how we perceive things. When something that I perceive as shocking or upsetting happens, those are the moments of grace I give myself to remember to take a beat and to let the information move through my nervous system. Then I ask myself, *Has this happened before? Have I lived through anything, any feeling like this before? Have any of my ancestors? Is there precedent?* Things get less scary when your perspective includes a wider focus.

Ancestry isn't just about the bad stuff, it's also about the good stuff too. What breadcrumbs can be found, and can we ask our ancestors for help, and support?

This is the root of our individual magic and power. It's our physical DNA that evolved over generations. The ancestry of our consciousness is the soul. The deeper (extra-credit) work is considering what gifts may not run in your physical ancestry but may still reside in you. Those are your clues to your soul's origin. We live in an ordinary reality of tactility. When we entertain that consciousness has more than three dimensions, we can open up to the idea that maybe we have a lot more help than we thought. Maybe we know a lot more than we think we do about our purpose, our past, and our progress toward the future. Maybe we *can* level up.

Preachers, Pagans, and Astronomers

My great-great-grandfather, John Oke, became a circuit preacher after grappling with alcoholism. Addiction and redemption. I know this because he wrote it down. I have his journals and I also have a copy of his amazing eulogy. It told me the stuff you tend to learn about people only at their funerals. *He was a man of great humor and service who loved talking to people about the Holy Spirit.* One of John Oke's other descendants is John Beverly Oke. He was a famous astronomer, who was into quasars.

We'll take a quick trip to Nerd Town for this one. Quasars aren't on everyone's list of fun, but they should be. Quasars are the brightest known objects in the Universe (supercharge your next transfiguration session by using a quasar). Due to their structure, they produce massive amounts of energy. A quasar is always found near a supermassive black hole, and this seems to generate extra power. Quasars can produce up to one hundred times more energy than our home galaxy, the Milky Way. John Oke preached about the Holy Spirit, the Divine Light, and in many ways so did John Beverly Oke, who discovered that the fuzzy halos around some quasars were actually starlight from the galaxy that's hosting the quasar. John's son, Leroy, my great-grandfather, was a character who would dress up in costumes and wigs to sing and dance. He was the manager at a bank and survived a heist by bank robber and murderer Red Ryan. A love and curiosity for space and Spirit *and* survival courses through my veins, but so do costumes, a real lineage of light workers here. My mother's mother brings her own magic. My grandmother and great-grandmother both spoke of fairies, angels, and spirits. They spoke of supernatural experiences, interactions, visions, and shared dreams. Clairvoyance runs on that side of the family. They were both also quite creative and (witch)crafty. My grandmother Jean specifically was a prolific artist who worked in oil paints. My grandfather John, the son of a preacher's son, surely saw the magic of light and creation in my grandmother. They both passed these gifts to my mum and my mum to me. Both of my maternal grandparents carry Scottish magic. On one side I descend from the Campbell Clan from the Isle of Skye. The motto of the Campbell's is "Ne Obliviscaris" (Forget Not). The "What We've Forgotten" portion of my own family tree was roughly one half.

My father's father was half Filipino from the Cebu province. My great-grandmother was a French woman he met in St. Thomas Virgin Islands. I didn't grow up knowing that I was part Filipino. Partially because my father isolated me from his family and partially because my great-grandfather probably had to do some assimilating in the United States to raise my grandfather and his sister, so us being of Asian descent wasn't a badge my family seemed to want to wear. We also blended in because we looked European, and had a Spanish colonizer last name. It wasn't until my thirties that, I finally saw a photo of my great-grandfather and found out where my last name had really come from.

After I finally went to the police about what my father had done to me, he did what most predators do when backed into a corner, he lashed out and attacked. Although being cautioned not to communicate with me while the investigation was happening, he sent me an email. In it, my father told me that I should change my last name because I wasn't worthy of it.

The irony. It ended with me for a reason. I'm the cycle breaker. Maybe you are too?

It's one of the biggest transmutations of my life. I will transmute the trauma of the name given to my family by colonial violence. This is the ten-thousand-foot view of my own trauma, the hard truth that I survived the violence he perpetuated and that part of it probably came from somewhere down the ancestral line. Uninvited.

It ran in the family until it ran into me.

My paternal Filipino and French grandfather married my Puerto Rican grandmother whose last name was Pagan. Literally, *Pagan.* When we ask for Spirit to make it clear, it really does its thing, especially from the ten-thousand-foot view. The breadcrumbs of my purpose and gifts were written into my instruction manual for Earth. I just had to know how and where to look.

As the energy of my trauma unfolded, so did the answers to why. I had brought light into the shadowy and cobwebbed corners of not only my story but my family's. I got my assignment through my own healing. I am a hereditary witch of earth-based healing, the great-great-granddaughter of a circuit preacher, and a descendant of Filipino ancestry, tying me to pre-colonial earth-based practices.

When I asked for my purpose in those dark nights of the soul, it found me. The rabbit hole is deep, but it brings great treasure.

Charting the Pain, Identifying Holy Wisdom

For years I said I would never share what my father did to me with my amazing, impish, glamorous artist grandmother, the one from whom I had no doubt inherited my sense of wonder. I couldn't imagine her having to think about it. I didn't want her to be hurt. She was so small, with a whip of white hair and always matching from her nails to her jewelry. She was in her mid-eighties by then, and I was worried that it would kill her. She'd already had a brain aneurysm and surgery to save her life after losing my grandfather. My mum assured me that my grandmother could take it. So I did it. I went over with some beautiful French pastries as if that somehow could make the horror of the news less sickening.

Remember what I said about chips? It applies to baked goods too. The pastries helped. I cut them up to share as we sat in her apartment at the dining room table that now sits in my home. At that table that held my family dinners, of magic talking about angels, memories of the good times that were safe and sound, I told her the horrible truth.

She took a moment to swallow the little bite she'd taken with her fork. Always a lady. Always doilies and dainty. She paused and reached out her hand to me. I held it. She told me two things in the moments that followed. The first, that she'd never liked my father. The second the words no one wants to hear, but all too often is the reply about this kind of trauma: *It happened to me too.* That she hadn't told many. It happened when she was very small. In that moment of the upset stomach, the unexpected news that *she too* . . . my world zoomed out.

I saw our lives on a map of time and I saw it. That I was raised by the daughter of a childhood sexual abuse survivor. My mother had likely chosen my father because the unhealed imprint was in my grandmother; she hadn't ever shared what happened to her, and her pain likely trickled down through my mum and to me. Not just scientifically speaking—I was an egg inside my mother when my mother was inside of my grandmother—but energetically as well. The vibration of being prey had stayed long after the abuse had occurred when my grandmother was just a tiny girl. Her abuser wasn't in our family. She didn't go on to marry an abuser, but she married another survivor of unhealed childhood trauma, just like her.

I felt my head nod at both her memories and the idea that the vibration of what happened to her, the unhealed trauma of her own abuse, may have vibrated through my mother, which attracted her to my father, and now, it ended with me. It wasn't just my mom's side of the family that carried a vibration, that carried these patterns. The childhood sexual abuse appeared on both sides. That's what happens when you don't heal. It spreads.

Working with survivors of childhood trauma is the core of my practice. Whether they come to me as children or adults, I meet them with the same commitment. We are not powerless in our lived experiences or our ancestral traumas. We can use our own gifts to work magic on the system of our family line. We don't have to leave it there. We can go back to go forward. We can remove the rotten parts and we can display them for future generations to see. We don't have to carry them as shame. We can put them in our war chest as reminders of how we survived. We can assign meaning and purpose to our pain. The secrets and low rumbles. Unanswered questions and mysterious departures. The fractures. It all shuffled into place.

I got something new about my life. I got the context, and I got the reason.

This was my ten-thousand-foot view. The map of time and space that doesn't just include my story, or my trauma, but the gifts and unhealed trauma of my family and my ancestors. It helped me process the things I've lived through, and it helped me understand *how* and *why*.

Love Collection

The ten-thousand-foot view of the relationship with my best friend Erin is that when she transitioned, our relationship didn't end, it changed. It became multi-dimensional. Erin passed away in 1997 and this particular scavenger hunt has spanned her time both alive and in the afterlife.

Erin was the first collector I ever met. Her one collection was the thing she loved the most. Pigs. You read that right. She *loved* pigs. Anytime she or anyone who knew about her collection found a pig figurine, candy, pin, whatever it was with a pig on it, she would take it for her collection. The collection was housed in a rectangular clear plastic container with a beige lid that had been wrapped in wrapping paper with silhouettes of little pink pigs on a white background. That was her treasure chest; she kept it sacred on a shelf in her bedroom.

I only ever got to see a few pieces of it at a time or whatever sacred pig happened to be pressed up against the clear plastic of the container. When we were kids, she told me that one day she'd have a little black-and-white Vietnamese pot-bellied pig. I didn't even know then that a pig could be Vietnamese or have potbellies. It was the eighties, so she'd clearly done her research—at the actual library. But Erin passed away before she could have the pig she'd always told me about. In our high school years, after reading *The Tao of Pooh* and *The Te of Piglet*, Erin took to calling me Piglet. She was Winnie the Pooh—the curious, tall, and happy bear—and I was more the little and anxious Piglet. Her calling me Piglet also meant she loved me as much as her beloved pigs.

After she transitioned, I kept thinking of her pig collection. Once or twice a year, it would pop into my head like an idea that wasn't mine. It was as if she finally wanted to let me look through it. After being nudged for years, I finally got up the courage to ask her mum, Inkeri, if I could see it, or even if I could have it. She said that I could but again years passed. I figured she had decided it was too important to part with, and that was understandable. It was Erin's treasure. I hadn't considered the idea that perhaps Erin sent a message for a time that just hadn't arrived yet. That maybe I'd just received a clue out of order on this part of the scavenger hunt; that's bound to happen when you're communicating through dimensions, right?

Along my path of reconnecting to Nature I'd become a bit of a wildlife rehabber (that's what happens when you plug back into Nature, it plugs back into you). I'd needed some guidance and expertise with squirrels, and I'd found a woman on social media who is a squirrel rehabber. I'd stayed connected with her on Facebook. About a year later out of the blue, she posted a photo of a tiny pig. All squirrels and then suddenly a pig. A little potbellied pig.

It was black and white. I felt Erin in my ear like a TV director from The Control Room. She wanted me to hold that pig. My thinking at the time was that maybe she would be able to feel it through me. So I set out following these breadcrumbs from my best friend who just happened to be in another dimension.

The wildlife rehab was based at a farm northeast of Toronto, so I planned to rent a car to drive up there and hold that little pig. I messaged the squirrel whisperer and asked if I could make a donation and come for a visit to meet the pig. She welcomed me and my weird plan. She told me that he was a runt of the litter, and he was with her because he wasn't thriving. She'd named him Groot. I made my way there, and as I spent time holding this tiny pig, I felt my best friend's joy. So did he. I'd put him down and he'd come right back. His little hoofs clicking on her wood floors. I heard Erin's voice in my consciousness, *Piglet and Piglet.*

"He likes you," she remarked, clearly impressed at my pig-witch prowess.

I held him for a long while that afternoon on the floor. I asked about the challenges he was having, as he seemed pretty spirited to me. He was just *so* tiny. He wasn't much bigger than a new kitten. I held him one last time before I left, and I told him I loved him in his ear as he nuzzled into my neck. I tried to imprint protection and healing onto him before I went home. I could feel Erin beaming.

As I walked outside the sun was beaming too. It felt as if she was saying: *Mission accomplished.*

When I got home from the drive, something struck me. I was stunned. I'd missed a clue. I bounded up the stairs to retrieve a box that holds some of my own treasures. My collection of Erin. Some of her hair that I scavenged from her hairbrush in the days after she left, photos of us over the years, cards, letters, and clippings from the newspaper from when she left the planet. There it was on paper. I'd never gone to the place where she transitioned. As if I wanted to reject it as a real place. I skimmed the addresses and detailed references in the clipping for the place where she'd left.

Although I already knew what I would see, I went down and typed the details into the computer. I needed to be sitting down. I entered the address of the farm where the squirrel whisperer lives. It was a ten-minute walk from where Erin left the Earth. I had driven by it without even realizing it. It felt somehow that she had sent me there to heal. I was amazed because of the wonder and magic. Because of the energy, but most of all, because of the love.

The Sisu.

After I processed the adventure, I posted a photo of myself and little Groot on Facebook. Erin's mum commented, and as I read it, I felt goosebumps all over my body: "I've got to get you the pig collection."

It was as if I had unlocked some kind of achievement. I was getting the treasure chest! A few days later, I saw a post that Groot wasn't well, and not long after, I heard he had passed away. As soon as I saw this, I felt Erin. I heard her. I saw her all at once. It was as if she had caught him through the veil. As if she set me up by imprinting with him. So she could bring him home when he was ready. She finally got her pig.

Thanks, Piglet, I felt Erin say.

I mentioned that sometimes we need a witness; this was one of those times. I called my mum and I told her what had happened. She paused as she was processing the energy, the story, and then she said, "She's got him. And she's grinning."

The pig collection is among my treasures (for now), and it begs the question—was the pig collection always some kind of special payment from her for Groot? Is that why she never let me rifle through it? Because who wants to ruin their own surprise? Did she know somewhere in her soul that I'd have plenty of time to look at it? I don't claim that Erin had this knowledge consciously when she was here, but did her soul know? I think it did. I think it does.

She is still teaching me, and she still knows what's going to happen before I do. She likes to make points with dates in her communications to me, like some kind of interdimensional exclamation point. She did that with her transition, she did it with her birthday (my friend Jason not only shares her birthday, his mum shares Erin's mum's birthday). She did it with her nephew Kellan who was born on the same day I lost my dear pug Dougie suddenly in surgery.

Kellan was born weeks early. It wasn't a week before the date of the anniversary of losing her.

It was as if somewhere beyond the veil Erin was saying, "She needs a new friend *right now!*"

She was right. I did. Getting that text from her sister-in-law Harmony that day helped me navigate a grief I wasn't sure I would survive. Before Kellan was a year old, he became magnetized to a photo of Erin, probably because he remembered. I didn't get to meet him in person until he was five. When it finally happened, he and I immediately had the same goofy spark Erin and I always did. Erin's mom and mine marveled because this time I wasn't two. I was forty-one and he was five. He told me very matter-of-factly in that first meeting that if I "had anything valuable" that I didn't need anymore, I could always give it to him. This was the breadcrumb I needed to know who was getting the pig collection.

Energy doesn't die. Love doesn't die. It transforms. It transmutes. It wraps around you if you let it. I would probably not be here, and I would definitely not be able to do the mediumship work I do without Erin's help. She is my sister in the stars. She helped me remember who I am and what I'm capable of, and she helped me reclaim my gifts by being the first one to show them to me. As above and so below. She still phones (now across dimensions) and I'm still answering the call.

Into the Wonder

You probably also have some calls to answer, or some breadcrumbs to hunt down, so now it's your turn. You're going to use the ten-thousand-foot view to look at your own moments. We're going to use your mind's eye to zoom all the way out and imagine viewing your own life as a timeline on a larger map (for some of you it *may* be a closer look if you're more of a big-picture person).

Imagine your life as a map, see your timeline, the year you were born, your childhood, moments frozen in time, and then the more you zoom out, the more you see. We'll notice what patterns or themes may have shown up in your life. These may be connected to experiences in your own life, or to your family (i.e., the unhealed trauma of your ancestors), or to your soul. You might be able to zoom out and see not just your timeline, but the timeline of your parents and their parents. Maybe you don't know a lot about them. That's okay, Source knows. Your soul knows. You may still get a vibration or image as you zoom out. You might see places on a map, and from there, you can ask with your intention, *What do I need to know? What do I need to see?*

In taking a wider look, what patterns or themes have shown up in your life's timeline that may be connected to family, your ancestors, or your experience? It's likely some of the patterns you're manifesting are part of your purpose.

Take note of anything that strikes that inner knowing. You might have to do this a couple of times. That's normal with new practices. We're just going to have a look. To get into that heart space, you may want to put your hand on your heart. You may need to use a few of your new practices combined to follow this path. That's the point. If you can't find the answer below, look for it above.

If we imagine that these points, these traumas, the wins, the losses, are all part of your soul journey and your soul purpose. That in your role within your family, there are probably clues about what you're here to do. As we're looking at this, try to just think about how this might connect to the work that you did in the first few rooms of The Temple. Where we thought about what kind of magic might be in your blood, what might be in your soul. Think back to where this journey through The Temple started for you, and what you may be seeing now that maybe you didn't see before.

As we're coming back and adjusting into the moment, did you have any moments of realization in terms of the ten-thousand-foot view? Maybe you had some thoughts or memories come through while you were looking at your map. What patterns or moments or themes could be related to your purpose? Does anything in there strike an inner knowing? That's what we're looking for. Notice and follow the breadcrumbs; consider what may be behind those moments to connect your own dots. Write them down. These are part of your very own multidimensional detective board. We track and follow the breadcrumbs. When it appears that the trail has ended in our ordinary reality, you may need to look in non-ordinary reality. You may have to do this practice a few times, so don't beat yourself up if nothing groundbreaking comes through the first time. You might have to check it out again. Be gentle with yourself, this is part of remembering.

Try to practice applying this idea of the ten-thousand-foot view in your daily life. Consider what patterns may exist, what threads, cords, or connections there may be to both the trauma and the gifts of your life or your ancestors' lives. When we bring these elements to light, we work to transmute their vibration. We recalibrate the trauma into triumph, and we can rebalance reality, *really*.

Creativity and divinity are inherently connected, and they are plentiful when we consciously and intentionally decide to invite them in. It's time to open the door and welcome the collaboration you've been waiting for into your life. We're going to leave The Observation Deck for now and move back into The Alchemist's Lab to co-create some magic. This time, new view.

CHAPTER THIRTEEN

THE ALCHEMIST'S LAB— UPPER LEVEL

CREATIVITY & DIVINITY

A s we move between the columns of The Observation Deck, we come to a doorway framed in light. Above the door is the sun disk, and below it a sign: THE ALCHEMIST'S LAB. It's glowing from the inside. It's as if the light from the Universe in The Observation Deck has filled the walls of this space if they're walls at all. They're the same meteorite columns from The Observation Deck, but here, they're wrapped in symbols and glowing from the inside. Thinking back to being in The Alchemist's Lab below, it didn't seem as if there *was* an upper level. It was two stories, but it was all ceiling. There were windows and light but . . . as we look down, we notice The Alchemist's Lab is below us. The floor is glass. Below us, The Transmutation Tent, the table, the potions.

We're standing atop The Alchemist's Lab in a room we didn't know existed. Fitting for a Temple of Wonder. Perhaps five dimensions instead of three. This wasn't on the map.

Where better than in this invisible room to discuss one of the most important principles of magic, the law of correspondence. Meaning that in order for *anything* to happen in ordinary reality, it must first happen in non-ordinary reality. On Earth as it is in heaven. As above, so below. As within, so without. This comes from ancient knowledge that precedes the holy texts most of us can name. It's said to have originally come from our friend in The Library, who may have been thrice born (Hermes Trismegistus: meaning *thrice great*); *The Kybalion*, an occult favorite, contains the seven Hermetic principles. Attributed to Thoth, the scribe.

In order to go deeper into remembering, we need to go back to one of the foundational principles of life itself—creativity. Creativity *is* a part of Spirituality. There is nothing without creation. There is only a place of nothingness. When we are in the valley of the shadow, darkness can permeate everything. We can feel as if there's no way out. I've come out of that valley myself enough times (sometimes once a day in my practice), to tell you that there *is*. We carry the light even when it feels as if our torch has no flame. We can bring it out of ourselves and light up the world. If we imagine being back in the Trauma Shed for a moment, we know how things feel when those walls close in around us. We also know now that the Trauma Shed is the door to Narnia. Sometimes the struggle brings the purpose. Sometimes the trauma even creates a real-life superhero origin story.

The Road to Narnia

We can blow the walls off it and do things like the high magic of one of our more famous modern magicians, Damien Echols. You may know this name because he was one of the West Memphis Three. One of three teenagers accused and then wrongfully convicted for the murder of three young boys in Arkansas in 1993.

Damien served nearly twenty years on death row before bursting himself out of it by focusing on Spiritual training (including becoming a Rinzai Zen Buddhist priest) using his gifts, rituals of ceremonial magic combined with good old-fashioned real-world action. He worked as above *and* so below. Damien worked his magical practice in prison while a team (including creatives like Peter Jackson and Eddie Vedder) worked for over a decade to help free not only Damien but all of the West Memphis Three. In 2011, Damien and the West Memphis Three were finally released. Echols, now an artist and author, has written about the role the practice of magic (or as he calls it, *Spiritual Sustenance*) played in his release. Along with his wife, Lorri, Damien has created works to share the gifts and practices (not to mention sigils!) to help others enjoy ancient and sacred practice, and their love story is also one for the ages.

With practice and effort, we *can* create ourselves right out of darkness. Imagine using your creativity in tandem with Spirit now, to transmute and recalibrate this understanding of what magic means and is. Magic *is* collaboration with Source for the highest good and best possible outcome, with harm to none. That is all magic was ever meant to be.

Remembering how to co-create is a crucial component to magic, to Spirit, *and* to life on earth, and I'd hazard a guess, it shows up beyond it too, in the afterlife. The element of Spirit doesn't have the same qualities as the other elements because Spirit is not physical. In cosmological models, Spirit is the material between the physical and celestial realms.

When we start flexing our visualization and creative manifestation muscles, we can get our energy moving more intentionally through our vessels, and people around us even start to notice. This is because Energy work improves our physiology since humans function better when in a state of connection. We raise our vibrations from mundane to magic. I'm not saying there's not going to be days where you need some mundane. Life on Earth can be as tough as it can be magical. It's okay to take a beat and close that third eye. Though you'll find as you move into a practice of consciousness, you will spend less time in those moments spun out on the side of the road (or crying in the shower, as was my go-to). You'll have shed (see what I did there?) the cocoon and begin to spend more time in The Temple of Wonder than behind the Trauma Shed.

The Cauldron of Creativity

High magic means we're on a path of healing to illuminate density. We have to admit as humans that we haven't always had the best perspective when it comes to

the big picture. As we practice, we get better at it. Using our gifts means it gets easier to do what a smart witch recommended we do about two thousand years ago: *Turn the other cheek.*

Remember we're all connected in this big Ocean of Consciousness, so it's best not to hit anyone. Creating a space where we can transmute is great, but creating a space where we can actually make something new and better out of the hurt is the real magic. Sure, it can sting in the moment to turn the other cheek, but when we have faith in the force of the unseen that surrounds us to light the way forward, we begin manifesting a change with Spirit. When we lean into the creative element of this action and intention, we can manifest things that can hardly be believed. When we try something we've never done, we tend to experience things we've never seen—or better yet, we get to go places we never dreamed of.

Clients often ask the exact same question as they start to come into their magic. *"How do I know I'm not making all this up?"*

I tell them all the same thing that I'm going to tell you. We're not that smart and we're not that powerful. Sure, humans are creative and intelligent, but most of the real brilliance and magic I've seen in my practice takes *two*. It takes you *and* divinity, an "as above" *and* a "so below."

Of course, that saying has multiple meanings, it's magic! We have to cloak sacred teachings in order to protect them. It's your job too now. We carry this knowledge, and we share it with respect to those who are ready to carry it because of who has carried it for thousands of years. That's part of the deal in creating with divinity. You get to choose where you put the energy to create. If we're really being honest (and trust me, I had to be honest about all this too), we weren't always ready. There were times in our lives when we'd have rolled our eyes at all this *and that guy in the tank top.* Let's not forget about him. We would have waved him off. We might have even pretended we didn't see him. Now we know he might be onto something, and the dude just wants to wear tie-dye while doing it.

Co-creation is in us all.

Quantum physics tells us that nothing that is observed is unaffected by the observer. That statement from science holds an enormous and powerful insight for magic. It means everyone sees a slightly different picture because everyone of us is co-creating what we see. The fifth element of Spirit, or if you want to get nerdy again, *Quintessence* (*the fifth element* in Latin), is the highest element. It's the underlying fabric of *everything*. In Western occult theory, the elements are seen as being hierarchical: Spirit, fire, air, water, and earth—with the first elements being more Spiritual and perfect and the last elements being more material and base, though no less special.

When we have these big epiphanies, typically it's because we've got a good amount of energy, or Spirit, moving through us. We're lit up like little light bulbs, and that light is running through the filament of our brains. While in the other dimension, Source creates by doing or performing rather than making. Some clues and breadcrumbs for our human instruction manuals. We need to remember *both* components must be included in order to successfully create. Let's think of it like this: We have the ordinary reality in which we live—the one where we can see, taste, touch, hear, feel, and smell, where we speak languages like English, French, Cantonese, and Mandarin—and then we have a non-ordinary reality that operates via a consciousness. It speaks less in words and more in colors, shapes, symbology, dreams, visions, synchronicities, and omens. The art of Creator.

Spirit Is an Artist

We're remembering how to connect those dots into a language of sorts. We are learning to weave together these two realities, or two worlds, if you will. The Spiritual realm is where we're planting seeds, the place we're making the wishes, because this is where we are now, in the upper level of The Alchemist's Lab. The one we couldn't notice before because we weren't ready. There's a physical place where the seeds grow: The Transmutation Tent, the table, and the shelves, the jars, the drawers of amulets. That is the lower level of The Alchemist's Lab. This *is* the law of correspondence, and it's a basic relationship found within two levels of existence. On Earth as it is in heaven. Body and Spirit. Intention and action. We need to consider correspondence in order to create anything in life . . . including babies.

Whether you consider yourself a creative or not, odds are you're creating all the time. If you're a human being, you're co-creating things, you likely already do it every day. It's just most of us aren't being conscious about it. As we get used to having our souls at the wheel, we're going to start flexing our visualization abilities, our creative and manifestation muscles, in order to really get our energy moving. We should have a bit more of that in the system now since hopefully we're doing less ego apology tours these days.

We can't talk about creativity without addressing something rarely discussed but really important. Creative arts like music, dance, fine arts, and dramatic arts are no different from the healing arts. In fact, they're often combined. Earth-based healers are known for their art, their songs, their dances, and their stories. We all know that the arts can heal. We've all had experiences in life where a piece of art has connected with us so deeply that we felt it in our bones. It may be a symphony, or a Lizzo song, or both. We don't just experience art with our five senses, we experience it energetically. We feel its energy. Creativity has the capacity to move our Spirits.

Ask anyone who's a die-hard fan of *anything* to tell you why they love it, and they will always respond with energy, not just words. They will share their passion with you in the form of energy. There's a reason music and art are used in magic, Spiritual ceremony, and worship. There's a reason why human beings have danced, drummed, sang, chanted, and told stories in circles around fires since recorded history. It heals us, it helps us, it raises our Spirits.

Literally.

Humans are rhythmic beings: our heartbeat, our breathing, and our brain waves are all rhythmic. Our voices are sound waves. When you hear the term *oral tradition*, we always assume it only means storytelling. If we think about the correspondence of matter. We can imagine that one part of that is true, and that the other part isn't about storytelling. It's about the vibration, or the current, of the sound coming from the being. We receive and we transmit vibrations using our voices in addition to our energy. When we hear music, or experience sound waves, we're not only processing the sound, but we're processing the energy.

The human brain and nervous system are hardwired to distinguish music from noise and to respond to rhythm and repetition. A breadcrumb for us as human beings is that the hearing is also the last of our ordinary senses to go when we transition. Those who are dying can and do still hear the voices and songs of our physical world. There are many more breadcrumbs to follow down the rabbit hole of sound, but we'll get more into how to utilize waves and frequencies when we get into The Archives. The foundation of music on this planet is tied to Source. It's *all* co-created content, whether it's Beethoven or Soundgarden that moves you (I'm partial to Chris Cornell). We can create with music, or we can invite music in to help us create other types of magic.

We have the ability to impact our reality *and* to choose (or create) the soundtrack.

Let's remember that we are on Earth to co-create, and that energy supports us in it. Co-creation with Source is our birthright. We know human beings can manifest. We see it around us every single day. Lots of people are having dreams and making them come true; yet there can be times when all of our worries, our stewing, our scenario-running and spinning takes us down a collective wormhole of self-doubt, shame, and stagnancy.

We've seen where this gets us . . . it's nowhere. It's not just into the muck, it's the end of the line. There is nowhere to go when there's nothing to see.

If we reframe the term *God* to *Creator*, we're in effect calling *God* an *Artist*. The *first* artist. Every time we create, we're honoring the system in which we live. We are inviting the divine to help us bring something new into being. We can *always* use our creativity or the creative gifts of others to lift us up. We don't ever create alone. Creator is the executive producer of all of our creations, whether we choose to add them to the credits or not.

Let Me Take You to Nerd Town

Whether we're singers or not, most of us know the vocal scale ("Do Re Me Fa So La Te"), what most of us don't know is that its roots are sacred. This vocal scale is known as Solfeggio and was adapted from an invention by an eleventh-century monk named Guido D'Arezzo. Another innovation included melodies that helped make it easier for monks to learn their necessary chants. Part of this was the development of the six scale, which was the basis of *all* Gregorian chants.

Music and sound *are* a universal language. They penetrate through our vessels and can impact our vibration. Sound can be synonymous with healing. We know from countless scientific studies that music can and does heal the body. Harvard Medicine conducted a study, *The Effect of Music on the Human Stress Response*. They noted that music seemed to slow heart rate, lower blood pressure, and reduce levels of stress hormones. The study showed it also provided relief for heart attack and stroke survivors and patients who were undergoing surgery. Research also suggests that music may promote the brain's ability to make new connections between nerve cells, perhaps working its magic through rhythms.

Collaborating with Creator

By consciously engaging in co-creation with Spirit, we're going to become more of a contributor to our experiences on the planet. Before ego chirps up from the back seat, this *doesn't* mean that hard things happen because we are *creating* it, or because we brought it on. It means they are part of life, just like in a video game where there's challenges and pitfalls. They're part of how we learn to use our tools. We're remembering our ancestry; experiences and purpose also inform what gifts we might have available to us on our quest. They're all part of how we learn how to maneuver ourselves through the adventure.

When we have good intentions, gratitude, and humility, we can influence things a lot more than we think. Remembering how to co-create brings a level of depth and purpose to our Spiritual practice.

Being in the flow of creativity feels amazing. The dots connect, we find our momentum, our synchronicity, and magic. We fall in love with it, and we feel the vibration of the idea itself. We can't stop thinking about it. This is what happens when we plug into Source and its power actively moves through us. It creates *with* us, and we have the opportunity to *experience* the power of creation. We become part of a tangible and physical expression to the divine. We can try to fold it over, tap it off, or constrict the flow, but it's *us* who misses out on the magic. The whole collective. The creative forces at work in the Universe are amazing; soak them up, see what they have in store for you.

Feed yourself with whatever craft lights you up. When we do this, it can create healing, not only within ourselves but the world because art travels through humanity really well.

Here's the thing about Spirit and creativity that I know all artists will confirm: Ideas and concepts are floating through the ether all the time. As human beings, we can pull them down from the celestial, partner with them, and use our intention to bring them into terrestrial being.

We can create something from nothing. Art invites more Spiritual (energetic) awareness, which is why engaging creativity is also its own practice; it reduces anxiety, depression, and stress. Through creative exploration and expression, we can also process past trauma with support and assistance from Spirit. If you do identify as a creative person, you know how surreal and disembodied the process of bringing a creative project to life can feel. It's like chasing a phantom. You can see it in your mind just out of the corner of your eye. It's a negotiation of sorts and there's this process of translating the idea into words, images, or sounds. It can sometimes feel as if we're channeling it and it's because we are.

If you've ever had a friend who is a musician, you know how many hours they spend in the studio, how hard it can be to rip an artist away from their desk, easel, or stage. It's partly because it feels good. The other part is we can lose time when we're creating, hours and hours can go by and feel like minutes. It's because when we're creating, we're entering the realm of Spirit, a realm outside of time.

Creating isn't always easy, but when you hit your stride, it feels so good you get lost in it; witnessing the co-creation process can be as moving as being the one bringing it into being.

We can have epiphanies and miraculous progress. The only thing we have to do in return is surrender. Co-creation comes with a healthy side dish of not knowing.

We can't control when and where, but we *can* steer the what. That's why our free will is so important. We can shape the idea, the thing we want to try to bring into being, but we don't get to decide how or exactly when it occurs. We have to release that control in exchange for the magic. Human beings don't get to be in charge of everything. And we've really proven why.

If you've ever tried to make anything creatively, you know you can't force the process of creation; it happens when it's ready. If it's not meant to come alive, it fizzles out. Just ask an artist about how many paintings or songs they haven't finished. Creativity is equal parts magic and Spirit, so it's not possible to pin it down. You can try asking Spirit to meet you at the same time every day to try to come up with something spectacular (*you can even send them a meeting invitation*), but that doesn't mean it happens. That's all part of the adventure.

The Magic of Conception

Some creators are so prolific you don't even know they're there, or that they had their hands on it. Some creators you can just feel their imprint. For example, most of us know what Tina Turner, or Taika Waititi, conjure without having to think too much about it. There isn't just a sound or a look, but a recognizable *feeling* to their works. A vibration. That's because creativity *is* a Spiritual practice. The energy is woven into the very fabric of the work.

Many ancient civilizations believed that creativity had its own Spirit; it was its own force. Creativity *was* divinity. The Romans called this Spirit a *genius* (this is where the concept of genies comes from) and believed that it was its own entity. A nonphysical energy that could assist us with the manifestation of big ideas. It was seen as being something *outside* of humanity. Who's to say creativity isn't *always* a solely spiritual collaboration?

We used to recognize creativity as Spirit itself. Over time as we disconnected from our Nature, we left this idea behind. We now find ourselves a few thousand years down the road feeling as if we're solely responsible for determining how to

creatively fix this bind we seem to have found ourselves in. It's time for us to ask the Source for some help with this brainstorm.

When we remember that creativity comes from Source, the idea of dreaming big about how to get the human collective out of this bind gets a little easier to manage and imagine because we don't have to single-handedly have the ideas. When we remember that, we can focus on the *what* instead of the *how* and *when*. Things aren't so insurmountable when we have help that is so, well, *experienced*.

Nurturing our ideas *is* energy work. Thoughts become things. One of the four female alchemists said to be able to produce the philosopher's stone was Cleopatra (not to be confused with the Pharoah). This Cleopatra lived during the third century AD and was a cauldron of conception. It's said that the alchemist who contemplates their work is compared to a loving mother who thinks about her child and feeds it. She was certainly a mother of invention. She experimented with practical alchemy and was also said to be an inventor. One of her many known sketches is one of an ouroboros with the words "The All Is One" inside the circle.

The work of hers that survived is likely the greatest hits. It's the best stuff that got repeated.

Not every creation is a symphony. Not every painting is going to be displayed. Some works are better than others, some manifestations more successful than others. This is part of alchemy. We have to tinker, we have to play with the ratios, this is how we set ourselves up for more success.

Into the Wonder

As we talk about creativity above the lab where it happens, maybe we can also plant some seeds here to sprout from below. We *can* do things to help raise our energy to manifest, to co-create, or just to get the Spirit of creativity moving. You may already do some of them subconsciously. Have you ever paced around the room when you were trying to think about what to do? Let's do that now, as we're planting seeds above The Alchemist's Lab. Let's walk the length of the room. A 2014

Stanford study found that creativity rose to 60 percent when walking. We don't have to co-create by sitting cross-legged with a cape in our rooms. We can do it in the world, in Nature, in groups. We can bring other energy into our Spiritual co-productions. We can ask for support from like-minded community. Join your local LARPing group, *if that's your thing*, lean into learning about your ancestral medicines, do what moves *you*. Raising power is integral to the work, and getting our creative energy moving is about the best way to do it. Remember, Spirituality isn't about doing things that make you uncomfortable. If you don't like dancing, chanting, or music, think about what you do like; what feels exciting to you?

Remembering our creative force is about reclaiming whatever ritual or creative practice it is that may connect you to Source. We get to build the bridge on the way forward. It doesn't have to happen in church; in fact, it's much harder to see Nature's synchronicities when you're inside. When we understand that these occurrences aren't coincidences, our voices and intentions become so much more important because there's *so much* power in our speech. When we align our intention to our purpose, and it's in balance with our soul agreements, we realize that we have an ability to shape reality, and that's where the magic happens.

The more we create in this vein, the closer we'll be to our own magic, unique gifts, and powers. It's kind of like *X-men* without the villains. In my experience, villains don't get to use real magic, and if they do, it's not for long. You don't get to wield real magic *and* be an asshole. The Universe suspends licenses and takes your keys when people misuse their power. That's why transmutation is important. I wouldn't bet against the Universe. Not a chance.

We can stop pacing now; it's time to start a creative collaboration we can all use. Since the field of energy is quite large, it would be helpful to create a place in our corner of space. This might help show our ancestors, guides, and helpers exactly where to send energy to help us in our practice. This is what an altar does, it's a physical manifestation of our Spiritual work. Let's do this as part of remembering our creativity. An altar is created with intention with objects often representing the essence of a Spiritual force or meaning; they are simply a space to focus the energy of a particular intention or practice. For example, a feather on the altar can represent the element of air and can also represent the medicine of a particular bird. Just as a stone, crystal, or tree bark can represent both the element of Earth and whatever specific type of medicine from which the offering came.

Every organic being that exists in our biosphere carries a medicine and meaning. We aren't meant to abuse them. We can use these to represent manifestations in our magic. The apple can represent knowledge or abundance. The altar itself can represent the stability of Source. In magic, everything carries a meaning, and that meaning is imparted by both Nature and your intention. Nature brings the medicine, and we bring the intention. As we're manifesting and co-creating with Spirit, maybe there's also a ritual you can create to go alongside something that you're trying to manifest in the world. What objects might represent something you're hoping to bring into reality that can go alongside your wish list?

We can set intentions on the altar in words, and in objects in ritual. Offerings on the altar represent abundance, and just as the ancient Egyptians left food and tools that may be needed in the afterlife, people all over the planet still do similar acts for their loved ones. We show the ancestors where to come. It's a beacon through space and time. We can all create that using what works for us (*Erin's pig collection is admittedly a pretty weird altar, but it works*).

When I'm doing important manifestation or ancestral healing work, I always make an offering to the ancestors. I also often talk to their photos. I talk with them as if they can hear me, and most of the time, I feel as if they show up so much that I *know* they heard me. Without wonder, I wouldn't have the deep and often profound connection I have to them.

Their creativity courses through my veins as much as their survival and service does.

Let's take what we've learned in our ten-thousand-foot view. What objects might be of use to represent in creation of an altar? In this writing and intention practice, you'll use your magic book (*and your creativity*) to communicate more with your soul, with the Universe, or with your higher self. Write down your wishes, prayers, or something in a petition format to assist in making sure the Universe knows *exactly* what you're looking to co-create in life. You may want to ask for something bigger. Whether it is healing for yourself, or your ancestry, or for humanity.

Remember this is not about bending anyone's free will in any manner, this is about *you* and the highest good. Part of this practice is listening to our soul, not telling it what to do. You may need some quiet space. You may need to do this in two parts. You may need to do some ritual first to create an altar. Part of remembering is using our natural intuition.

Imagine that the energy and vibration of what is needed is being combined with the intention of bringing it to fruition. We can use our energy to convey our wishes and let the vibration of our chosen words combine with the intention of the physical act of writing to bring momentum. Once you have it, read your wishes aloud. Imagine the air carrying the vibration of your voice and intentions as far as they can go for the highest good and best possible outcome for all with ease and grace. Harm to none throughout time.

Place that order with Source. See Source carrying it forward. It will figure out how to maneuver around any obstacles that may exist, in any reality. Release the collaboration and let it do its thing. See it happening below us in The Alchemist's Lab.

Creating Reality

Imagine how it will feel to have it come into being. You may be moved to leave what's been written on your altar. If you're trying to manifest something that's not just for yourself but for the world, you may want to work with a group to hold space. Many hands *do* make light work. Spirit is going to determine whether the wish is in alignment with your purpose or not, and when to deliver it. Sometimes you may feel as if you're stuck on repeat with a manifestation. Here's the reminder to confirm with Spirit that we got the message, or that we appreciate it. This is where the offering part of the practice can be helpful. It's as much part of the work as the work. To say thank you and offer things to Nature as a representation and recognition of the assistance or being seen. We leave a thank-you gift because that's good manners for collaborations. Offerings are meant to be natural things, bird seed, apples for deer, nuts for squirrels. It may be cleaning up some trash outside that isn't yours (*because you wouldn't do that*), it may be volunteering for a coastline cleanup. Whatever it is, just make sure to do it with heartfelt thanks.

Sometimes people think that because they know what they want, they don't need to write it down. I'll say the same thing now that I say to them. *YES, YOU DO.* The physical act of writing, the vibration, and the intention in tandem with the words coming out of your body is the correspondence that we're looking for in magic. Our words carry a sound wave and a current. It all matters, because here in ordinary reality, it's all matter.

In order to make magic, we need to use our intention to bring it to being in *both* realms. As you start co-creating, there will be new breadcrumbs to follow, new scavenger hunts to explore. This is what comes with remembering, living a more Spirited life, as we shed new light on the old ways. Since these ways are so old, we don't make them come to us.

We go to them. It's that time.

We're going to return to the room that almost drew us in first. The one in The Entryway protected by Anubis, the guardian of the gates. It's time to head into The Archives to view the knowledge of the ancient ones and visit The Hall of Records. You're welcome to bring a cape, or a tie-dyed tank top. Or just your magic. Your choice. No shoes. Cool shirts. *All service.*

CHAPTER FOURTEEN

THE ARCHIVES

EVERYTHING IS ENERGY
& EVERYTHING MOVES

As we move through the doorway from the upper Alchemist's Lab, we come to another long hallway. This one is also made of glass. We must rely on trust and surrender. As we step from the lab and onto the glass floor, we realize we're moving above The Hall of Secrets and into the upper balcony of The Archives. What's above The Hall of Mirrors? Nothing. Because there's no room for wonder with ego.

Each movement we make over The Hall of Secrets is met with the floor adjusting its opacity, moving from transparent to opaque as we pass over it and toward The Archives.

The space we're entering is open, and toward the edge of the room is a walkway that runs the span of the front of The Temple. From what we can see, glass doors at the far end of The Archives seem to open up to the upper level of The Library. From our vantage point on the upper level, we can lean over the railing. When we do, we see a massive space lined with shelves. The shelves hold not books but scrolls. In the center of the room are narrow chests of high drawers that look like card catalogs. Giant filing cabinets. There's a vaulted ceiling down the length of the space with a view of the heavens. It's like a dining hall but without the food. Statues of deities and archetypes line both the upper Archives and the space below.

Looking into the center of the room below, it looks as if someone has already been here. As if someone has already pulled some selections from the stacks. Boxes of books, reels, scrolls, and maps surround a huge globe in the center of the lower level.

We see it now, it is a dining room, but *the food is knowledge.*

As we move to the right, we notice the stairs leading to the lower level tucked neatly beside a statue of a jackal. This time Anubis is laying down like a sphinx. Anubis has sometimes been known as a god of the underworld, but just as the *Book of Going Forth by Day* is known as the *Egyptian Book of the Dead,* the Underworld is actually the inner world. Spirit world. Anubis went before us to pave the way into life everlasting, as faithful a companion and guide as any dog you've ever known. Just a *lot* bigger. He knows how to sniff out the clues and breadcrumbs around the tree of life, and he knows how to walk between worlds and protect us during our transformations. He is a guide through awakening, and through The Archives.

As we make our way down the stairs and to the main level, the scale of the documents and boxes becomes real. There have to be millions of them. There is a doorway toward the back of The Archives that's aglow. You recognize the smell immediately; It's coming from The Sanctum.

We didn't notice that The Sanctum had more than one entry and exit when we were there. *You didn't have your ten-thousand foot view yet.*

The incense permeates The Archives, and we realize where the items on the shelves in The Sanctum must have come from. The books, the relics, the sacred objects, they would have been brought to The Sanctum from The Archives. Some have called this room the Akashic Records, or a filing cabinet for souls. *Akasha* is the Sanskrit word for ether, sky, or atmosphere. Spirit. These are the records of Source. They can also be known as the Book of Life, although as we can imagine life is massive and there are many books, documents, and scrolls. If everything that has ever existed (or will exist) is made of the same thing—Energy—it means we can access it here, forever.

You're a Natural Mystic

Everything that exists in the natural world has energy moving through it. Yet most of us spend so much of our energy trying to anticipate the *what if*s and the *I can't*s, so zoomed in on the minutiae, that we forget where we meant to go in the first place. We can lose our perspective completely. We don't just forget our energy, we forget who we are, and what we're part of. We know this because we've been remembering. Sometimes we require a total reset in order to be reminded that there is in fact a whole other view. An entirely different way of doing things.

We can recalibrate our own viewfinders or we can contact our local light worker and wisdom-keeper to help with remembering and reigniting our sparks. Remember your training. When we begin to utilize our energy, and the movement it can bring, we can start to connect the dots in our own lives. As a side effect, we share the stories and experiences of our connection and remembering. We share the wonder, and that encourages others to explore the current. Sharing our experiences of Source with others is like when you're the first one in the water. It's your duty to say: *Come on in, it's fine!*

The magic we bring into the world as individuals isn't *just* for us. It's for our family, our friends, our colleagues, our community, and the wider collective. There is enough energy for everyone (*this is not a human-made power grid*). One person *can* have the ability to change everything.

Let's talk about how.

What if the world right now was so full of anger and divisiveness because not enough light was getting through our collective being? What if we'd all been thinking about such dense and heavy things, and been focused so tightly on the horror that it got too dark to even navigate? What if we as a collective got stuck in the muck of the conditioning, and these systems of oppression, that we forgot about the bigger picture, that we literally oppressed and suppressed our own energy? The windows got dirty, filthy even. What if in closing off to Spirituality, we all lost our connection to the lightness of being that we're born with? What if

the answers had been simple this whole time? What if all these Spiritual thought leaders and prophets throughout history were all just saying the same thing? What if they were all just trying to convey the key to everything this whole time was light? That keeping our hearts light, and our beings fueled with it, is the key to *everything* we need to know about being human on Earth. As Rumi said, "The only lasting beauty is the beauty of the heart."

When we zoom out with our ten-thousand-foot view and see ourselves as a species, we think about all the things we know about ourselves. The real science of it. We know that we can't explain consciousness as a physical concept without using energy. Energy is crucial to *everything* we do. Not just what we are, but *who* we are. So why are we all so afraid to talk about it? We're made of the stuff. All organic matter was produced originally in stars. So whether we believe in a Creator, a God, a Spirit, or nothing—we happen to be living in a world where everything we know, everything we touch, everyone who we've ever known, who will ever live, is connected by energy. That's not just Spirituality, it's science.

Energy Flows Where Attention Goes

Everything is connected to that light. That force. That system. Artist #1. All these stories about people describing a tunnel and going toward the light in near-death experiences, all the similarities in those who have experienced healing crises, or catastrophic events. What if we all saw the same kinds of things because that's our Source? That when we leave here in the human experience, we go back to being what we were before we got here? That we go back to the source of our being?

What if all these previous civilizations in history had built the same complex structures as a grand gesture to us. What if the pyramids are perfectly aligned to the cardinal directions, because of magic? What if all the measurements are perfect because they were given to us? What if the land told us, what if we all heard the same thing? Entertain the idea that all these great civilizations, from the ancient Egyptians

to the Aztecs, wanted us to know that everything we ever needed was up there, in that light.

With our ten-thousand-foot view, we can see connections from a new vantage point, and we can more easily engage our sense of wonder and purpose. The magic of being here at all.

As we think back to The Observation Deck, about that blue-green ball in space in our mind's eye, let's imagine that everything that is, is somehow connected to a web of light (or life, if you prefer). We can imagine these are threads, or strands, all coming from the same source and extending outward. As if we're all part of one giant woven fabric of light. The first building block of this ancient knowledge is that *everything is energy,* and *everything vibrates.*

When we think about energy moving, we have to accept that everything is energy. Whether you can see it or not, everything is made of it. It's not just food that makes us go—that's caloric energy—we're talking about life force, that infinitely possible part of us. If you're having a hard time with the tangibility of this one, let's start by imagining the element of air, it's all around us, and just like air, we can't see it physically. We sometimes feel it when it brushes against us, or we may smell something carried in it. It may cause goosebumps, just like energy. We've just lost consciousness around it. We're remembering that Spirit is included. We are in fact three very real parts.

Modern science has started to recognize what ancient mystics have told us for hundreds, if not thousands of years: *that everything is in a constant state of vibration.* Everything. Down to the smallest particle to the things we cannot perceive (yet) with our limited senses.

If everything in the natural world is energy and it's also in constant motion, that means that nothing in the Universe is at rest. Everything vibrates. That means we need to acknowledge this in our practice. As everything is moving and everything is energy, we can use the term in magic of *sealing things eternally* or having something *take effect throughout time.* When we speak of *sealing something throughout time,* we can imagine something being hermetically sealed, meaning it's airtight, it's closed, and it's complete, like vacuum packs of magic.

When we speak of *sealing something throughout time*, it means it's like vacuum packs of intentional magic. When we ask for something to take effect throughout time, we are referring to past, present, and future. If we're working on transmuting or transfiguring ancestral traumas, we would want to have it take effect throughout time in order to reach all timelines. This is our acknowledgment of the constant expansion of time and space, combined with our intention for the highest good and best possible outcome of the light work we are doing. This is what is really meant by vibes. Vibrations are a side effect of movement. Positive movement creates positive vibrations. Do the opposite and you'll get the opposite, and as you know, it's best not to work with a limited source.

Don't Let Anyone Tip Your Kayak

When I first learned to kayak, I took lessons. I've learned through my experiences of trying new recreational things, such as skiing through a barrier into a set of ski racks, that my gifts are more magical than they are physical. It may have looked intentional as I sailed into the safety fence, but I can assure that it was *not*.

My kayaking instructor made a point about tandem kayaking in the lesson. He joked that like in relationships, autonomy is important in kayaking. He said he'd seen some pretty bad tandem kayak arguments and that codependency in a little vessel like a kayak can be deadly. Literally. Wear a helmet. From that moment I started to realize all the moments in my life where I was in a metaphorical tandem kayak (with humans, not Spirit. Spirit doesn't need a seat). I thought about all the times I'd served others before myself. The times when the emotions of those around me dragged me under, took me through rapids, or sent me right into the rocks.

I was letting other people lead or trying to be of service in ways that weren't healthy to me. As a survivor of childhood sexual abuse, there's a hard fact in here: We are programmed for service. We are literally manipulated into not considering ourselves, because it's how they succeed in hurting us. Autonomy and sovereignty are a part of our human experience. They are also crucial to the practice of magic and Spirituality.

This perspective has helped change the way I respond to moving through the rapids of my life, and it's helped my clients begin to navigate theirs more powerfully, knowing we are all in this Ocean of Consciousness together, as alone as we sometimes may feel. In my experience, "God" as a construct is not some guy on a throne in the sky (or in a kayak), they are an all-encompassing, omnipresent, omniscient energy system. This also helped reframe how I viewed my own empathetic Nature, and as a result, I realized I could hold space for others without having to take it on myself.

We can still kayak together. We just don't need to be in the same boat. We can hold space and be there as people we love go through the rapids; we don't have to go through them too. We can be there to help pull them to the surface or give them an oar if they need it. We don't have to risk drowning in the rapids for others. Because we can't be of real service to others if we're drowning too.

Going All In with Source

I know it's not easy, but ideally because we're doing this in The Archives, and since we've now been through the majority of The Temple, we've seen how much intelligence is around us and how much love exists. Hopefully you've felt it by now as we've begun to practice and engage in the rituals of wonder. If I asked you to consider surrendering to an unseen force as soon as you got that invitation, some of you would have just closed the book. No adventure. Maybe those of you who liked *Star Wars* would have (but the rest of you, not so much).

Now that we're here, and the magic has been moving through The Temple and into us, you may feel a little more comfortable with the idea of letting go and surrendering some of that control to an all-knowing and yet mostly unseen force. Consider that allowing this Spirit into the driver's seat (and seating ego in the back) was the first part of surrendering. Now, imagine pushing in the rest of your chips and betting fully on yourself—that's the surrender.

Imagine it now.

How does it feel? For me, the best description of what I felt when I did this was sweet relief. My muscles loosened on my bones, my jaw was less tense, suddenly I wasn't solely responsible for my mission on planet Earth. I had backup. We all do. All we've ever had to do was send our own invite and make room.

When we surrender to the idea that we *are* in fact vessels through which energy moves, and that energy is moving *all the time,* we can imagine there's a flow. There's a "way" to life (a current, if you will). We are remembering to move into a state of being that enables us to operate from this place more easily. We can move downstream in our vessels without struggle. When we begin to perceive situations as part of a whole versus as an independent and disconnected moment, we can perceive emotions as temporary cycles, or states of being. This is akin to seeing this life as a flowing river of consciousness versus a stagnant pool of murk. When we know we're in the river, it becomes much easier to paddle through the rapids, even if we get knocked around a bit. We know a bit better now how to get the being back into the vessel.

This flow is also known as the Tao: *the way things are.* Taoism is the following of the way. It doesn't mean we're denying the conditions we may find ourselves in. It means by recognizing that everything is energy, and everything is moving, that we can more easily accept that it *will* pass. When we employ (or deploy) this foundation, we'll have less barrel rolls in our kayaks. We won't be dragged so often under with the weight of other people's emotions, or expectations. We'll get to a point where we won't be so willing to let just anyone or anything tip your kayak. And if it does happen, it won't be for long.

The recovery time will be faster, spending less moments of life struggling and more soaking it all in. Of course, we should go kayaking with other people, enjoy life with other people, but we'll be able to maintain your autonomy. Just as in any relationship, including the one we have with Spirit, we can hold space without codependency or holding ourselves in the same emotional state as those who need us. Many hands really do make light work. Talk about a double entendre. As we're moving deeper into these shelves and stacks of antiquities, we realize we're not alone. More hands have joined us. Standing beside a wall of rolled up maps of plans stand a statue of Anubis. He looks as if he's glowing. There's a familiar hue of blue light, just like the light of the Universe coming through the wall of window in The Observation Deck. Just like the light above The Alchemist's Lab, but this time it emanates from Anubis.

The Lightsaber Is You

As we move toward him like magnets, it's the same feeling we felt when we got pulled toward The Archives in The Entryway. We *recognized* him. We felt what it was like to be reunited with an old friend. The biggest (and most adorned canine) we've ever seen. He feels like, and glows like, home. You're remembering, this is not the first time we've been here, seen this, felt this. As we stand frozen in awe and wonder at the discovery of remembering this place, we notice the statue holds a scroll. It's tiny in his hand and as we take it, it is still illuminated in that calming blue light. In trying to open it, we realize the scroll isn't a scroll at all, it's a baton.

Anubis passed it to us. We hold the baton now because we've remembered how to walk in light. When we do this, something amazing happens. It's something that we should have been taught in school. It's kind of the most important thing about being a human being. *We become responsible for our own energy!* Hooray! The positive side effect is that we become change agents, conduits of its magic. When we remember this, we begin to gain support, making it easier to navigate even the most challenging currents of our lives.

It shows up all around us, both as above *and* so below.

This *is* magic.

We're all part of the same big (*and dysfunctional*) human family. You may also be part of a smaller, and more immediate circle of dysfunction too (*most of us are*). Consider this good training because this is where I tell you that no matter how much magic is in our lives, how much we zoom out, there's likely still going to be

a pack of jerks. (They do travel in packs, don't they? I certainly did.) We're going to accept this as fact. One day, maybe even in the not-so-distant future, we won't have this problem. Eventually this consciousness will permeate. May each human become responsible for their own energetic being and its wellness. That's how we'll change the world. Fast.

We can use our new tools (transfiguration and transmutation) to recalibrate to help us deal with jerks. We imagine that those vibrations can create an impact on the energetic field just as we see in the science of cymatics. That's the study of visible effects of sound and vibration. By sending sound waves through matter such as sand on a plate, or a cornstarch and water mixture, various geometric patterns can emerge depending on the frequency and amplitude of the sound being played. If we imagine that, imagine what tones do for our cells. This is why people do toning. This is why monks chant, and why I mentioned trying to do this during transfiguration to see how sound impacts our Spiritual practice, whether you can see it (as in cymatics) or not.

Vibration is a current; it moves through everything and when there's a disturbance in the current (the force) of our community, family, friends of humanity, we feel it even if everything on the surface looks smooth—yes, like *Star Wars*, *the force* runs through *the field*.

Ready to head back to Nerd Town?

Let Me Take You to Nerd Town

There is a whole arm of physics and study around this quantum field theory. Since we're in The Archives, we'll just pop into the entryway of this particular rabbit hole. In physics, there is something called the Casmir effect, which is based on an experiment in which two conducting plates are brought parallel to each other with an electromagnetic field held between them. The gap between the plates can't sustain all frequencies of the electromagnetic field, particularly those wavelengths that might be comparable to the plate separation. As a result, this creates a zero-point pressure on the outside of the plates. A small force that is trying to push the plates together, to close the gap.

This is called the *Casmir force*. It increases in strength the closer the plates get to each other but vanishes once the plates actually make contact. The *Casmir effect* is often cited as evidence of a sea of zero-point energy in existence throughout the universe. For more on this rabbit hole, I highly recommend the book *The Field* by Lynne McTaggart. If there is a force or a field that connects us all, we can assume that when we experience hurt, it moves through the web of life, and someone else may feel it somewhere down the line. It's important that we learn how to surf the waves of being human without separation.

Without feeling the collective, we end up disconnected, and most of us already know what that feels like.

Our whole biological system works on frequencies and vibrations. The heart beats, the brain waves. Our brains function through waves of activity. Those patterns are measured in cycles per second in hertz, or Hz. Different Hz have different characteristics, and as human beings, we all have the ability to enter into different levels of consciousness. We do it all the time subconsciously. The trick is learning how to do it voluntarily or intentionally. To be more present at the controls during our normal waking consciousness.

Being a practitioner of magic, a practitioner of light or Spirit, means we use our energy consciously. We can't manifest without employing the force. Being a magician, a witch, a wizard, an alchemist *means* you're in a state of conscious intention. Since we're in The Archives, we can take a little dip into this ocean together and learn a little more about the waves of our brain and how this corresponds to magic.

The Alpha and the Omega

In terms of our brain waves, the higher the wave, the more alert we are, the lower the wave, the closer we are to sleep. Human beings typically function at a beta level (between 12 and 30 Hz), which shows we're awake and we're alert. This is the level

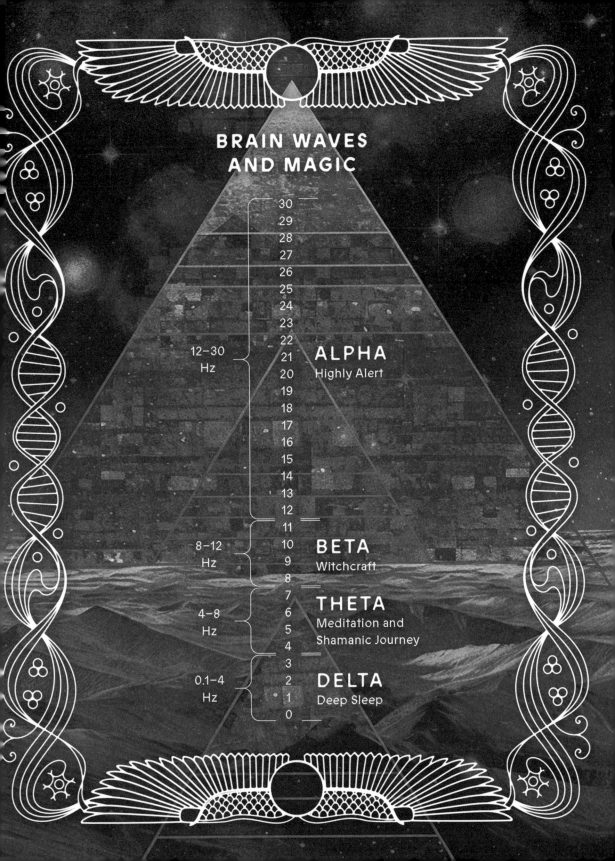

BRAIN WAVES
AND MAGIC

30
29
28
27
26
25
24
23
22
12–30   21   **ALPHA**
Hz   20   Highly Alert
19
18
17
16
15
14
13
12
11
8–12   10   **BETA**
Hz   9   Witchcraft
8
7   **THETA**
4–8   6   Meditation and
Hz   5   Shamanic Journey
4
3
0.1–4   2   **DELTA**
Hz   1   Deep Sleep
0

of consciousness that deals with things like math and left-brain logic. It's the engaged mind. Studies have shown people with high levels of beta activity have more positive thoughts and can generate ideas more quickly than those with lower levels. In most cultures, we've rewarded this beta state as being of greater importance. This is because typically when a person is focused and alert, they also tend to be *productive*. Beta has been a required state for The Uninvited, but we can't operate in beta all the time. We aren't machines, and we aren't meant to be.

This is where the other waves come in. The alpha state (8–12 Hz) is one where we are relaxed but aware. The most common state of alpha happens when we daydream. When we watch something without actually watching it, we're in alpha. Alpha is a place of accelerated learning, increased memory, psychic ability, and intuition. We may find we get an idea, intuition, or insight while getting acupuncture or a massage. When we practice ritual, or spell work, we do this in alpha.

This is the witch wave.

In a meditative state we are in theta (4–8 Hz). Theta enables us to enter a state of deeper consciousness. That is where we can enter a trance state. We can be so close to sleep that we can and often do fall asleep within deep journey work. When we get into a deep level of connection to the divine, it's in theta. We can experience things in our dreamtime, prophetic dreams, or vision. Deep insights can happen, and it can also be a state of physical ecstasy, where we can feel that we have transcended beyond the body.

The lowest level wave is delta (0.1–4 Hz), which is the wave of deep sleep. When I go deep into the channel work, I don't necessarily remember what I said but I may remember what I saw. People who don't get sufficient levels of delta sleep are the same ones who suffer from sleep deprivation. We need this wave. People who have chronic pain, or who have survived trauma, sometimes have a hard time with sleep or getting into the deeper waves of consciousness. Listening to tones can help open to that wave.

There are also states and waves above beta that are intriguing. Above that are gamma (30–150 Hz), linked to improving mood, concentration, and even athletic performance. When time seems to slow down during an important or traumatic event, we are likely in gamma. This can also be referred to as battlefield consciousness. Spiritual experiences such as moments of epiphany or divine inspiration can occur in gamma. This is also likely why these moments of inspiration and connection to the divine can feel so brief—they're meant to be. Our brains can't and shouldn't sustain gamma for lengthy periods; we'd burn out. If I knew magic had so many numbers, I probably wouldn't have failed grade 10 math.

The Mathmagicians

Galileo said, "Mathematics is the alphabet with which God has written the universe." We know from our adventure through The Temple so far that math is a key component of energy, and therefore, there *is* magic in numbers. We see it in every form, and sacred geometry has appeared throughout human history, Christianity, Islam, Hinduism, and Buddhism to name a few. Breadcrumb alert. Pythagoras was the leader of the Brotherhood of Pythagoreans, a secret society that studied mathematics. *All Is Number* was their sacred motto. The Pythagoreans explored the "magic 3-4-5 triangle." This triangle was called "magic" because any triangle with sides of 3, 4, and 5 units always creates a right triangle. What symbol was chosen by the secret order of Pythagoras to represent them? They used a pentacle inside a pentagon.

Phi, the golden ratio, appears in the pentacle. It is a powerful magical and mathematical symbol because: Math *is* magic, and magic *uses* math. One could not exist without the other. The ratio within the pentagram is itself holy. It also represents both the micro and the macro, the as above *and* the so below, through all the triangles it can be broken down into. The foundational shapes of Nature are math. Since we're so close by, you may want to walk back next door to The Library to have another look at all those amazing patterns and repeating shapes in Nature. Fibonacci!

Sacred geometry is often referred to as the *architecture of the Universe*. These are the building blocks in the universe of shapes, used in the design and structure of mosques, altars, churches, and temples (including this one). They've been deeply ingrained into so much of our art and culture. In scientist Nassim Harmein's paper

"Quantum Gravity and Holographic Mass," it is shown that the 3-D pattern known as the flower of life can be used to describe the gravitational field of any object, filling any sphere (a proton, a planet, or a galaxy).

The use of symbology and sacred geometry in magic is rooted in simplicity. We can represent the Universe simply by using these in our practice, on our altars, and as symbols of light and protection. Harvard mathematician Shing-Tung Yau expressed a belief in the centrality of geometry in 2010: "Lest one conclude that geometry is little more than a well-calibrated ruler . . . geometry is one of the main avenues available to us for probing the universe. Physics and cosmology have been, almost by definition, absolutely crucial for making sense of the universe. Geometry's role in this may be less obvious but is equally vital. I would go so far as to say that geometry not only deserves a place at the table alongside physics and cosmology, but in many ways, it *is* the table."

If you've ever experienced psychedelics, you'll know that often during the trip, patterns emerge. It's as if we're seeing behind the curtain (*through the veil?*) and viewing the fabric of life itself. Here's the good news, you don't need psychedelics to see it or feel it. Just as you don't need ayahuasca to have a shamanic journey. For some, this is the way the door opens; for me, I exist in a reality these days where I want to have as much memory and consciousness around my relationship with Spirit as possible. If we've done any ceremony together, you'll already know processed foods and alcohol are both discouraged the day before, the day of, and the day after the work. This is as much for me as it is for you. Working with someone else's energy when they've been imbibing adds a more challenging current and the transmissions aren't as clear, for me or for them. Processed things tend to be much lower vibrating.

If we think of energy in pure form, it's unprocessed, so when we're working with Source in ceremony, we want to give it a clear line. Changing consciousness is an art and is a core part of healing arts, the magical arts. It's the only real physical ability necessary to reclaim our mystical wonder and being able to change your own channels.

We're going to find that as we acknowledge this and begin to practice living a life where we acknowledge the intelligence of the Universe, sometimes when we poke Spirit with our consciousness, it will poke back.

Full Circle

Two years after Jennifer's trip to Egypt, I found myself in ceremony with Daniel. As we moved through this session, I would for the first time walk with him on this journey for parts of my soul. This time we both brought back my power. The first piece was far back in time and the first thing we both saw were the columns, seventy feet high. We were tiny standing among them. We were both being guided through gateways and into a dark room. Making an offering to a statue in that room, there was me from another life.

I knew as Daniel described what he was seeing that he had no idea where we were, but I knew it in my bones. I could see it. It was Karnak.

As we left that room in the Temple and journeyed back through space and time looking for any other pieces of me ready to come home, this newly retrieved ancient piece inside of me insisted on going with us. We moved together through darkness and desolation to get there. Crying together, we looked for her—this tiny girl with the overgrown bangs. I could see her hiding behind a stone. A rock. I could feel her there. The wonder, brightness, and the magic of my childhood.

I could see these pieces of me through the veil. A priestess and a child holding hands. Walking back home to me in the here and now. It's time.

As we came out of the ceremony Daniel asked me, "Where was that?"

I said, "It's Karnak, and that statue was Sekhmet. I'll send some photos."

I recounted Jennifer's story as Daniel leaned back, sitting with the wonder and magic. The instant physical reaction is to give it lots of room. So we did. When we closed the session, the first thing I did was to email him photos of Karnak, of Jennifer's photo of Sekhmet. Then I researched the statue of Sekhmet at the Royal Ontario Museum. Every piece of my body started to vibrate as I read about its origin. Then the lights flickered, and again it was like something I already knew, something I *remembered*. The statue came from the temple of Karnak. Now I could understand why I wanted to touch everything, why she'd told me herself that I could touch her. Why she had roared with laughter about my visuals of being escorted out of the museum by security guards. In some iteration of my soul's life, I had already touched them.

I went deep on the breadcrumbs, when I finally determined the origin of the scene featured in the papyrus Chanda and Jennifer had both brought back for me from Egypt.

It all made sense. The image depicts a scene from the tomb of nineteenth-dynasty queen and priestess Nefertari. Nefertari is making an offering of magical oils to the goddess Hathor. The goddess Hathor is known as the ascended Sekhmet. She has the head of a cow. The dairy cows across the street from our house flashed in my mind. #20. *Of course*, these two women in my life brought me back this same image. Both divine mothers in their own right, they delivered these to me because they saw me in it even when I didn't see it in myself.

From the Mistress of Dread to She Who Heals with Magic, I had undergone an initiation; I had come to the planet remembering. Nature spoke to me, helped me find the clues that would lead me back home.

Synchronicity is the wink from Nature, or energy itself, that you are on the right path. If we weren't, the clues wouldn't line up so beautifully. I realized it was time to make a change after so many years of fighting for my life. I would make a commitment to lay down my sword for a saber of light. Sekhmet had made it clear she had it covered.

It was time for me to focus on moving into my Hathor years.

Into the Wonder

We'll continue with a little transfiguration practice. First, let's go back upstairs to the upper level of The Archives. We can settle into one of the couches, away from the shelves of scrolls. Let's give our brains a little break.

As we move back up the stairway to the upper level of The Archives, we're going to imagine settling in on one of the plush couches. Want to lie down? Lie down. Do whatever makes you most comfortable as you take a moment to ground yourself. We're moving into this private space in our consciousness. A little room of your own for the soul. Try experimenting with adding some toning or sound as we move into this transfiguration practice.

We're going to imagine vibrating our own cornstarch into beautiful patterns, and vibrating our own cells.

To begin, we're going to drop into our heart space. Put your hands on your heart if you like and allow yourself to focus only on your breath. As you inhale, try to imagine that you're allowing the energy that surrounds you, that light and vibration that moves through everything, all the time, to move into your lungs, and through your nervous system. Imagine that you are in the current and in flow with all there is. Imagine that you're floating through the Ocean of Consciousness (*maybe you're in a kayak*). Totally safe, totally held in love. You are home. *Welcome home.* As you float in your mind's eye, try to imagine that light source you used with the transfiguration, or if you like, try a different one. If you used a star in the night sky, you may want to try to use the sun. You're going to imagine that as you connect to that light, just as we reconnected with Nature, you're going to reconnect with the Spirit of everything. Source. You're allowing that light to move through your being; it could be coming down from the very top of the universe to the tips of your toes. You may imagine it's flowing down on you like a fountain. If it moves out of you, it just comes right back up again and through you.

Just notice how your nervous system reacts to being in balance with the natural order. What changes, how does it feel? Try to imagine that anything that feels as if it may be weighing you down, anything that you may want to let go of on this day, in this week, or from this life, is lightening up. Release it for transmutation. Ask for your load to be lightened.

If there's other people popping in as you connect to Source, if there's other people weighing you down, allow the light to reveal them. Maybe there's just not enough source light getting through some people's windows. Maybe their windows are kind of foggy and they don't even know where the Ocean of Consciousness is. Our job is to shine the light, shining so bright that eventually they know where to go. Light clears fog. We don't need to get out of our float, we don't need to go over and yell at them to clean their windows. We just need to imagine that the same Source you've remembered and found inside of you is moving through them. Wave to them and tell them the water is *fine*.

You may want to take a ten-thousand-foot view, and maybe you'll see some areas of your life or those of your ancestors. Maybe the work so far has shown you something that needs illumination? Imagine that you're sending a wave from your corner of the shore to theirs, with love. With ease and with grace for the highest good and best possible outcome. With harm to none through all time. See yourself as a channel, a vessel carrying this beautiful light of the source as you become the star, and as we zoom out, we see the full web of life. We can ask what we can do to help at this time on Earth? What can we offer? Might there be a spot within the web of life (light) that needs some lighting up? Is there a place you can be shown or see that you can feel a connection to?

Stay in this state for as long as you need and bring yourself back using toning. As always, take a moment to write down anything that may have come through your field of energy. This practice will be much more fulfilling than worrying—and with *way* cooler results. As the world expands and systems change shifting under our feet, we can stay connected to the greatest foundation there is through our own Spiritual practice.

How did it feel to connect to the field, the force? How did your system react? As you write down your practices and track this connection to the web of light over time, note what might be changing in ordinary reality because of your non-ordinary work. Write down any insights or messages in your magic book to help you remember. This is also helpful to track progress as you deepen your practice.

When you've finished your transfiguration and writing practice, we can move off the couch and continue our journey farther down the walkway, along the balcony that runs along the length and perimeter of The Archives. As you walk along, we notice a small door. It's tucked into the wall before the balcony opens into the door at the upper level of The Library. This little door isn't curtained, and it doesn't seem all that magical. We almost walked right by it, but it has the same kind of plaque found in the rest of The Temple, so it seems to be part of this adventure.

It reads:

THE CONTROL ROOM

Sign aside, it looks more like the door to a supply closet from middle school. A utility closet of some kind; maybe The Temple has a furnace? The door isn't wood or meteorite. It's metal and gray and utilitarian. From beneath, we see a blue glow, maybe a faint sound, a buzz, or a hum. We lean against the door, and hear it, it almost sounds as if there's a hive. Something is humming, and since we've been hearing all about vibrations and toning, we're intrigued. Reach for the handle and open the door.

CHAPTER FIFTEEN

THE CONTROL ROOM

THE SYSTEMS

A s the door opens, the blue light spills from The Control Room and onto the balcony around The Archives. The room is much bigger than expected. This is *not* a supply closet.

The first thing we notice is a full wall of different kinds of monitors and screens running the length of the back of the room. Rows of long tables lined with chairs face the wall of screens. Each of these seating areas has smaller rows of screens built in above the table. Each seat has a tablet device laid on the desk. It reminds you of the cockpit of a plane, or NASA's mission control. The room's hum, or tone, is coming from the dozens of screens. Displayed on the screens appear similar views to the ones in The Observation Deck. There are galaxies, star systems, and planets. The monitors also show all kinds of measurements and visualizations. A bit of the moving codes from *The Matrix* but instead of feeling as if it's a room of surveillance operations, it feels more like a light show. Behind the veil, there is magic. It's not a simulation, it's a living organic system that responds and reacts. It is alive.

An ocean of intelligence surrounds us.

This place *is* a control room. It's also the place in The Temple that we can return to whenever we want to remind ourselves of the grandiosity of the systems that are in operation at any given time. To remind ourselves that Source has it covered. This room is one big wonder meter. It's a place where we can come to recalibrate and have a look at all the systems we are a part of. This room is a reminder of all the tools and systems available to assist us on this now five-dimensional journey we've found ourselves on.

As we move closer to the screens, we notice another hum coming out of what seems to be some kind of server cabinet beside the monitors. Maybe they're processors that are running all these monitors and supplying the current from Source to whatever amplitude is required to keep care of this Control Room. The Temple does kind of have a furnace, it's just not like any furnace we've ever seen. The supplies in this "closet" are fueled by magic.

A galaxy dances across one of the screens. There is a blip moving and vibrating almost like a radar screen that somehow seems to be slowly transforming into a planet. This is a monitor into creation. We're like the astronauts we heard about "Earth gazing." Let's slide over some chairs so we can get closer to the wall of movement. It is a literal symphony of breadcrumbs, and the conductor is Source. As we sit down, the images on the monitors in front of us begin to change.

It's you and then your family and your ancestors. You're not just seeing them, you're feeling them. *We* are feeling them. It's as if you've sat down at a 360-degree interdimensional viewfinder, we're moving through all the breadcrumbs of your life. We are moment collectors. You hear the voices of everyone you love almost at the same time. You're even feeling the impacts of the work you've been doing in The Temple. They begin to roll through like waves. You are retracing your own steps. The transmutations, transfigurations, and rituals. The screens refresh and your impacts and energy are radiating from you and emanating through the collective itself. We're being shown our own adventure. There are oceans of emotions and the magnificence of being able to measure this is settling in. There has been a transfer of energy.

Monitors of Creation

As we begin to process what's happening, each screen in the room begins to show a part of the same image. Slowly the image becomes clear. A giant keyhole is displayed in front of us. Every monitor has one.

When the student is ready . . .

We know what to do. We've been practicing. We raise our vibrations into a state of transfiguration. We extend our hands outward and create a key with our energy. You know that in magic the essence is *the same* as the object. This isn't a philosopher's stone, it's alchemical gold, it's the key of life. The light coming from Source, through us, down our spines, through our nervous systems, it conducts through our extended arms—the mind wide open—it's Us.

The Ankh. The Key of Life. The Artist Formerly Known As . . .

As we sit in The Control Room, we're unlocking not just our potential but a place in the stars. We are *part* of the system, and every time one of us unlocks this knowledge and remembers it, we catapult ourselves and our circles into a new realm of being. We're Spiritual Olympic gymnasts! Feel free to imagine whatever costume you like for this visual; mine has a cape that stays out of the way for my moves on the pommel horse. Our coach, Artist #1, was literally at the first Olympics. They've also been part of *every single win* since the dawn of time. That's who we trust to tell us where to go, when to turn on the heat, and when to take a break. This is who we can always trust to get us home. When we remember to open ourselves to a state of deep listening and surrender, we allow ourselves to be in a state of flow. This is when we are truly at the controls because we're at one with the systems. Athletes get into a state of being and flow when they make room for their body and energy's intelligence to lead the way. It doesn't mean we aren't focused; it means that we can nail the landing from the pommel horses by letting our practice do the work. And with an amazing dismount, it's us *remembering our magic!*

TA-DA!

Unlocking the knowledge to walk in light brings both freedom and responsibility. At this moment the tablet in front of us on the desk begins to reveal handwriting. As if someone were seated next to us, passing a note, slow and painterly script appears:

> **"Take ye this wisdom and heed it, listen to my voice and obey.**
> **Follow the pathway to brightness, and thou shall be one with the way."**
> **—THE EMERALD TABLETS OF THOTH**

A scrawled postscript appears: "Translated into English by alchemist Sir Isaac Newton."

Tablets of Knowledge

The Emerald Tablet is another occult favorite and is attributed, again, to the smartest guy in any room across dimensions and timelines: Hermes Trismegistus (or Thoth). The Tablet's origin stories are cloudy, but it's rumored it could be around thirty-six thousand years old. The origin story goes that when it came time for this version of Thoth to depart from this part of the Universe, he wrote his wisdom on the tablets. One theory is that the originals were lost during the burning of The Library of Alexandria (*thanks to The Uninvited*). No wonder he keeps coming around trying to point us in the right direction. Throughout the tablets, humans are referred to as children of the light. That means us, sun child. Sun of Source. Sun of Light. Human beings *are* children of the Light; we come from it, and we return to it.

We're here alive on the planet right now because our souls wanted to help rebalance these scales. We all chose this. We came back as a consciousness to help right the ship, not just our own kayaks.

It's time that those of us who've collectively pulled up a chair lift the veil and help reveal the truths that others have obscured. We *are* on a journey of transformation and awakening. Sometimes in order to grow, we have to start again. The systems oppressing us are collapsing and the systems that have supported our evolution are ready to pick up the slack. We are going to vibrate right out of this bullshit. Sometimes, being a change agent is dim and murky work, but we have Spiritual flashlights to get us through this, and we have help that knows exactly what to do once we are clear in our wishes and intent. It's already been written in the big book of life.

This is why we're in The Control Room, learning more about the controls that make us more competent pilots of both our vessels and our collaborative spaceship Earth. Part of leaning into the Systems available to us is remembering that this thing is ancient. That means there's always a precedent. We can count on it. Literally.

We track our breadcrumbs, our moments of synchronicity, of magic and manifestation, of our interactions with the divine. So we can chart and track the precedent (in your magic book). So that in the moments of despair, we'll remember we have help, that Source will show up for us. As my friend Jen Pastiloff would say: *We get to have this.* And if it's aligned with our purpose and if it's going to be of benefit to others, we can also ask for help in manifesting [insert wishes and dreams here]. Source loves us even when we may not love ourselves. That's the beauty of the systems of magic, they're all built on a force of love. Why else would all these ascended masters spend all this time trying to help us get the message if they didn't care? If we weren't worth it? I'm sure there's some amazing things happening in whatever dimensions they're in, but they keep checking in on us. That's love. *Real interdimensional eternal love.*

What I have experienced is that if you're being a jerk or not following the rules, or not leading with love, magic doesn't show up in the same way. Why should it? Sometimes I think when we got going on Earth, there was some advanced civilization out there who co-signed for us *(like an apartment)*. Maybe they're out there right now at an intergalactic divine council meeting trying to change how things have worked out, so that we don't lose their deposit.

Maybe that's why we haven't met anyone else in the Universe yet, maybe they're too busy having meetings *about* us.

When we're at the controls, working in partnership and following the rules, things change. When we know the systems, and acknowledge them in our practice, we can not only find more moments of synchronicity, but we tend to find others more easily too. So many of my clients talk about how as they practice the work, amazing people show up in their lives. They describe how they feel as if they've become some kind of beacon for like-minded people. I remind them that they are, and that practices like transfiguration do in fact bring with them a beam of community, and that's coming from me, an introvert! Finding the others is crucial to our collective remembering. Congregating helps ground the healing.

We need more connective tissue to heal the collective so by learning the systems and restoring balance we can literally change the world. What happens at a micro level is just as important as what happens at a macro level. The intention here in The Control Room is to become aware of what we know about the systems of the Universe, and of course, magic. Whatever reality, or whether you're an ascended master, the laws seem to apply to everyone.

You may have heard of, watched the movie, or read the book *The Secret*. Those weren't new systems; they are much older than *The Secret*. This wisdom, these systems, provide a combined knowledge of both the physical and Spiritual world. This knowledge or *tradition* was given to us by, and has been attributed again to, our Ibis-headed pal. The "Hermetic tradition" refers to alchemy, magic, astrology, numerology, and related subjects.

These arts were given to us by Source and have been passed through time by a series of initiates. If we imagine that Thoth is an initiator into the mysteries of divine science, maybe he did carve the principles. The second Hermes has been said to be the actual teacher of Pythagoras. Whether it was him, or just his texts, we know from our little adventure here that Pythagoras was a math-magician. Maybe this explains why? The third Hermes was said to have been the first teacher of alchemy. Another explanation is that Thoth was referred to as *Trismegistus* because of his praise of the trinity. He is known in Egyptian mythology as a king maker in his own right. Isis and Osiris would never have had Horus (the trinity) without Thoth's negotiations for Isis and Osiris's parents Nut and Geb. Without Thoth, Horus (and Anubis) may never have even existed.

Hermes Trismegistus isn't just found in metaphysical texts; he's also found in Islamic, Baha'i, and Christian writings. In those traditions, Hermes Trismegistus has been associated with the prophet Idris in the Bible. This knowledge has been

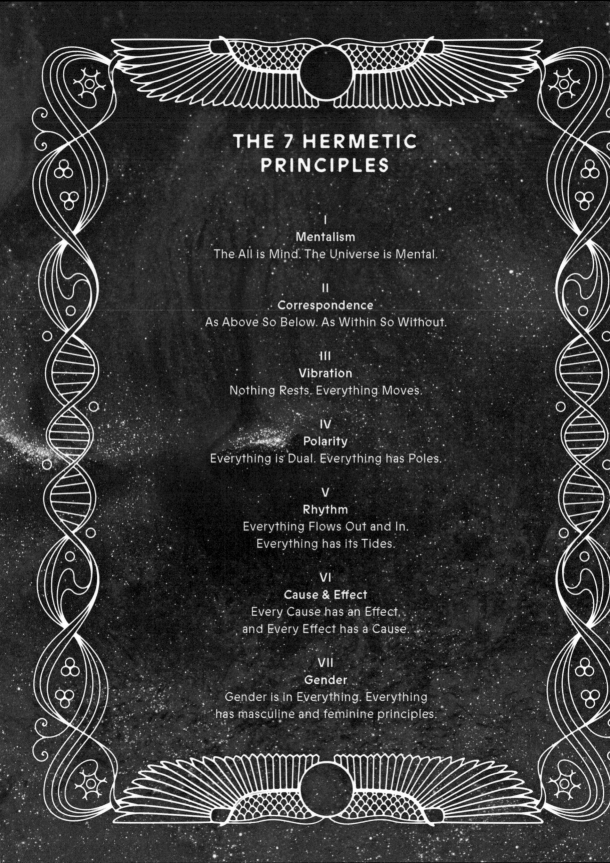

THE 7 HERMETIC PRINCIPLES

I
Mentalism
The All is Mind. The Universe is Mental.

II
Correspondence
As Above So Below. As Within So Without.

III
Vibration
Nothing Rests. Everything Moves.

IV
Polarity
Everything is Dual. Everything has Poles.

V
Rhythm
Everything Flows Out and In.
Everything has its Tides.

VI
Cause & Effect
Every Cause has an Effect,
and Every Effect has a Cause.

VII
Gender
Gender is in Everything. Everything
has masculine and feminine principles.

protected behind seals and riddles in books and laws, hermetically sealed for safe-keeping. It's said in occult circles that he put his students in charge of guarding and protecting the knowledge and passing knowledge down through generations. It's believed these students became the high priests of ancient Egypt and passed the knowledge to ancient Roman and Greek philosophers and so on. These traditions are still foundational teachings among many of the world's secret societies. Secrets and mysteries are part of the wisdom.

When we speak about these higher intelligences, whether they be gods or god-desses, angels, or ascended masters, it's always important to remember that, ener-getically, they all come from the same Source, they're all in service to the same thing. Light. We have a lot of interdimensional experts in lots of specific areas because we *need* them. There's a lot of us. Life has a lot of moving parts, and it's ancient stuff. So we need good, experienced representation. When things get tough or I feel overwhelmed, I like to imagine them all at the same (very long) table. That's a board meeting I'd like to sit in on. Talk about competent leadership and corporate governance . . .

We've got some more numbers coming but this one is an easy one to remember as it's already got some connection to divinity. If you're a fan of the Pixies (or Pythagoras), you'll already know that seven is the number of Spirit. In Pythagorean numerology, the number 7 means Spirituality. God stopped on the seventh day. In Hebrew, the number 7 has the same consonants as the word for completeness or wholeness. In Judaism, Christianity, Islam, Hinduism, and various other world traditions, 7 also represents divinity. No surprise there are seven hermetic princi-ples, laws, or systems.

We've already (magically) covered three of them.

1. **Mentalism:** That Source, or the All, *is* Consciousness. Everything is energy.

2. **Correspondence:** As above and so below. So within and so without. That there are always two components to how the Universe works. Ordinary and non-ordinary. Inner. Outer. Upper. Lower. Everything in life has correspondence.

3. **Vibration:** Nothing is at rest. Everything moves.

4. **Polarity:** Everything is dual, and everything has poles.

5. **Rhythm:** Everything flows out and in; everything has tides.

6. **Cause and Effect:** Every cause has an effect and every effect a cause.

7. **Gender:** Gender is in everything. Everything carries masculine and feminine principles.

We know that everything is energy, everything has correspondences, and everything vibrates. We also learned a bit about the law of polarity. There are two poles in everything and when we remember this, we can begin to accept that opposites are only extremes of the very same thing. The only difference between the two points is degree. Positive and negative. Hot and cold. Light and dark. Where warm becomes cold or hot is by degree. When does light become dark? On our planet, this happens slowly as the sun sets and the moon rises. We can practice seeing energy in the same way. We can feel when something is negative, and we can see it as a pole. We can use our practices to make adjustments. For example, we can use our Spiritual, or magical practice, to recalibrate a negative emotion to a neutral emotion. We don't have to fall in love with the jerks in our lives, or in the world, but we can begin to accept the fact that we are inherently connected via Source. We can do our best to neutralize the annoyance, anger, shock, or dismay we may feel when we see someone who is asleep at the wheel energetically. Transmutation is inherently a part of the system of energy. It's built in.

Let's imagine now these laws have seven dials, and maybe they also have associated monitors in The Control Room. We can check in on these things in our lives, in our manifestations, in our moments before bed, when we typically would have been on our phones checking social media and looking at someone else's life, or worse, worrying.

We're going to start with your dials to determine where you might be needlessly expending your energy. You'll find all kinds of illuminations about how you are tuned in and to what channel. Whether its resentment and anger, or comparison and judgment. We'll be able to take a little look and determine whether we've collected enough of those.

Dial number 5 is the law of *Rhythm*. We know this inherently from physics, rhythm is classic momentum transfer. If you think about Newton's cradle, one of those little stands with silver marbles on it that when you drop one into the rest it impacts the other side and then for as long as the momentum transfers, the cradle moves. A pendulum is always going to swing the same amount to both sides. Whether in Nature with the tides, or in the sunset and sunrise, The All's got rhythm. This puts those videos we've seen of people being swept up in the Spirit, whether through ecstatic dance or a church service, in a whole different light. Rhythm *is* a dancer. It *is* a soul's companion.

We're already going to know the next dial because most of us learned it in school, it's science, but also because we've all felt it in our own lives. I call them the twins. The twins who can bring magic or malice: *Cause and Effect*. Whether we want to see them as conjoined twins or as a tag team, they're forever connected. We can't have one without the other. We often refer to waiting for the other shoe to drop. Typically, it's Effect's shoe, or sometimes it's a very heavy boot that can feel more like an anvil.

Every cause has its effect, and every effect has its cause. It doesn't matter what dimension we're operating in; nothing escapes the laws of Nature. *Nothing*. That's what Karma really is, what it really means. It's a cause eventually having its effect. Energy doesn't always move fast but it has *perfect* aim. How long it takes to come back through the field is up to Source. We may even have effects we're experiencing from past lifetimes of our soul, or from our ancestors, or both.

Tracing the Roots

As we follow our own breadcrumbs and patterns, we'll begin to see how a root cause in the past could bring an effect to our lives, whether positive or negative. Our energy is our responsibility and how we wield it can hurt or help. This is why becoming responsible for it can and does reverberate through time. Not only can we heal the wounds of our ancestors, but we can also impact the future. I work with so many Remarkables (as I like to call them)—survivors of childhood sexual abuse. When we do the work to trace the cause, we always seem to find the same thing. The cause of our abuse is the same as the effect: trauma.

In my practice, I have also experienced that those who grew up with events of childhood trauma are actually more wired for sound when it comes to energy work. A positive effect of a horrible trauma. I believe this is in part what helped keep so many of us alive. If we didn't have our connection to Source, we may not have had the energy to survive. These traumatic experiences that impact the soul somehow also create an initiatory response where survivors, or Remarkables, are initiated to become incredible teachers and magicians.

We seem have a predisposition to be able to see through the dark, that's part of our origin stories.

Transmuting on the effect does also impact the cause. By using our voices, by telling our stories, by not carrying the shame or secret of the abuse, especially in our families, sends a wave of effect that knocks out the cause. It means those who break the cycle also break the chain. We transmute trauma into truth, and we remove the veil of darkness. By speaking it and sharing it, we remove the places where it can live in our families, and in our lives. Sometimes I think that's why a lot of us can't remember everything. Maybe in the span of time and healing, there's a world where we can wipe our own memories to help ourselves survive. We can recalibrate the system to catapult ourselves out of ancestral trauma, but we have to use all the gifts available to us. We can be motivated to do this work by remembering that with intergenerational healing come *gifts*.

I have also had the honor of working with Indigenous women who carry the compounded wounds of many generations. Imagine wading through life with the unhealed trauma of all of your ancestors and living in a world where the atrocities continue, as ancestors are literally being unearthed again, as with Canada's residential schools. In addition to carrying the wounds, they carry the power, medicine, and gifts of survival. We can transmute that poison to medicine. Some of the most powerful ceremonies I have been part of involve witnessing the cutting of those old cords and the transmutation of the pain to power.

This doesn't mean we are lessening the meaning of the experience; it means we are asking for adequate help to carry its weight. These things are too heavy for humans to carry so we need Spiritual reinforcements. We are asking for the effect to bring a new cause. If we are descendants of colonizers, immigrants, and all those Settlers who benefit from living on stolen land, we have a sacred obligation to transmute this on *both* planes of existence. We *can* go back to go forward. We can make an impact with our energy—not just in ordinary reality by getting involved, actively educating ourselves, and making reparations, but also by using our Spiritual practice and inviting our ancestors down the line who may have caused trauma to help rebalance the scales. If time is elastic and everything is connected, we can go back and flood the system with light, asking for the best possible effect after so many generations of pain.

Control Room Goals

Dial number 7 is *Gender.* Gender manifests on all planes of existence. Every being carries both masculine and feminine principles. Spirit, Source itself, *is* nonbinary as are so many of the souls coming to and living on the planet right now. This is not a coincidence. The farther the polarities of male and female are gaping apart means the larger the energetic tension. Nature won't break, but it will bend.

The farther humanity moves into the fifth dimension (meaning using all of our gifts and capabilities), the closer we move to the nonbinary. The neutrality of poles will balance, and dissolve, and we will further develop our magic by rebalancing gender in the world. This will likely be the point where we are finally granted the intelligence we have struggled to understand for thousands of years. The solution was always simple. The struggles we are experiencing are because these limiting

systems cannot survive the shift needed to ascend humanity. They must fall away for us to move ahead. We're meant to be recalibrating how we see and understand gender. Most of us have grown up in a system where there are gender roles. We know what role gender played in the Witch trials and continues to play in the ongoing persecution of women and queer folks around the world. Of 344 alleged witches in New England, 78 percent were female. Most witches persecuted were women because witch hunts were aimed at pursuing those most powerless in society to defend the allegations. Exhonerated now or not.

When men did face allegations of witchcraft, it was because they associated with the accused women. The few men tried for witchcraft were mostly the husbands or brothers of alleged female witches. This is probably why so many men are still nervous about witches (*just ask one for a lock of their hair, you'll see*).

The essence of all human beings is our Spirit. The human Spirit is nonbinary in the same way that Source is nonbinary. The human being has been referenced in so many religious and Spiritual texts as having been made in the essence of Source. It never meant we looked like Spirit on the outside. The soul is not material; it doesn't need organs for biological reproduction because it doesn't have a material body. In working with energy, we have to consider both facets. When we're in the physical world we should be doing the same. We can consider and honor both poles and all things in between.

When we consider all these systems together, we can begin to see a pretty clear picture of where things may be out of alignment, or where we may have one thing cranked all the way up. This will give us a clearer picture of where we may have lost some of our perspective, or where our own balance may be off. We're going to check in now and have a look.

In this visualization practice, we'll imagine a visit to our own control panel. We are going to look at all of our little dials and knobs we have access to in order to be the captain of our lives. We're going to have a look at the dials. We can imagine that it's like a stereo. You're going to see yours. Are your dials at the top? Right? Are you in rhythm? Are you not? Are you trying to grab a wheel from the universe? Are you ignoring any aspects of your life?

This is what we check in on.

Into the Wonder

From now on, when you're feeling out of balance, this is what I want you to try to do. If you feel as if something's off, you're going to imagine that you're looking at the controls. You're going to imagine that these are your seven dials. Are you out of balance in any of these areas? We'll go through them now, together. First, the All. We know that energy is everything and everything is vibrating, right? Are you holding on too tight or stuck? Or are you moving in flow? Is there something happening with polarity? Are you on one side of the dial more than the other when it comes to perceptions, perspectives, or relationships? Are you out of rhythm? Are you trying to set too many plans that aren't in harmony with the tides? Is something happening in your life because it's the twins in action? Cause and effect? Are you trying to avoid an effect that happened because of a cause? The last, dial 7. Are you recognizing all aspects of yourself and situations, the space between the feminine and masculine?

Look at the controls. If they're out of whack, you can imagine putting them back into the middle. You can imagine that those dials represent something specific that you're trying to achieve or perhaps you have specific dials for big manifestations or important relationships in your life. Maybe it's the intention you wrote down or maybe it's something you've been actively working on. And again, just note where the dials are. You may want to check in later and do this for a few different things in your life. Just have a look. Where are things at? Is the family part of my life out of balance? Is it my part that is out of balance? Is this attached to something else?

When we're feeling as if we need some adjustment, this is the first place we're going to check. You'll likely notice if you repeat this practice enough that some of your controls may be slipping around more than others. Take note. Your soul will let you know where the work is. Sometimes these patterns are breadcrumbs that can even relate to your soul purpose. What parts of ourselves may we be back on Earth for another go so we can graduate to a new domicile?

The goal with The Control Room is that eventually we're able to identify when something is needing attention and deal with it in the moment.

If you're up for it you may also want to check in on your utilization, maybe there's some apps, or relationships, you need to force quit. Maybe you're holding a bunch of space for something, or someone, that you didn't realize before. Maybe you're harboring a lot of anger after a period of grief. Whatever it is, you can imagine putting a lid on it. Putting it to the back and moving some more efficient and positive things to focus on into the front. We can cap off our time dealing with challenges that we have put to bed. For example, how much more reality TV do *I* need in this lifetime? Probably none (but some is "good" too).

This work in The Control Room is akin to taking our vessels in for maintenance. You may begin to do this as a weekly or monthly practice. You may decide to align it with a certain number of miles on your system. Some clients like to do it before going to bed, trading it for a racing mind. Boundaries are a crucial part of our systems. When we're in The Control Room, we're in service. We get to determine how we use our energy. If you discover that you have some leaks in your vessel, or you discover that you have a stowaway, you can simply declare your autonomy in Spirit. You can first set your boundaries in Spirit to assist in the ones you'll see in the physical world.

Now that we've recalibrated our settings, we're going to do some work around the protection of our vessels. Think of it as a protection package typically sold to you by the dealership. The good news is that this one comes at *no extra cost*, there's nothing confusing about it, so when you're finished with making notes about this maintenance visit, let's move to the upper level of The Library.

We have a little more remembering to do.

CHAPTER SIXTEEN

THE LIBRARY— UPPER LEVEL

THE PRACTICE

As we move out through the doorway of The Control Room, we're again surrounded by the majesty of The Temple. The buzz and whir of creation that flooded The Control Room is gone. It's like coming out of a hive as you adjust back to the ancient smells coming from The Archives. We're in what I like to refer to as the processing stage of our adventure.

It's as if we're getting a software update, or for some of us, there may be a lengthier series of systems upgrades. This is part of being an energetic being who is having a human experience who may not have been connected for the automatic updates. This is normal. You're for the moment, just like a computer or a PlayStation.

There are going to be times in our lives where we may feel as if we need a minute. In our world, this is also known as *winter*. Nature doesn't just power through times of growth. It rests. It takes a beat. We get to do that too. We don't need to call it a mental health day, and we don't need to let it get to the point of a breakdown on the side of the road. We can wave—and not just our arms to the people in our lives—but we can wave our energy. We can ask for a tether, a tow back to home base. We know exactly where to go and what to do if we're feeling caught up in the muck (or in the spins). We have a checklist now. We're going to use it, but we're going to make sure the ego is buckled in.

We're going to check into the web of life and see where the feeling or wave might be coming from. *Is it you? Is it someone in your network? Is it the collective?* We're going to use our magic book to track the breadcrumbs as well as the WTF moments, which might just be currently unidentified breadcrumbs.

When we are in that level of alignment, we deepen our magical, or Spiritual, practices, acknowledging the systems we're in, and beginning to receive transmissions, or downloads, from divinity. When we get into that level of connection with Spirit, it becomes a direct revelation as we remember how to decipher the transmissions.

Whether it's journeying, meditation, or ecstatic movement or dance, we can begin to be in moments of alignment with Source where we raise our vibration enough to meet it. When this happens, Source itself begins to become our teacher.

The Foundation of Magic

By growing our practice and connection to Spirit, and in effect magic, we will touch the stars and weave together the two realities from which we've come. As above and so below. Always look for the higher perspective and remember to examine the ten-thousand-foot view, sometimes it's where the breadcrumbs (or treasures) are hidden.

As we stand on the balcony of this library, we remember there are two parts to everything in our lives. Sometimes we are the students and sometimes we are the teachers. This *is* the practice. This is what is meant by becoming *our* magic.

As we move across the balcony into the open doorway of the upper level of The Library, we already see down below back to where we met and started this adventure. The place below where we first came through the curtain from The Entryway. We see the table with the Deity Decimal System carved into it. This is a ten-thousand-foot view moment. Let's stand here for a second and take in all the things that have begun to transpire since we started our adventure. Consider and honor all the seeds we have planted and begun to nurture, all the energy that we've released and reset. All the things we've begun to recalibrate and remember. The rituals, the magic book, the things, and moments collected along the way through these halls and in life.

We've *just* begun to sew together the foundation of the most important part of this story—your own energetic practice.

Remembering wonder is as much a practice as magic is. When we reconnect to our own medicine, we begin to interact with the world in new ways. The side effect of a continued practice is that new pathways, doors, and rabbit holes open *all the time*. We're going to have lots more adventures, because life does become a wonder-driven scavenger hunt where we get to be on a team with the greatest intelligence there is. There will be times where the veil between the worlds can feel and seem so thin that we can experience literal miracles. Where we see things that can hardly be believed. Leaving us standing in a state of wonder and gratitude with the only words possible to utter being, *"Can you believe it?"*

Or far more often, *"Wow!"*

We call it a practice because that's exactly what it takes. Practice. It's no different from learning to play an instrument (*remember, recorders?*), this time it's you. You're the instrument.

In Taoism, there's a parable about a traveler on a journey who comes to a fork in the road. There's a wise person standing at the fork so the traveler asks, *"Which way should I go?"*

The wise person replies, *"Where are you headed?"* And the traveler, unsure of their purpose and destination, replies, *"I don't know."*

The wise person answers back, *"Then it doesn't matter what path you take."*

To obtain guidance we need an intention; it's up to *us* to set the intention now, to lean into the practice, and find our purpose. It's up to us to know where we're trying to go, even if it's a feeling. My own journey started with the quest to feel peace. When we're in alignment, it becomes much easier to determine which path we should be on. We spend less time looking on Google for clues, and more time in our lives interacting with the best search engine there is.

Let the Light Shine In

Spirit can help us get there. Our ancestors can help us get there. If it's in alignment, the Universe *will* get us there. It finds a way. It's up to us to follow the breadcrumbs. It's up to us to ask. It doesn't have to be writing a book, or changing the systems at schools so that kids don't have to learn to play the recorder anymore, it can be as simple as what kind of dynamics we are or aren't willing to have in relationships. We can set intentions in our practice, and we can make space in our lives for wonder, the room (or rooms) for magic to happen. We *can* see the timing of the Universe as a series of gentle surprises. We *can* think of synchronicities as a wink or pat on the back from the Universe. But being a change agent can be hard. It means we're doing some major remodeling and heavy lifting, especially if you're in a particular edge of the web of life that may not have had magic running through it in a while.

As we continue to build the practice, and as we continue to be responsible for our own energy as we move into the ancestral lines, we *will* see the positive impacts of our practice. We will see positive shifts, breakthroughs, and growth happening in our immediate family and human family in this reality. We return to real community. There has never been a time where I have not seen that happen when people lean into the work. This is *real* magic. It's not a stage show, an illusion, or pageantry. It's a deep, omnipresent, and collaborative force.

It doesn't hang with people who aren't ready to wield it with the respect it deserves. They're like Santa, it knows when you've been bad or good, and the only difference is Spirit can make every day feel as if some magical elf is dropping off gifts—and it doesn't need milk or cookies. Just *take care* of Nature.

We're not going to go all the way down the rabbit hole here, but the original Santa was a shaman. That's a breadcrumb you *can* follow on Google.

As you continue with the practices remembered in The Temple, we'll witness dynamics changing and shifting as we begin to purify our own energetic toxins. This may still sound bizarre when we think about the more dysfunctional or dense beings in our circles, but they're made of the same stuff we are. I have been a dense being and trust me, eventually, it permeates. There's no way around it. We can't stop energy from moving no matter how hard we try. We don't have to be in the room with these people to hold space to fix the problems. We *can* shine our light at those dirty windows, Care Bear-stare style.

I've asked my own teacher, *"Do I need to have challenging people around my clients in ceremony in order to bring light back into their being?"* The answer is *no*, eventually in our practice and maybe even the practice of others, light is going to wrap around them. That's exactly why transfiguration is so powerful. We can simply work with Source light to call it forward on the planet. Again, for those in the back, this *isn't* doing magic on people without their permission. This is flooding ourselves with the light of Source and then running it through the web of life, which happens to also include some dense energy bopping around inside people. We're simply seeing all humans in their light-filled perfect form. Transfiguration is a great way to get into a state of vibration where we can move more deeply into our own practice.

Being in a transfigured state while doing ritual, manifestation, or divination work will bring more energy to the practice. Try experimenting with working outside in Nature, whether it's while sitting on a park bench or getting out into the forest and notice how it impacts the practice. This is what makes your practice unique. There is no wrong way to hold sacred space with Source at the table.

Custom Builds

As we hone in on our practice (or customize our builds), we really begin thinking about all the things we want to do, accomplish, and achieve. What do we need for ourselves and how can it benefit the collective? Where in our lives might we want to slow down? Where might we want to make more room?

It can start by identifying areas or relationships in our lives where we need more light. We can ask for support and change. We can ask for love and care as we move through initiations or energetic growth spurts. We can ask for ease and grace. I often frame it by saying, *Please show me the right way. Please show me which path to take for my intention.* Surprisingly, or not, when we hold the intention, you'll find you will know what path to take. It becomes *very* clear.

When we're feeling untethered, or having challenges with our purpose, our ancestors can be especially helpful. Whether we had an existing relationships with them or not, our collective ancestors want the best for us. They want us to use our gifts. They want us to use the tools of the family line. It's an honor for them when we call on them and ask for help with life. *Help me to remember to slow down.* They *can* help do those things because the odds are that the pace of their lives was likely slower, especially the further back we go. They don't necessarily have to be our close ancestors, maybe they had trauma, or maybe weren't close.

This is the beauty of the ten-thousand-foot view: we can go farther back, and we can ask for helpful loving support from the bloodline itself. Healing, success, connection, and abundance are part of our ancestors' playbook. We can explore your own and bring into being a Spiritual practice that honors them, if this is something that resonates. The ancestors can really help us slow down. We are not meant to be moving this fast, especially in a state of disconnection. A huge side effect of the COVID-19 pandemic was humanity being slowed right back down to Nature's speed. There's really no Spiritual reason for us to live at this pace. There is no rush hour in Nature because there is no capitalism in Nature. Nature moves in balance with the rhythm of life. This is part of our practice. The faster we adopt new systems based on mutually beneficial outcomes, the faster the planet will heal from damage caused by our apathy, entitlement, anger, and pain.

With our transmutation practice, we can move into a state of being in a better state of balance with our energy. The Universe seems to support us in this, as if there's some kind of amazing reciprocity engine at work. The ultimate algorithm. The benefit of being in alignment energetically is that we can get to a point where we can receive downloads or transmissions from Source. A voice memo or text message from the Universe. We can suddenly have a knowing or an idea that feels beyond our capacity.

It's also why I recommend writing things down in your magic book. You can't track or confirm your predictions if you don't write them down. Same goes for dreams, times, and dates. We can develop these gifts by practice. As you do you will begin to recognize when you may have hit a roadblock, or hurdle, and when you're wired for sound.

Part of the adventure is experimenting with different practices and facets of magic based on what lights us up. That's how it works. Magic, or a Spiritual practice, isn't meant to be something we don't want to do. Some witches I know (*maybe me too*) dance their faces off, and that's where their practice is rooted. Some witches sing (*maybe me too*), and the power they raise comes from their voices. Some make jewelry, or incense. Our practice is ours. Anything with heartfelt positive intention can become a Spiritual practice. We are in charge of how we inject our medicine and magic into our lives and realities.

Your Team in Spirit

Our helpers in our practice are what show up for us. They may be power animals, angels, ascended masters, ancestors, or transitioned Spirits serving in light. Those beings who serve in perfect love and perfect trust. That is our intention. I always recommend finding a trusted practitioner for deepening the practice of working in Spirit. This does two things, it helps for the current to be passed, but it also helps to feel less as if we're full of it. Witnesses help show us that we're not making this up.

When we have a human teacher who can provide insights and also see between worlds, it helps with those bigger quests. I would not have been able to do this work without my teacher helping hold the flashlight in the moments where I felt as if the whole world had gone dark.

Deep journeying work *requires* helpers, otherwise we'd just be stuck Googling, wondering what was supposed to happen next. Helpers are our translators. They're who help us in Spirit at the forks in the road, and they're the ones who help carry us when we feel as if we're without purpose, or direction. They're the ones who can fully understand the language of Spirit to help us translate it into human.

Next, we're going to get a little closer to the Earth to ground the adventure. We'll take the stairs and come back down to the main floor of The Library. As we walk down the stairs and back onto the main floor of The Temple, we can feel a vibration that we probably wouldn't have been able to name, let alone feel, when we first arrived. It is ancient. It's home.

We're going to come back to the place where we first took a seat.

If we think about our own practice so far, how has it been working? How might magic have already begun to show up and impact your life since the first things you wrote down about it? If you've been through The Temple before, how does this time compare to the last adventure? What did you notice that you hadn't before? You may want to note what may have already changed. You may want to take a walk around your vessel. How are you operating now that you've begun to remember and create space for practice? You may also want to track how some of your bigger wishes for the collective, or the Earth, are shaping up. Have there been any movements, transformations, or changes with regard to any of your bigger wishes, or things you may have seen or experienced in the ritual work we've been doing since you started the adventure? In order to track the progress of our practice, we sometimes need to take a ten-thousand-foot view of it too.

Moment Detective, Building Cases

The core of my work has been working with Spirit to make a case that the energy that creates cycles of trauma is uncovered so we can remove it. That oppressive Uninvited energy that has created the predators among us be illuminated and brought to divine justice so that we can properly protect children. It's as if we're all little lawyers arguing our cases before Source, and I'm taking mine to trial and in doing so, reporting this to the proper Universal authorities. In my own life, I've found doing both the "as above and so below" to be a part of the work of healing. Reporting to both Source *and* the local authorities has been instrumental in my own rebalancing of the scales. But I didn't do both at the same time. I started with Source until I had enough power to one day walk into an actual ordinary reality police station. Maybe one day we'll be able to do it the old-fashioned way, a place where perpetrators are escorted out of the collective. Eventually, the world will deal with this the same way the Universe does.

No child should ever lose the autonomy of their being at the hands of an adult. I believe this world has become a safer place for survivors like me to come forward in the time I've been doing ritual and building my case to Spirit. The needle is moving. I've watched it happen. So have you.

I trust the powers hearing my cases because I have seen the kind of power good wields. It is magnificent and spectacular. You may want to think about where you're putting your energy. Where might you lend your intention? What cases are you making and what evidence or examples can you bring to Spirit for resolution and healing? We can release our conflicts to our highest selves, and highest Source. We can ask for more intelligence. We can stand in front of the divine council of energy and ask for change. The Universe loves change. Just don't forget the ease and grace.

To think that our little rituals are not having an impact on the Divine whole is simply against Nature (and science). We have the capacity to co-create and we have the capacity to back up other people's intentions. There's an army of us out there, and each time one of us Remarkables (and our allies) step into the light, another is safe to come out of the dark. I believe in high magic. I believe in the power of Source, and I believe we *can* remove this kind of evil from the planet. That's what it is. I haven't used that word yet here in The Temple, this is to whom it applies. The more we flood the system with light, the better the odds of chasing out the darkness on this planet, whether it be in the systems of oppression, or the people who commit the crimes.

We can fix it, repair it, with action and energetic practice, but we also have to protect it, especially if we're working to change the world. We can ask for that and then notice what comes through. Remember, energy moves but it moves at its own pace. When a season changes it doesn't all happen in one day (though if you're Canadian, there are times where it feels like that).

Protecting Your Magic

We have to acknowledge a crucial part of our practice is protection. Unfortunately, not every place is safe to be in our magic and not every space is sacred. We may be all high vibrating and doing Spiritual work now in The Temple, but we *do not* have to enter every situation in life with our sacred gates open. We need to remember we're on Earth and everything isn't as gentle right now as it can be in Spirit. Sometimes things in Spirit aren't gentle. Sometimes we have to deal with toxicity. Sometimes we have to deal with those who inflict trauma, but we don't have to come to those situations without protection. It's a field of energy just like the other ones. Since we don't typically drive our vehicles around with our doors wide open, we don't want to do that in our vessels. We want to keep ourselves safe from falling out, from jerks getting in, from other people's things getting inside.

It's the same in our practice, we want to have a field of energy around us. Imagine that you can put a gate around your vessel. Maybe it's even a moat, a perimeter, an electric fence (but one that doesn't hurt, only warns). When we need to protect our energy, we can do it simply with intention and vibration, but also, we're going to learn to close the gates. And in fact, there may be people who never get a key.

I used to have my gates open all the time. It didn't occur to me that I could close them. I *do not* recommend this energetically or otherwise. Maybe one day the world will be back into balance, and we'll have transmuted enough of the anger and density out of the collective, but for now, secure your drawbridge. Our energy matters especially when it's a hard time. Maybe we're feeling extra sensitive and need to make ourselves a little nest of energy, maybe it's a real nest too—do what thou wilt. This is the concept of a magic circle. This is why the circle surrounds the star of the five elements; it is the protection and sacred space. Sacred geometry indeed.

We already have a field of energy around us. We can imagine it's like the egg Mork had in *Mork & Mindy*. Mork and Magic. If this is new to you, I highly recommend it as a show, and as a lesson in being human. Since we're in The Library with Thoth, we're making an energetic egg.

As if on cue, a book flutters down from the ceiling as the feather did before. It lands on the table.

The Cover reads: *The Cosmic Egg: Global Cosmogonies.*

There's an illustration on the cover. It's an Egg with wings, a snake. As we're processing this the book is already gone. Is the Egg another winged disk? The sun of ascension? Creation taking flight? The snake medicine of transformation and rebirth. You feel Thoth again in your consciousness, repeating the same thing as the first time we were here.

"What came first, the Ibis or the Egg?"

We know the answer now. Both happened at once, because "as above so below."

They were created in tandem. We feel as if Thoth has clapped his hands, remarking with a knowing smile, *"It's time to close the gates around our vessel."*

Into the Wonder

Imagine in your mind's eye that there is an orb or oval of light or energy around our body. We can visualize it wrapping around like the great cosmic egg (we're basically Mork). Imagine that we're adding a gate around the entirety of the egg. You're putting in a little (or big) perimeter, or circle, around your vessel. In whatever form you want to protect our energy and our vibration. It might be a moat, it might have fire, or ice. Whatever you see is what it is. We can do this very simply with your intention. We can ask our helpers, our angels, our guides, the elements, whatever feels right to patrol the perimeter. We can set that as an intention and ask them to let you know if someone is at the gates from whom we may need protection.

There's going to be times where someone is already inside the gate. There might be times where someone slips in because something stressful is happening, there may be times in relationships where boundaries are new, sometimes people aren't who we thought they were, or we might just find someone unknowingly, subconsciously rummaging around in our consciousness. We have systems we can implement to help us navigate these spaces, as we're likely going to be increasingly focused on our breadcrumbs and new views. We can ask for help for patrol and we can close the gates. We can imagine our helpers escorting them out with kindness or throwing them out if they've already been asked nicely. We do no harm, but we take no shit.

We can use our energy more effectively and efficiently if we use all the tools available to us. So much of what we typically are used to doing in ordinary reality can be done in non-ordinary space by transmuting or transfiguring the energy. You may end up doing both. We don't need permission to recalibrate energy in our own lives, or to see those in our lives in their perfect highest form, even when they're being low-level jerks. We can also use our breath to help us remember and create that circle of protection. We can pull up that energy out of the earth and we can protect our energy by using the fourfold breath. We can pull in our light, and as we breathe, we can imagine that we're filling up the bubble and our vessel with light.

As we breathe, the light stays in as the air goes out. As we breathe in for a count of four, and then breathe out for a count of four, we can help move energy through our vessel and cleanse the system ourselves when needed. When things are painful, when emotions are not so pretty, we can rely on our breath. Remembering that Spirit *is* to breathe, we allow it to move through our system. We set the intention to recalibrate ourselves to safety by protecting our energy.

This is one of the keys that we've forgotten; we need to remember to protect our magic. Especially when we're going to be shining so brightly with all of our amazing practices. You may want to create your own ritual around how you can expand your protection? How can you honor and protect your space? Again, bring in your medicine. How might you be able to work with Nature in this regard? How can Nature help protect our spaces? Notice what comes through and write it down. How has our practice already changed the way we consider inviting or allowing energy in our daily life? How have our boundaries changed as we're remembering?

When you've finished with this practice, we're also going to take a look at *what your* practice has transformed. To do this we'll need to head through The Greenhouse and Garden, and back to The Reflecting Pool.

As we turn to the doors leading out to The Greenhouse, we already notice something that wasn't there before.

CHAPTER SEVENTEEN

RETURN TO THE REFLECTING POOL

REMEMBERING

For the second time in this quest, we step back down the few stairs into The Greenhouse. The smells remind us of the reconnection we did with Nature. The rituals and magic we've invited into our being and consciousness. We remember how stark a contrast it was when we last crossed from the arched door of the fairly bare Greenhouse compared with the lush greenery in The Garden. Now though The Greenhouse has been overtaken with new growth. Vines have grown over the windows, the walls, and the floor. There are seedlings *everywhere*. The smell of soil and the vibration of life itself. We can feel the hum coming from them.

The sound from The Control Room wasn't processors, or computers at all; it was *life* vibrating in its highest form. How else could all these plants be growing so quickly? We *just* planted these seeds. It has to be the light.

Not just the light of the star that is fueling the sunshine, but the life force in you. The Temple continues to expand and meet us with boundless connection and magic. These plant beings surrounded by the protection of The Greenhouse aren't just new growth; they are a by-product of our practice. *Your* work, *your* practice, is having an impact not just in your life, but in the web itself.

As we practice in ordinary reality, as we grow our transfiguration work, we are planting seeds of change, growth, and transformation. They stand here as a reminder of ourselves.

We're the seeds. We're the new growth.

We're the miraculous architects of a new age. We *are* the children of the light with the power of Nature coursing through our veins. We can no longer mistreat ourselves, our cohabitants, or our planet. We've got to stop punching ourselves in the face. Just because we can't see anything with our physical eyes beyond the dark matter in the night sky doesn't mean that nothing's there. Maybe we humans are actually contained in some kind of focus group (there's enough snacks for it). Maybe we can't see through dark matter because other intelligent life hasn't decided to turn on the light yet to reveal the two-way window?

We can assume by what we've remembered that intelligent life in the Universe doesn't need to physically enter our reality in order to deliver messages. Why would it need to when we are surrounded with it? It is the All, it is everything, and it is for *us* to remember. We are the ones who slammed the door. When we open it, we are able to make our amends, reuniting not just with a force like no other, but with each other. We are the ones who can make the reparations, not just in Spirit but in this world, the one you are reading this book in right now. We have a lot of work to do so it's good that there's so many of us, and that we have such growing numbers. Some of our work will be done with energy and some of it must be done with physical labor, emotional labor, our bodies, our money, our time. We are the change, and we correct the imbalances. We bring the reharmonization. We own the horrors of what has happened on this planet.

We must make reparations with wisdom-keepers; Indigenous peoples all over the planet are owed. Not only for the violence, but for the injustice of what The Uninvited have stolen and to the ideologies that could have saved the world twenty times over by now.

We must recognize that the ancient knowledge provided has always been the way forward. We can and will again live in harmony and in communion with the land, and the beings who serve it. This is remembering. This is what lights the way forward.

As we stand in the midst of this new growth, we notice that one seedling in particular is standing out. It's as if the sun is shining a pointing finger. Let's bring it into The Garden, we can plant it on the way to The Reflecting Pool. As we move, light seems to trace its beam to the door of The Greenhouse.

It Was Written

We head through the doorway and are standing back in The Garden. As you hold the little seedling, you can almost feel its excitement about its newfound home. This time as we step into The Garden, we both stop. We can feel all the energy of the beings who live there. Everything feels more alive than it did when we started. Everything feels more vibrant and connected. It's as if this reconnection is not just to Nature, but to the old ways and practices. They have not only caused new growth in the garden, but more life. Something has shifted in The Garden because something has changed on the planet.

There is an ancient prophecy about this time, about the change we are welcoming by remembering. The Prophecy of the Eagle and the Condor is an ancient Indigenous tale from the Amazon. It speaks of human societies splitting into two paths, that of the Eagle, and that of the Condor. The path of the Condor is the path of the heart, of our intuition, of the feminine. The path of the Eagle is the path of the mind, of the industrial, and of the masculine. It can be seen also as a division of North and South, or Eastern and Western thought and culture. It was predicted that the Eagle would begin a five-hundred-year period during which the Eagle people would become so powerful that they would nearly drive the Condor people out of existence.

The colonialism of the Americas brought murder and oppression of Indigenous peoples for five hundred years. The prophecy says that during the next five-hundred-year period (which began in 1990) that the potential would arise for the Eagle and the Condor to come together. That one day again we would fly together in the same sky. This coming together would complete the circle and bring healing to what was once broken.

By doing this, by reconnecting and coming back together it was prophesied that we could have an opportunity to create a new level of consciousness for humanity. It was said that from a union deep in the hearts of the Eagle and Condor people, we would be able to grow with a mutual collaboration. That a renewed relationship with the land would reunite humanity once again with their original knowledge, strength, diversity, and connection to the earth. This would signal a new *"Pachakuti,"* a time of reconciliation, reunification, and healing of the land and its peoples. The old ways are what unite us. Continuing to shut out our Spirit will be our demise; opening up our own floodgates is how we will begin a new era. A golden age for humanity can happen, as it has already been written.

As Oglala Lakota Medicine Man and Warrior Heȟáka Sápa, Black Elk, so beautifully described in *Black Elk Speaks*, "I saw more than I can tell and understood more than I saw, for I was seeing in a sacred manner the shapes of all things in the Spirit and the shape of all shapes as they must all live together as one being."

Here's the thing about prophecies, we have to account for free will. So the prophecy speaks only to the *potential* of a vision. It is up to humanity to activate this potential and to ensure that a new consciousness is allowed to rise. It's up to each of us to make the room and reconnect. As we move farther into The Garden, we notice something new.

Lust for Light

"What shall I take with me? Will I let nothing behind me over the earth? How shall my heart act? Is it that we come in vain to live, to sprout over the earth? Let us leave at least flowers, let us leave at least songs."
—NEZAHUALCÓYOTL

As we make our way to The Reflecting Pool, we move through the rock formation where we notice something shiny. A sign with a poem has appeared on the side of the rock where we did our grounding. Let's honor the ritual we did when we

started in The Garden. The one where we reconnected to Nature. The one right in the circle of cedars where we plugged back into the *real* power grid. Remember it now and let's try doing it again with our transfiguration practice.

Move toward the circle of cedars and stand on the solid foundation of the ground that has anchored them. The ground that anchors us. Let your vessel vibrate with the Earth. Imagine the sun is creating beautiful new growth inside of our hearts. Focus on expanding that love light outward from our heart space. Let it dance with the leaves, let it hover with the dragonflies. Let it rise and touch the clouds. Feel the depth of the roots and the strength of the trees. The tall ones. The soil beneath our feet, the stones lining the path under the archway. This is part of remembering, realizing that for the majority of our lives most of us have just touched the surface, we've barely begun to track all the magic and power we have access to. Imagine what that is going to look like?

A world, a human collective that has actually woken up to the magic and remembered. It is Eden, without The Uninvited. It is us in perfect form. Light beings for the win.

If we *are* light, it's our job to stay light. Meaning, being in our Spirit, but also keeping our hearts light. Treading lightly. Doing light work. As we move out of the circle of cedars, we see the path of stones leading to the stone circle. We follow the stones like breadcrumbs.

In the *Book of Emerging into the Light*, the heart carries the vibrations and imprints from our existence, recording all the good and bad deeds of a person's life. It was seen as the center of emotions and memory and was said to help reveal a person's true character, even after death. The recording device of our human vessel. The heart really is the driving force of our bodies, and probably why we tend to point to it when we point to ourselves.

The Ancient Egyptians felt that the heart could not lie. It was this belief that had them leave the heart in the body during the mummification process. In Spell 30 of the *Book of Emerging Forth into the Light*, it provides instructions for making a heart scarab. The process of mummification included putting a scarab in between the wrappings to further protect the dead during their journey. Closing the gates *and* leaving an amulet. The sheer volume of these amulets recovered in Egypt helps confirm the significance of the heart, both in life and in death. Upon death It was believed the heart could travel with the soul to *The Duat* (the realm of the dead ruled by Osiris). It was on this journey from death to the underworld that the human had the accompaniment of Anubis to The Hall of Ma'at. The goddess Ma'at personifies order, truth, and justice and presides over The Hall of Mirrors. *Surprise!*

Wouldn't that be nice if that's who gets to decide our fate, a reasonable lady who enjoys ostrich feathers? That the way we acted in the world and the way we acted in our Spiritual practice lined up with the principles of Ma'at, and that any disturbance in cosmic harmony could have consequences, not just for the individual, but for the community through which we were all connected? So, if it's our job to keep our hearts light, we want to keep things moving because we don't want it to be heavy. This is where I tell you that we already know Ma'at's husband. We met him in The Library.

Upon arriving into the Duat, the soul of the dead showed up for the ceremony outlined in Spell 125 in the Egyptian *Book of Emerging Forth into the Light* known as *the weighing of the heart*. The ceremony was enacted to determine the fate of the soul. The heart was said to give evidence for, or against, its owner, and was then weighed on the scales of justice against the feather of Ma'at. The spell even appeals to the heart not to weigh down the balance or testify against the deceased. If the heart was successfully balanced with the feather, the soul was presented to Osiris and granted access to the *Field of Reeds*, an eternal afterlife in the heavens. The light. After judgment, Thoth, always the scribe (*and helpful husband*), writes down the name of the soul in the book of life. You already know Source keeps good records.

If the heart was heavier than the feather of Ma'at, and the deceased was weighted with sin, it would be immediately consumed by the goddess Ammit. Yes, I know we're processing that in Egyptian mythology, the judgments are handed down by the *women*.

Ammit is a badass mix between a crocodile, hippo, and a lion designed for consumption. The soul would be destroyed forever. No reincarnation, no resurrection. Just destruction, transmutation, and then purification of that energy back to the light, back to Spirit. Ra.

The ancient Egyptians had a deep conviction of an underlying holiness and unity within the Universe. The belief was that cosmic harmony was achieved by practicing both a strong public *and* Spiritual life. Any disturbance in cosmic harmony could have consequences for the individual as well as the community. The idea of doing unto others is much, much older than we've been told. The concept of judgment after life appears in most holy texts so we have to assume there's got to be some truth to it if all these prophets and seers wrote it down (so many times in so many ways and in so many languages) for us. All cautionary tales.

So many Spiritual practices and teachers have tried to help us understand that what we do and how we live in this reality affects the next one.

Whether or not we believe in this description of what may come when we transition, I will tell you what I know from my own practice. Out of all the survivors I have worked with who have been harmed by predators and real evil, when those who commit crimes against children leave the planet, when those beings pass, there doesn't seem to be anything left. Especially when testimony of their crimes has been given to Spirit. They don't get to come back. The Universe takes care of it. Most of the survivors I work with who've had their abusers leave the planet also report that they stop having their abusers in their nightmares. The imprint is gone; that's a side effect of energy work and their total destruction by Source. Again, it might take some time, but Source always has perfect aim. Donald Trump's indictment was a prime example of universal justice's divine timing—and what felt like one hell of a big wink from Source. A man who has been labeled as evil by so many was actually indicted during Holy Week. Not too shabby, Spirit.

Regardless of what you want to call him, Trump is clearly not someone who follows the golden rule (Gold maybe, rules definitely not). And to add to it, as one of the most well-known members of The Uninvited, he was taken down by a case centered around a woman who is both a Remarkable and a witch. The Universe has a sense of order *and* a sense of humor. For someone who likes to abuse the term *witch hunt*, perhaps he didn't realize that this time, the witches were leading the charge.

Our Own Medicine

There are too many people getting hurt and too many of the people responsible still being free to hurt others. We all know how long it took for Harvey Weinstein, R. Kelly, Bill Cosby, Jeffrey Epstein, and Donald Trump to be labeled predators. Some are *still* debating it. We also all know how many people are still arguing about it. Predators have a very distinct imprint, that's what this should show us. Not all predators show up in a van with darkened windows. Some of them do, but most of them are hiding in plain sight.

We can leave no stone unturned and nowhere for them to run. In the early days of humanity, when tribes had councils and we lived in community, there were ways to hold these kinds of people accountable. Elders and wisdom-keepers knew the ways. Perpetrators of this kind of violence would be brought to council and given a chance to defend their actions. The women of the community would typically be asked to vote on whether they believed the person to be responsible for the accusations. If they were deemed responsible, the perpetrator would be forced to have their hair cut off by one of the women in council. The perpetrator would then be ejected from the community. Cutting the hair was a way to identify those who hurt people in other communities. It was a sign for those who would encounter the person that they were not safe. The length of time the hair took to grow ensured the person couldn't hide their status and would ideally be rejected by society.

As we light up the world we will see less and less of these kinds of human beings in the world. We can shine our collective light into every corner of the web. We can light up all the segments to bring back the magic. All we ever had to do was ask. All we ever had to do was remember.

As we center in this, we begin to walk back toward the stone circle as we near The Reflecting Pool. We stop among the stones. Before we head on, let's each choose a stone. As we hold it, we can think back to all the struggles and challenges of not only ourselves but our ancestors. We can imagine that we are honoring them and leaving them behind in this stone. When you're ready, imagine

tossing them over our shoulders. As we do, we set the intention: *May the hardest times be at our backs.*

This is an inherent part of the challenge as human beings living on the planet (especially today, because jerks). It's that we have to learn how to move these heavy things through our beings without letting them sit on our heart. We have to learn how to keep our hearts light and how to let our emotions move through our vessels. Feelings like anger, fear, pain, grief, or even jealousy are heavy, and these things can weigh down our hearts if we hold on to them. If we don't process them. Loss, grief, and pain aren't as heavy or dark when you have the light on inside of you. If we don't actively work to keep our energy moving, our hearts get heavy, we get stuck, and eventually we can get sick, or out of alignment.

We can either allow these feelings to move through our beings or we can have them set up shop in our hearts. This is how we heal this state that we all seem to have found ourselves in. We have to remember, and we have to pass it on. We have to tell the others that *the water's fine.* We need to pass the current itself, so that everyone is getting the same message from the same source. This current that runs through us all, that lives inside of us that have been awakened by remembering. The current is growing. Just like the seedlings.

As part of honoring our own journeys here—the adventure we've taken through The Temple—we're going to choose a place in the circle to plant our seedling; yes, the one you almost forgot you'd been carrying because we were talking about some big existential stuff. As we arrive at the circle, it doesn't seem to be much of a circle. . . . *Was it always more of a heart?*

Perfect for planting.

Once you've found a place for your seed in The Garden, try to imagine infusing it with your light, your vibration. You may want to transfigure over it. Do whatever little practices you've been developing along the way. You're going to imprint this little seedling with your special brand of magic. You're going to plant it. You can come back to The Garden whenever you like and visit it and track its progress to help yourself remember to nurture your own being. Give yourself plenty of light. Make sure you take time for food and water. Play some music, speak as gently and kindly to yourself as you would to a growing seed. Yelling at seeds doesn't make them grow.

It won't help you either. You may want to name your little seedling, or you may want to give it a blessing before we continue through the hedges to The Reflecting Pool.

As we move through the hedges, we see The Reflecting Pool. The water is vibrating with a slight current, glistening in the light from the windows. It seems to be dancing. As we move toward it, we take a seat together again in the Gazebo to reflect.

Into the Wonder

Remembering what we have forgotten is an ongoing practice. In order to do it, we have to go through it and pick up our own pieces. It's good practice because who knows if we may be back here on Earth doing it again one day. This *"you only live once"* stuff is pretty debatable, but it doesn't mean we shouldn't *try* to make our dreams come true in *this* life.

Life is meant to be fun; we're meant to collect moments of beauty and connection. Don't worry, no one else is going to take your clues or surprises because they're only meant for you. Try talking to someone about a synchronicity they experienced, you will never feel the same excitement or magic as they do, no matter how awesome it is for you to witness. That's because it's *theirs*. It's *their* treasure. Just like they won't be able to feel the shivers you do when Spirit gives you a wink or a nod. Because it's *yours*. It's sacred and it gives you goosebumps because it's between you and Source. Just like on the cover of this book. It's you. It was always you.

You are the keyhole, the key, and the door.

When we have the light of the Universe moving through our vessels, it makes it much harder to get lost, or off track, as we find that the great spotlight coming from Source is so bright and immense that we will *know* the way. This light is so big and immersive that it has no trouble finding us or shining like this for us all. So, before we leave here, we're going to do one last visualization and transfiguration practice. This one will serve to help light the way to the place in the Universe where we're going to put those keys. We don't want to lose them again.

As we're sitting on the bench near The Reflecting Pool the vibration of the water begins to hum. Almost as if a tone is coming from it. *Ohm. Ohm. Ohm.* As the pool hums, the water begins to vibrate in patterns, circles inside of circles. It dances. As you look into it, you notice the sacred spiral. It's as if Source is painting over the surface of the water, gently and elegantly. As you look into the pool, you notice it's the web of life there. So many strands and threads. Whisps and points of light. This massive interconnected system of everything. In it, you will find the place where you will hang your keys. A place to park your vessel. This place in the light. You can imagine that you may also want to put a copy of this book there. You can imagine that everything you've learned so far, everything that you haven't learned so far, any homework you did or didn't do, you can just put it there. You may have more interaction with this place. The manual of *What We've Forgotten*. This is a private home for your magic, a sacred place where you can put your bread- crumbs, a place where your dear ones can find you in the Ocean of Consciousness one day long after you've gone home to the stars.

This is how we will remember everything for the next time. This is a place that you can imagine going when you need to remember what you're made of. This will be your safe space in the light. This is our inner landscape, our light body.

To end, I'd like to imagine sending back a little wave to yourself and the col- lective. A little light wave of love and light back to yourself and all of us at this moment in time.

As you do this little wave, this little current gently brings you back through the web of life. You're sitting back on the bench and looking over the surface of the water. As we ground this transfiguration and visualization practice, you may want to write down what you experienced and what you felt. What did you notice about this ritual? What did the space look like? You might want to draw it. You might make your own map. You may want to write down any colors or objects you may have seen. You may want to follow the breadcrumbs about what you saw and what the medicine means. We know that part of this system is that everything carries meaning. What Easter eggs might you find in your experience as you hang up your keys?

Walking Each Other Home

This last practice is one that I know works both in this reality and the next. I have had the honor of working with people who are leaving the planet. I had reminded my Grandmother Gee how to journey and not long after my mum felt something was coming. She was moved to go stay overnight with Gee, and it was that night that Gee collapsed. She went to the hospital and never went back to her apartment.

As she declined, she was moved to palliative care. She was no longer able to speak but I knew she could still hear me. I started speaking to her consciousness. I told her we were working on breaking her out of the hospital, that if she wanted to hold on to leave from a hospice she could, or that she could go when she was ready. It was her choice. We were okay. We loved her, and we were ready if she was. We didn't want her to be in any pain; we wanted her to be at peace. The next day when I woke up, I knew it was the day. I got word from my mum that the nurses felt she would pass that day. As I drove to the hospital in the car, I could already hear Gee in my head. *Three o'clock,* she said. It was about 1:00 p.m. by then. I knew she was telling me what time she would transition.

When I arrived at the hospital and entered the room where my grandmother was, I told my mum she would be here until three o'clock, and that we should take the time with her, maybe call a chaplain. My mom made a call for the chaplain, and we all talked about my grandmother as she seemed to hang between the veils. Between life and death. As above and so below. I held her hand, her breathing was shallow. Not long after, the hospital chaplain arrived. If there's one thing I can say about my grandmother's Spiritual practice, it's that she liked the King James version of the Bible. Not *any* other version. As we talked with the female chaplain (*which Gee would have loved*), we spoke of her favorite verses. As the chaplain started reading, I felt It, our heads had been bowed but I looked up at my mum. We locked eyes. In this holy moment, we were both trying not to laugh. It was *not* the King James version being read.

We were both hearing my Gee, "This is *not* the King James version."

Though tears were streaming down my face, inside I was smiling at the gift of this work, the magic of this life. As my mum and I held my grandmother's hands, my very first best friend on the planet, on opposite sides of the bed, I could feel we were getting close to her soul breaking free.

I stood up and muttered something about going to get a blanket. We already messed up the version of the Psalm, so I at least wanted to make sure her body was warm. I wanted to make sure she would go from one warm consciousness to another.

As I came back with the warm blanket, I began to lay it over my Gee. And as clear as day I heard it, *"What is this? . . . The shroud of Turin?"*

I looked at my mum, her eyes worn from crying for days, and she looked at me, not sure what to make of the expression on my face. Through tears, I started to laugh as I repeated what my grandmother had said. We both laughed through tears. The ugly cry of grief. I know about the shroud of Turin *because* of my grandmother. She had books about it, printouts, newspaper clippings. My grandmother had a special relationship with Jesus. She saved clippings as if he were family and she were making a scrapbook. She loved everything to do with him. So, through this mention of this relic of his life on Earth, she had also predicted what was next. She was leaving. The Shroud, also known as the Holy Shroud, is a strip of linen cloth bearing the negative image of a man who was crucified. It has been rumored this was the cloth Jesus of Nazareth was wrapped in after his crucifixion. My grandmother, laying there on her death bed, unable to speak and seemingly unconscious was making *jokes*. She was my grandmother after all.

I tucked the fresh blanket over my grandmother's tiny vessel as I could already feel her beginning to float around the room.

It was just before three o'clock as Gee's breathing grew less frequent, shallower. Then it came, the voice.

Help her pass.

It was *Him*. My Mom said it out loud as I heard it. I nodded.

We both took Gee's hands again from either side of the bed and looked at each other.

"How do you want to do this?" my mum asked as if we were trying to parallel park a car or put a trailer on a truck. My grandmother took a deep, rattling breath, which in any other circumstance would be comedic, as if to say, *"Hurry up."*

"Let's just take her to Him," I said without mentioning His name. There was only one guy my grandmother would want to see first. Jesus (then my grandfather). Her other longtime crush Harry Belafonte was still singing "Day-O" on planet Earth.

My mum and I both closed our eyes.

Jesus, Take the Wheel

My grandmother was still breathing but infrequently. I closed my eyes, my mum was already there, on a journey without a drum, holding on to my grandmother's hand and Spirit. I was holding one side of her being and my mum was holding the other. I was calling him, as I had done *so many* times in my own life. I was vibrating at the highest version of myself as I always do when I visit him, or any other ascended master. I felt him then, as I had so many times before when I had asked for comfort, or to help me move into a state of forgiveness about my trauma, who better to teach, to guide through the act of forgiveness, than the big JC? Now here I was handing my grandmother over to him.

I always feel him before I see him, and then, there he was, like a light I cannot explain. A force so magnificent and bright, total, complete, unconditional love. As I felt him, I felt her. I felt my grandmother's awe, her wonder hanging in space, as we lifted her out of her body and toward him. Hanging between worlds, she was looking back at us as both in total wonder and amazement, as my mum and I motioned for her to go. That it was okay. I felt her joy. I felt her love. Then I felt her oneness with him. I opened my eyes, and I looked down at my grandmother. She was gone.

For the second time in my life, I'd walked a best friend into Spirit.

It hadn't been five years since we lost Gee that I got a call from my bonus sister Katy. It wasn't many months after Jennifer had called me about the broken statue of Sekhmet. When Katy called me that day, I had been on the phone with my mum. She told me to take the call, so I clicked over to the other line, and as Katy and I started talking, I saw my mum's text pop up on my phone, always the psychic.

"It's Jennifer."

And it was. I got a few minutes to process what might be coming before Katy told me the terrible news. Jennifer had fallen ill. Terminal cancer. It was everywhere. My grief would wait. I went into shock and then into service. *Did I date her son because I was meant to be of service through this? Not just me but my mum too?* My mum had trained as a death doula not long before. I thought about Jennifer's experience with Sekhmet in Egypt. The gifts she'd brought me from Egypt were all part of the story. I held pieces of the pyramid in my hands as I rode the tsunami.

The Lioness, the Witch, and the Whole Globe

Jennifer was someone you would consider to be Spiritually gifted. She was strong and she was a survivor and she was full of light. It wasn't her first war with this illness, but this time, it was ravaging her. She wasn't afraid but she was exhausted, and the pain was taking over *everything*. As much as I wished we could have stopped it, as much as I'd like to tell a story of a miracle that she survived, she chose the date of her transition through medically assisted end of life.

2/2/2022 at 2 p.m.

Two is the number of inner peace, harmony, *and* divine purpose.

Before her transition, I reminded her how to hang her keys, and then how to help her find them when she got home through the veil of life. It was the last ceremony we did together and the last time I saw her in her body. As I prepared for it, I'd held the smooth stones from the pyramids she brought me from Giza. The amulet of Sekhmet on my lap and the papyrus framed behind me. I was surrounded in protection and magic of the place I hadn't yet been, but which had been with me through it all. Before the last session with Jennifer, I wanted to get some earthly housekeeping out of the way. I had offered to bring some of her ashes back to Egypt. We'd talked about going together, this just wasn't what either of us had expected. I wanted to make sure I had the details for this important part of the quest. This woman who opened her heart to me when her son brought me home, just I was now helping to bring her home.

Sekhmet, who had delivered me safely through so many initiations, flashed in my consciousness. I was to bring a part of Jennifer back to her in Egypt. Before the end of that last session together I asked her if she'd like to meet the next week in Spirit at the same time and same place to check in after she transitioned. Without missing a beat, she said *"Yes."*

We confirmed exactly where we'd meet but both of us already knew exactly where we were going. She flashed it in her consciousness, and I flashed it back. Her soul had begun the transition. I put the non-ordinary reality appointment in my very ordinary reality calendar. I knew I would be doing it from the depth of my grief, the very next week. When they say what a difference a week makes, this is probably what they meant. When I went into the ceremony the next week for Jennifer, I did something that we hadn't planned on. I brought Katy. Katy had done *What We've Forgotten* as a retreat a month before her mum left the planet, and part of that felt as if Jennifer had set us up. The ceremony wasn't just to check in with Jennifer's Spirit. It was to check in with her daughter's.

As I started the ceremony, the air changed, and I could feel her energy around me. I could feel Jennifer's excitement about Katy being a surprise guest. As I started to rattle and move between worlds, I shared with Katy what I was seeing. I could see Jennifer there, outlined in white light, her hair more of a halo than ever, transfigured among the columns of Karnak.

"We're at Karnak," I said to Katy as I led us toward her mum.

I could feel the impact of energies as Jennifer felt Katy's presence. Surprise and delight. Jennifer too has brought a guest. She stood small beside the towering Sekhmet. Jennifer grinned. It was hard to grieve because she was *with* the ultimate warrior healer. Remarkable. As I checked in with Jennifer's Spirit, I could feel Katy too. In the midst of such grief, a bond of love was unbroken across dimensions. When I closed the ceremony and checked in with Katy, I asked if she could still feel her mum. She did.

We'd all been feeling her after she transitioned. There were waves of change and love. As if she were up there settling old loose ends for us all, as if opening floodgates of wonder, and as a result, the waters around us all became extra clear. I joked that she was already at the table with the powers that be negotiating. I told her before she passed that I could see her trying to bring the whole illness to divine council to obliterate it from humanity. I had no doubts that she was working on it. I could feel it. I think the world will feel it soon too. She was a successful business-woman, and I had no doubts she'd been up there making her case and presenting evidence at the tables of divinity. We all felt that way. If anyone was going to make it their mission, it would be her.

Less than twelve months after her transition, in the fall of 2022, the news reported that they had found a viable vaccine for cancer. The seemingly positive side effect of so much investment in pharmaceuticals from COVID-19 brought progress for treatment of the disease that took Jennifer. She walked a totally organic path, and yet, she got her COVID vaccination to receive treatment for the cancer. The irony of the vaccine felt like a wink from her through the veil.

If This Is It, Please Let Me Know

Jennifer was already busy poking us, sending synchronicities, signs, and omens, and reminding us that love doesn't die. The energy was palpable and still is. When we feel loved ones like this, it doesn't mean they are having trouble transitioning, sometimes they're just not finished watching the show. We can imagine them as if they're just watching through a window from their dimension. They're sending communications in signs and symbols, moving into the language of Spirit as they continue to transform in the stars. I also felt her commenting on *everything* just like a bonus mum should.

Oh Amy, I could hear her voice in my consciousness. The familiar laugh. She was already delivering tremendous connection. In life, she was a born networker, a fast friend, and a community hub, so in Spirit, she was already dropping breadcrumbs like wildfire.

My mum had been looking to move for years and suddenly a perfect place opened up a few blocks from Katy in her small town. And as if to make sure we were all clear, to get to my mum's new place, you had to literally turn onto a street with the same name as the street of the house I bought with Jennifer's son fifteen years before. Jennifer was making sure *I knew* I would always be connected to that street. She knew what a nostalgic noodle I was, she was too. We both held on to things, cards, letters, journals, moment collectors. Now she was making sure we were picking up every breadcrumb she put down. Katy was also having amazing experiences, including her car radio being turned up on her way into the city on an annual industry weekend event known for Jennifer as quite a party. The same industry organization who posthumously named her a Hall of Famer. There's no better term for her, I see her as a Hall of Famer on how to live. She always loved to talk about frequency and vibration. *Now she was one.* She was conducting a symphony of synchronicity through dimensions—and turning up the music as she did it. That was her medicine. *Jennifer was fun.*

That doesn't end just because you leave your body.

People may transition but their energy goes on, and typically the breadcrumbs and synchronicities they give us from other dimensions are still imprinted and recognizable as being *inherently them*. People showing up in Spirit doesn't typically mean they're not at peace, it means, *they love us.*

I see so many clients who have lost loved ones who see me just to confirm that the things they are experiencing are really happening. A lot of times my work as a medium, or witch, is to be a fair and neutral witness, whether it's someone who is departed, someone in a coma, or with a brain injury that leaves them unable to communicate in the traditional sense, they are still there. Consciousness doesn't need the brain. It needs the soul and the heart. All it needs is light.

I'd thought my gift from Jennifer was this book being published, since she was so excited about it, but it was a done deal before she left. Like most mums (*bonus or not*), she wanted me to meet my person, and would ask about my love life. Within a few weeks of her passing, *my consort* knocked on the window of my consciousness; it felt as if she'd had something to do with the timing. True love found me and it's a love for the ages. I could feel her beaming through dimensions at us, and she was there when we decided to make it official (so were Erin and my Gee).

But Jennifer still wasn't *quite* done. By late summer I started to feel a nudge from her, a twinkle in her (now starry) eyes every time I visited my mum and Katy in their small town. I'd been in the same place in Toronto for sixteen years in the same house I bought with her son. I'd healed myself there and I'd never intended to move, but if I knew one thing about Sekhmet, she *loves* change. And it was crystal clear she was on this journey too. As the due date for this manuscript neared, I found myself in the midst of my own adventure. Somehow, I'd followed the breadcrumbs she was dropping to find my dream home, a sanctuary of healing.

"This is it!" I yelled out to my mum for the first of dozens of times during our first visit. And this particular scavenger hunt was really picking up. I ran down to the garden surrounded by cedars as my mum yelled after me, "Amy! *Wait for the real estate agent!*"

But I was finding one clue after the other. I was *inside* synchronicity; it was as if time had stopped. *Maybe I was traveling at the speed of light?*

As I finally made it to the front door, I was faced with a *lion's* head knocker. As I walked into the living room, I saw a sculpture of a *dancing bear* on the mantle, a symbol of my teacher, Daniel. My mum and I caught eyes as I looked at the wall across from where she stood. There was a painting of a Holstein dairy cow looking over a fence.

"Number 20," I shrieked to my mum, who, like many people close to me, is wide-eyed about just how much synchronicity follows me (or do I follow it?).

"This is it," I said again.

And so it was. A week later, it was mine.

The Hathor healing years, dedicated to number 20, have indeed begun.

Within a few weeks of moving in, Raccoon showed up again. This time, new crossroads, new trade. I was walking near the circle of cedars with my mum (*because witnesses*). This time, a skull lay at my feet. I already knew. Raccoon. It may have been six years later but it perfectly fit the lower jaw on my headdress. Even my osteologist bone expert friend said "It shouldn't be, but it is." So it is.

Into the Wonder

As we stand to leave The Reflecting Pool, this time, we both reach in to touch it. As we do, it's almost as if we're soaking it up through our fingers, this elixir from this ancient place, sustenance of Source. *Holy water.*

This is the story of your remembering, but also, the story of mine. Because it's also how I found this place. This Temple. It's how we find each other and I'm so glad we made it. Typically, this is the spot where I sing a whole song, and people get uncomfortable, but you'll just have to use your mind's eye to imagine that one.

To leave The Temple, we can exit back through the doors and travel back through time like we did when we got here, or we can just lean in and take the plunge into The Reflecting Pool and let it take us back to our life through the Ocean of Consciousness.

We both lean forward, right before we jump in with both feet, we whisper: *"Remember me."*

CONCLUSION

No matter how much work I do with Spirit, or in Spirit, or how many times it shows up for me, it never loses the magic. It never loses the full-body goosebumps from feeling like Source whispered in my ear. I still feel the excitement, surprise, and delight in ceremonies with clients. As much as I've learned, as much as I've experienced and seen (*talk about views!*), as much room as I've made, it still remains a sacred miracle to me. It is *still* a mystery.

What other secrets and mysteries are contained in these walls? We have only scratched the surface. Please come back when you're ready for another adventure, maintenance, or just to look a little deeper. Witches, alchemists, medicine people, and wisdom keepers do love their symbols and codes!

Where the collective goes from here is up to us now. We can and will prevail over egotism and narrow-mindedness. We *can* choose to work together as a collective again, or we can continue to sow seeds of division, but they will grow like walls between us. We aren't supposed to be perfect in human form, if it was about perfection we'd never have needed to be born, our souls were perfect before they got here. It's about our intention, it's about our effort, our effect. Our intention *is* the medicine. It's about our journeys both as above and so below. We can choose a future where we grow together with ease and grace, and where we begin to learn more secrets of the Universe *from* the Universe itself. Where we get out of our bullshit and get into our star stuff. Enlightenment, or Transcendence, isn't a destination. Ascension is just the beginning of the journey. Our intention is what matters most, we can choose to hold it so close that it only lights our lives, or we can hold it up high so that others can see it.

How much light can we bring the collective? How much magic can we return? If we used all of the intelligence available to us, what would we know? What might we remember?

When we remember who we really are, and what we're made of, we become who we are meant to be. You're just getting started, the world needs you. It's a part of why you're here. I can't wait to hear about your scavenger hunts. Enjoy all the prizes and treasures you collect along the way, and make sure to share. You've already begun to remember. How fast we move to the phase where we bring the tools to practice for the collective is up to each of us. It's not a race. It's not a contest. It is a quest of wonder—and it is the biggest gift we could ever have received.

When we reunite and reconnect the circle, we will and can soar on the winds of our own breath. You have the keys now. It's time to choose *your own* adventure, and then it's time to find the others.

ACKNOWLEDGMENTS

To Spirit, Source, Artist #1, Creator, the Tao, the Neteru, The Temple of Wonder, and all of the wisdom keepers walking the planet and beyond. I thank you for the privilege of remembering and hope I've done you proud. May we all remember the magic we have forgotten. Thank you to my helpers and all the prophets and ascended masters who serve in perfect love and perfect trust. To the wisdom keepers and shamanic ancestors, I humbly share and offer my deepest gratitude and service. Without the protection of the knowledge, this book would not exist.

My consort, my creator companion. My magic man. Thank you for the soundtrack, the omens, the gifts, and surprises. Thank you for walking me through the Temple, room by room, so very patiently. For being everything, everywhere, all at once. Thank you for fanning my flame and supporting me in every way and in every dimension. I'm so glad I'm yours, my hero, my best friend, my world without end.

My mother Heather, my grandmother Jean, my great-grandmother Margaret. I love you. My very own triple goddesses. Thank you for making me a powerful creatrix, encouraging my magic, my jokes, my shows, my healing, and my visions. Mum, thank you for your support, your acceptance, and most of all, your love and strength. To my grandfather Jack Oke who flew in the Lancaster during WWII to push out the fascist Uninvited. To Leroy and John, I hope the publishing of this work is felt by you writers. I hold your memoirs close. Thank you for always valuing the word and its power.

To all of my ancestors and relations. I hope I have done you proud. May the line be clear and full of light and magic through all time.

To Erin Muckle, my sister. My balance. My scales of justice. Thank you for showing me how to live. This book would never have been without you, and my mediumship would never have been as strong without your guidance and translation. I love you through space and time forever. Thank you Inkeri for your permission to include Erin, and thank you Kellan for all the snake stuff and encouragement.

To Daniel Leonard for being my brother, teacher, cheerleader, and friend. I would not be standing where I am without your guidance, dignity, grace, elegance, heart, and example. Thank you for mentoring me through this adventure, reminding me of what I carry, and for the medicine you bring to the world. Thank you for allowing me the honor of being your student and for helping me out of the Trauma Shed. I love you. Sorry about all the snakes.

To my animal companions and familiars. Thank you for the honor of caring for you. Thank you for teaching me and choosing me across the world and across time.

To my bonus mum, Jennifer Grant, for allowing me to share such an amazing scavenger hunt, and for helping me see the light I carried long before I could name it. Your remarkable Spirit will never be forgotten. To my bonus sister Katy Groves, thank you for allowing me to witness your interdimensional love and for welcoming me into your heart.

To Sandra Ingerman, for reading an early version and asking the questions that helped lead me here. Thank you for helping me to remember and for the absolute wonder, joy, and light you bring to the world with your immense Spirit. Your work and medicine for the Earth are testaments to the kind of service we can all aspire to.

To Paul Reubens, thank you for your friendship, your magic, and for inspiring me to know that I could have a big adventure too. My bonus Dad, the timing of your transition propels me forward and you remain a gift in my life.

To my friend and soul sister Kristen McGuiness. I could never have imagined that I'd ever meet anyone as committed to creating moments of connection and change in the worlds we inhabit (hot tub worlds). Thank you for being such a fiercely compassionate and fearless leader, thank you for shepherding this book into the place where it came to live, and thank you for believing in the work so much that you wanted to give it a home at Rise, and with you. I am grateful for all 20,000 years of experience you brought to this process. I'm also grateful for you as a witness to the absolutely astounding magic that came with this book. Thanks to Tere, Ella, and Dylan for making sure this process wasn't too business-y. Things are less stressful when there's pizza, and kids.

To my family of friends and inspirations: Chanda Chevannes, Lee Harris, Jason Ford, Aimée Tobolka, Chris Cornell, Harmony Lynds Muckle, Charlene Dinger, Nada Yousif, Ben Ferguson, Naomi Nichols, Teri Walls Fiore, Bryan Walls, Ken "Pepper" Macy, Krista Muir, Allison Berry, Jessica Westhead, Elisha Seaton, Heidi Kidd, Kritty Uranowski, Michelle Van Manen, Deborah Laforet, Deborah Glassberg, Peter Roth and the Geologic Family, Rusty Blazenhoff, Serena Oakley, Pastel Supernova, Opal Gamble, Lisa Labute, Eric San/Kid Koala, Tony Parisi, Erik Muckle, Jen Pastiloff, Heather Matarazzo, Jumpin' Jack Frost, Chuck D, Shaun Hatton, Ryan M. Cohn & Regina M. Rossi, Leonard Fong, Katerina Lamere, Karly Richter, Elaine Li, Gloria Ui Young Kim, Rob & Lisa MacDonald, Madison Harview, Roselby Rodriguez, Nick Groves, Spencer Wilson Wynne, Maggie Boxey, Ashtyn Ford, Maranda Bell, The Gatehouse, Arthur Lockhart, Gabriele Dinardo, Dr. Donna Akman, Michael M. Hughes, Cindy Gallop, Brittany Chung Campbell, the Grooms, the Macorittis, the Muckles, the Wilsons, the Custodios, RZA, Tina Turner, Eddie Vedder, Public Enemy, Soundgarden, Vinyl Syndicate, and all of the next generation of magicians in my life: Adelaid, Austin, Chelsi, Chris, Dylan, Elijah, Ella, Fiona, Grace, Gursaacha, Henry, Isaac, Kayla, Kellan, Liam, Maya, Neely, Nicky, Phoebe, Rebekah Joy, Tai, Willa, and Zion.

Thank you to my fellow survivors, the Remarkables. The founding members and all of those who are in the process of reclaiming your power. You've found the others, and we're bringing the band back together—globally. It's our time. Keep coming forward, keep speaking up, keep sharing your stories. The more light we bring, the less places they have to hide. I love you and I'm listening.

To my healing community and clients. Thank you for the way you show up not only in sessions and ceremonies but in the world.

To my team of business affairs magicians: Rick Krozonouski, Warren Sheffer, Heather Whitten, Fred Guzzi, and David Whitten, thank you for your guidance and counsel.

Thank you to Nic Taylor at Thunderwing for bringing the mystery and magic we needed to the artwork and collaboration. I am so grateful it was your medicine in these pages.

To the What We've Forgotten community, all the alumni, you are the people who are helping to weave the light of change back through the fabric of our existence. My snake family. My Medicine Circle family, My Lunch Inc. community, Rise Books community, the editors, copyeditors, and production team at Neuwirth.

To all of the witnesses and magicians who appear in this book. Thank you for your willingness to share your stories, magic, creativity, and wonder.

In love, gratitude, power, and light,
Amy

BIBLIOGRAPHY

Ainsworth, Thomas. "Form vs. Matter," *The Stanford Encyclopedia of Philosophy*. Edward N. Zalta (ed.), 2020. https://plato.stanford.edu/archives/sum2020/entries/form-matter/.

Anderson, Micheline R. *The Spiritual Heart*. Columbia University, 2020.

Andrews, Ted. *Animal Speak: The Spiritual & Magical Powers of Creatures Great and Small*. Llewellyn Publications, 2002.

Ayangat. "Rooted Messages." (n.d.). Rooted Messages YouTube channel. Retrieved July 20, 2022. https://rootedmessages.com/ayangat/, https://www.facebook.com/watch/?v=2212307645587157, https://www.youtube.com/@rootedmessages3459.

Apostol, Virgil Mayor. *Way of the Ancient Healer: Sacred Teachings from the Philippine Ancestral Traditions*. North Atlantic Books, 2010.

Avicenna, et al. *Liber medicinalis*. 1400.

Baclawski, Kenneth. *The Observer Effect*. NorthEastern University, Boston, 2018.

Barks, Coleman. *The Essential Rumi: A Poetry Anthology*. HarperOne, 2004.

Betro, Maria C. *Hieroglyphics: The Writings of Ancient Egypt*. Abbeville Publishing Group 1996.

Beverley, J. A. *Holy Laughter and the Toronto Blessing: An Investigative Report*. Zondervan, 2015.

Baragwanath, Nicholas. *The Solfeggio Tradition*. Oxford University Press, 2020.

Black Elk. *Black Elk Speaks: Being the Life Story of a Holy Man of the Oglala Sioux*. Excelsior Editions, State University Press, 2008.

Brînzeu, Pia. "Hidden Esotericism: Postmodern Witches and the Cauldron of Intertextuality." *European Journal of English Studies*, 2011.

Buckley, R. P. *The Night Journey and Ascension in Islam: The Reception of Religious Narrative in Sunni, Shi'i and Western Culture*. (Library of Middle East History), I.B. Tauris, 2012.

Bull, Christian H. *The Tradition of Hermes Trismegistus: The Egyptian Priestly Figure as a Teacher of Hellenized Wisdom.* Leiden, 2018.

Casta, Ange. "Un Certain Regards." Interview by Enrico Fulchignoni with Amadou Hampâté Bâ, 1969.

Chia, Mantak, North Kris Deva. *Taoist Shaman: Practices from the Wheel of Life.* Destiny Books, 2011.

Chittick, William. "Ibn 'Arabî." *The Stanford Encyclopedia of Philosophy.* 2020.

Choim, Charles Q. "Humans glow in visible light. The human body literally glows, emitting a visible light in extremely small quantities at levels that rise and fall with the day, scientists reveal." NBC News, 2009. https://www.nbcnews.com/id/wbna32090918.

Christianto, Victor, Kasan Susilo, and Florentin Smarandache. *Roles of Cymatics & Sound Therapy in Spirituality & Consciousness.* University of New Mexico, 2020.

Constable, George. *Mysteries of the Unknown: Secrets of the Alchemists.* Time Life, 1988.

Critchlow, Keith. *Islamic Patterns: An Analytical and Cosmological Approach.* Bear & Co., 1999.

Curl, John. *Ancient American Poets: The Flower Songs of Nezahualcoyotl.* Bilingual Press, 2005.

Donner, Richard, and Dave Grusin. *The Goonies.* Film. Amblin, Warner Bros. 1985.

Echols, Damien. *Life after Death.* Plume, 2013.

Einstein, A., B. Podolsky, and N. Rosen. *Can Quantum-Mechanical Description of Physical Reality Be Considered Complete?* Physical Review, 1935.

Eliade, Mircea; Willard Trask, (trans.). *Shamanism: Archaic Techniques of Ecstasy.* Princeton University Press, 2004 (originally published in 1951).

Ellis, Eugenia. *Ancient Mathematical Origins of Modern-Day Occult Practices.* Journal, 2007.

Emoto, Masuro. *The Hidden Messages in Water.* Atria Books, 2005.

Faulkner, Raymond O. (trans.); Eva von Dassow (ed.). *The Egyptian Book of the Dead, The Book of Going Forth by Day. The First Authentic Presentation of the Complete Papyrus of Ani.* Chronicle Books, 1994.

Galford, Christophe. *The Universe in Your Hand: A Journey Through Space, Time, and Beyond.* Flatiron Books, 2016.

Galileo, Galilei. *Il Saggiatore/The Assayer.* Opere, 1964.

Garner, Rob, ed. *James Webb Space Telescope Science.* National Aeronautics and Space Administration, August 3, 2017.

Gilbert, Elizabeth. *Big Magic: Creative Living beyond Fear.* Westminster, 2015.

Gingras B., G. Pohler, and W. T. Fitch. *Exploring Shamanic Journeying: Repetitive Drumming with Shamanic Instructions Induces Specific Subjective Experiences but no Larger Cortisol Decrease Than Instrumental Meditation Music.* National Library of Medicine, 2014.

Greene, Brian. *The Fabric of the Cosmos: Space, Time, and the Texture of Reality*. Vintage, 2004.

Grillo, Paul Jacques. *Form Function and Design*. Dover, 1975.

Grossman, Pam. *Waking the witch: Reflections on Women, Magic, and Power*. Gallery Books, 2019.

Haramein, Nassim. *Quantum Gravity and the Holographic Mass*. OSF Preprints, 2019.

Hawking, Steven. *A Brief History of Time. Updated & Expanded Edition*. Bantam, 1996.

Hoff, Benjamin. *The Tao of Pooh*. Penguin Books, 1983.

Hornung, Erik; D. Lorton (trans.). *The Ancient Egyptian books of the Afterlife*. Cornell University Press, 1999.

Hossenfelder, Sabine. "Maybe the Universe Thinks. Hear Me Out." Time.com, 2022. https://time.com/6208174/maybe-the-universe-thinks/.

Huffman, Carl. "Pythagoras." *The Stanford Encyclopedia of Philosophy*, 2018. https://plato.stanford
.edu/archives/win2018/entries/pythagoras/.

Hunt, Tam. "The Hippies Were Right: It's All about Vibrations, Man!" *Scientific American*, December 15, 2018. https://blogs.scientificamerican.com/observations/the-hippies-were
-right-its-all-about-vibrations-man/.

Ingerman, Sandra, and Hank Wesselman. *Awakening to the Spirit World: The Shamanic Path of Direct Revelation*. Sounds True, 2010.

Ingerman, Sandra. *Soul Retrieval: Mending the Fragmented Self*. Harper One, 2006.

Ingerman, Sandra. *Medicine for the Earth: How to Transform Personal and Environmental Toxins*. Harmony, 2014.

Jung, Carl; R. F. C. Hull (trans.). *Synchronicity: An Acausal Connecting Principle*. 2010.

Kauffman, George B. *The Transmutation of Silver into Gold*. Department of Chemistry, California State University, 1983.

Kaur, Valerie. *See No Stranger: A Memoir and Manifesto of Revolutionary Love*. One World, 2020.

Khait, Itzhak, Raz Sharon, Ran Perelman, Arjan Boonman, Yossi Yovel, and Lilach Hadany. *The Sounds of Plants—Plants Emit Remotely-Detectable Ultrasounds That Can Reveal Plant Stress*, 2018.

King James Bible. E-book edition. Project Gutenberg, 2011 (originally published in 1769).

Kobayashi, Masaki, Daisuke Kikuchi, and Hitoshi Okamura. *Imaging of Ultraweak Spontaneous Photon Emission from Human Body Displaying Diurnal Rhythm*. 2009.

Laozi, Mitchell Stephen. *Tao Te Ching*. Frances Lincoln Limited, 2009.

Lindon, Stanton J. *The Alchemy Reader: From Hermes Trismegistus to Isaac Newton*. Cambridge University Press.

Lindsay, Jack. *The Origins of Alchemy in Graeco-Roman Egypt.* Barnes and Noble, 1970.

Matson, John. "Fact or Fiction? Lead Can Be Turned into Gold." *Scientific American,* 2014.

Matt, Daniel C. *The Essential Kabbalah: The Heart of Jewish Mysticism.* Harper One, 2009.

Mendoza, Lily S. *Back from the Crocodile's Belly: Philippine Babaylan Studies and the Struggle for Indigenous Memory.* CreateSpace Independent Publishing Platform, 2013.

Merkel, Ingrid, and Allen G. Debus (eds.). *Hermeticism and the Renaissance: Intellectual History and the Occult in Early Modern Europe.* The Folger Shakespeare Library, 1988.

Milonni, Peter W. "The Casimir Effect: Physical Manifestations of Zero-Point Energy." *Physics Today,* 2003.

Morck, Nemo. *Connected: The Emergence of Global Consciousness by Roger D. Nelson.* Journal of Scientific Exploration. 2019.

National Aeronautics and Space Administration. James Webb Telescope News, 2022. https://webb.nasa.gov/content/webbLaunch/news.html.

Nelson, Roger. The Global Consciousness Project. *Explore,* 2006.

Newton, Isaac; William R. Newman (ed.). *The Chymistry of Isaac Newton.* 2010.

Newton, Isaac. *Newton's Principia: The Mathematical Principles of Natural Philosophy.* D. Adee, 1848.

Nono, Grace. *Babaylan Sing Back.* Southeast Asia Program Publications, 2021.

Perkins, John. *Eagle and the Condor: A Prophecy for Our Time.* Pachamama Alliance.

Perry, Bruce, and Oprah Winfrey. *What Happened to You? Conversations on Trauma, Resilience, and Healing* (unabridged). Macmillan Audio, 2021.

Pinch, Geraldine. *Egyptian Mythology: A Guide to Gods, Goddesses, and Traditions of Ancient Egypt.* Oxford University Press, 2002.

Pomar, Juan Bautista de, "Relación de Pomar," in *Poesía Nahuatl,* by Ángel María Garibay K. México, 1964.

Roberts, Alison M. *Hathor's Alchemy: The Ancient Egyptian Roots of the Hermetic Art.* Northgate Publishers, 2019.

Rossi, Corinna. *Architecture and Mathematics in Ancient Egypt.* Cambridge University Press, 2007.

Sagan, Carl. *Billions and Billions.* Ballantine Books, 1998.

Sagan, Carl. *Cosmos.* Ballantine Books, 2013.

Scalf, Foy (ed.). *Book of the Dead: Becoming a God in Ancient Egypt.* Oriental Institute, University of Chicago, 2017.

Shadyac, Tom. "*I Am.*" Documentary. Universal Pictures, 2010.

Strogatz, Steven. *Sync: How Order Emerges from Chaos in the Universe, Nature, and Daily Life.* Theia, 2003.

Tesla, Nikola. My Inventions. *Electrical Experimenter Magazine*, 1919.

Thoma, M. V., R. La Marca, R. Brönnimann, L. Finkel, U. Ehlert, and U. M. Nater. "The Effect of Music on the Human Stress Response." *PLoS One,* 2013. doi: 10.1371/journal .pone.0070156.

Three Initiates. *The Kybalion: A Study of the Hermetic Philosophy of Ancient Egypt and Greece.* The Yogi Publication Society, 1908.

Turner, Ben. "Quantum 'spooky action at a distance' lands scientists Nobel prize in physics." *Live Science,* 2022.

Van der Kolk, Bessel A. *The Body Keeps the Score: Brain, Mind, and Body in the Healing of Trauma.* Viking, 2014.

Vazza, F., and A. Feletti. "The Quantitative Comparison Between the Neuronal Network and the Cosmic Web." *Frontiers in Physics* vol. 8, 2020. https://www.frontiersin.org /articles/10.3389/fphy.2020.525731.

Warber, S. L., S. Ingerman, V. L. Moura, J. Wunder, A. Northrop, B. W. Gillespie, K. Durda, K. Smith, K. S. Rhodes, and M. Rubenfire. *Healing the Heart: A Randomized Pilot Study of a Spiritual Retreat for Depression in Acute Coronary Syndrome Patients.* Explore, 2011.

Winkelman, M. J. *Chinese Wu, Ritualists and Shamans: An Ethnological Analysis.* Arizona State University, 2023.

Wohlleben, Peter. *The Hidden Life of Trees: What They Feel, How They Communicate—Discoveries from a Secret World.* HarperCollins, 2016.

ABOUT THE AUTHOR

AMY MIRANDA is a wonder witch, medium, and Spiritualist who demystifies the mystical. Before being called to service in healing work, Amy spent over twenty years working in media as an internationally awarded executive producer and creative. Amy's focus on digital technologies and experiential media were always indicative of her comfort in Nerd Town.

A few years into the launch of her creative company, Lunch, Amy began to follow her personal breadcrumbs and examine her own ten-thousand-foot view. In working through her own healing journey, she finally named her trauma and transmuted poison to medicine in pursuit of justice and change. Amy likes to say it ran in the family until it ran into her.

After receiving a call to service to do healing work, Amy pressed pause on a successful career and trained in Shamanic healing and Reiki and began to trace her own lineage. Amy is the great-great-granddaughter of a circuit preacher, the great-granddaughter of colonized Filipinos, *and* a hereditary witch. This unique background brings a fresh and wonder-filled perspective to Spirituality by shining a new light on the old ways and bringing a new lens and creative perspective to our collective connectedness.

Amy conducts creative healing workshops and ceremonies with clients around the world to help remind them how to reclaim their magic and authentic power.

In her practice, she specializes in working with creatives and survivors of childhood sexual abuse. Her wonder workshop and retreat version of *What We've Forgotten* is described as "life changing," as Amy brings together the cosmos and the collective. Her invitation-only traveling Sacred Supper Club is described as "holy dinner party!"

Amy enjoys animals, nature, creating, magic, music, singing, kayaking, making jokes, *and* changing the world. She and her partner share a home with their three fur kids surrounded by forest and wonder outside of Toronto.